Olivia Conde

Stone Ship

Stone Ship

Author: Olivia Conde

Copyright © 2025 Olivia Conde

The right of Olivia Conde to be identified as author of this work has been asserted by the author in accordance with section 77 and 78 of the Copyright, Designs and Patents Act 1988.

First Published in 2025

ISBN 978-1-83538-466-4 (Paperback)
978-1-83538-467-1 (E-Book)

Book Cover Design and Book Layout by:
    White Magic Studios
    www.whitemagicstudios.co.uk

Published by:
    Maple Publishers
    Fairbourne Drive, Atterbury,
    Milton Keynes,
    MK10 9RG, UK
    www.maplepublishers.com

A CIP catalogue record for this title is available from the British Library.

All rights reserved. No part of this book may be reproduced or translated in any form or by any means, electronic or mechanical, including photocopying, recording or by any information storage and retrieval system without written permission from the author.

The views expressed in this work are solely those of the author and do not necessarily reflect the publisher's opinions, and the publisher, as a result of this, disclaims any responsibility for them.

Contents

I. LOVE POEM

II. SANDCASTLE

III. TOMORROW IS HOPE BUT NEVER A PROMISE

IV. RAIN OF LEAVES

V. PHILOSOPHY OF THE UNIVERSE

VI. LEARN TO FLY

FLYING BELOW THE RADAR	1
THE ECONOMIC TIGER	2
IS SOMETHING REAL?	3
THE CULTURE OF WASTE	4
IN A WORLD OF BUBBLES	5
THE OTHER SIDE OF THE SKY	6
THE MEMORIES OF THE SOUL	7
THE DIVINE TREASURE	8
THE WAY OF PEACE	9
THE SPIRITUAL SUBSTANCE	10
GOLDEN CIRCLE	11
CHALLENGE RAIN	12
CAUGHT IN A STORM	13
THE INVISIBLE THREAT	14
CIRCLE OF FIRE	15
BEINGS OF THE SKY	16
THE UNLIMITED POWER	17
ANDROID LIFE	18
CASHLESS WORLD	19
ACTORS OF THE DIGITAL ERA	20
THE WISE BEAUTIFUL NATURE	21
A FLOWER OF SLEEPING PETALS	22

- THE MELODY OF SKY AND SEAS 23
- WE LEARN TOGETHER 24
- LEARN TO DIE 25
- SUCH A NOISY WORLD 26
- SABRE TOOTH TIGER 27
- A MAGICAL PATH 28
- THE DOMAIN OF SPACE 29
- FOOD OF THE FUTURE 30
- DRUG ADDICTIONS 31
- THE THOUGHTS 32
- THE BIBLE WRITTEN WITH LIGHT 33
- BUTTERFLY 34
- THE TEACHINGS OF KING DAVID 35
- CRYPTOCURRENCY 36
- OVERCOME ANXIETY 37
- CHILDHOOD WOUNDS 38
- COLONISE MARS 39
- SHARK SCAMS 40
- A CONTRACT WITH THE SOUL 41
- THE THREE HEAVENS 42
- SLEEP TIME 43
- INFINITY 44
- THE HIDDEN MYSTERIES 45
- NIGHTMARE OF THE FUTURE 46
- CRUEL CIVILISED WORLD 47
- LOOKING FOR HAPPINESS 48
- THE COSTUME OF FANTASY 49
- PHARMACEUTICAL BUSINESS 50
- THE CRISIS OF COMPARISON 51
- ISLAM STEALING ILLUSIONS 52

A BOX OF SURPRISES	53
AMAZON IN DANGER	54
A DIALOGUE TO WAKE UP	55
A CLOSE EXPERIENCE	56
PASSENGERS OF DESTINY	57
THE SPIRAL OF ATTRACTION	58
PLAY WITHOUT LIMITS	59
LOOKING FOR FOOTPRINTS	60
VALUES AND OBJECTIVES	61
THE SHORTNESS OF LIFE	62
THOUGHTS ARE THINGS	63
GAMES WITHOUT RESTRICTIONS	64
OBSERVING LONELINESS	65
TRAINING THE MIND	66
NEVER TELL YOUR PROJECTS	67
ON THE JOURNEY OF LIFE	68
IMMERSED IN ADVENTURES	69
PARADISE IS NOT LOST	70
IN HEAVEN THERE ARE NO BORDERS	71
WITH A FLOWER IN HAND	72
THE LIFE IS A PARTY	73
A FRIEND IS A WAY	74
LET THE CHILDREN SING	75
FREEDOM TO LIVE	76
EVERY DAY IS SPRING	77
TRUST YOUR INSTINCT	78
A BLUE UNICORN	79
WHEN THE SIRENS SOUND	80
THE ARROW OF LOVE	81
WE ARE DISTRACTED	82

START LIVING	83
THE STORY OF TIME	84
ABOUT US ?	85
MYSTERIES FOUND	86
A GAME WITH PHILOSOPHY	87
A PATH WITHOUT END	88
TODAY IS A HOLIDAY	89
THERE ARE PEOPLE WHO ARE LUMINOUS	90
WE CAN FLY IN THE WIND	91
WORDS ON A PAPER	92
YOUR FAITH IS YOUR FORTUNE	93
THE DARK DANCE OF TIMES	94
A JOURNEY TO THE BEAT OF THE COSMOS	95
THE CENTURIES OF THE NEW ERA	96
A BOOK WITHOUT A TRACE	97
REBIRTH OF HISTORY	98
THE SCREAMS OF THE SHADOW	99
PAPER WORDS	100
LEGENDS NEVER DIE	101
BECAUSE WE ARE HERE	102
LOOKING FOR A DIALOGUE	103
PASSING THROUGH THE DARKNESS	104
I'M STILL HERE	105
WEALTH IS BORN FROM THE MIND	106
A PALACE IN THE CLOUDS	107
WITHIN YOU IS THE POWER	108
A DOCTOR FOR THE SOUL	109
AN ABYSS INTO HISTORY	110
THE IDENTITY CRISIS	111
A SILENT TRAPEZE	112

ARTIFICIAL IDENTITY 113

VICTIMS OF HOPES.. 114

SILENCE CAN SPEAK 115

THE FUTURE DOES NOT EXIST 116

THE MAGICAL VIOLET FLAME.. 117

THE EMERALD TABLE.. 118

LIFE IS A TEMPORARY TEAR 119

MYSTERY 120

HIDDEN DOORS 121

IT'S TIME TO DECIDE.. 122

GOODBYE IS A CHOICE OR A SITUATION 123

SILENCE SPINS WITH WISDOM 124

I AM THE MOMENT THAT CREATES MY STEPS 125

TRYING TO LOOK FOR A SIGN.. 126

YOU CAN CREATE A NEW YOU 127

TALK LESS AND LISTEN MORE... 128

SAILOR OF LIGHTS 129

STOIC PRINCIPLES... 130

INFINITY HAS AROMA 131

A SLEEPING GIANT 132

STONE SHIP 133

Vll. WITHOUT LIMITS

Vlll. THE COUNTDOWN

lX. A WORLD OF MASKS

X. ON MY WAY

Xl. THE UNIVERSE DOES NOT SPEAK LANGUAGES IT ONLY SPEAKS ENERGY.

Xll. POEM FOR A FRIEND

Olivia Conde

Stone Ship

Material things do not provide happiness, only moments of pleasure. 👇✨

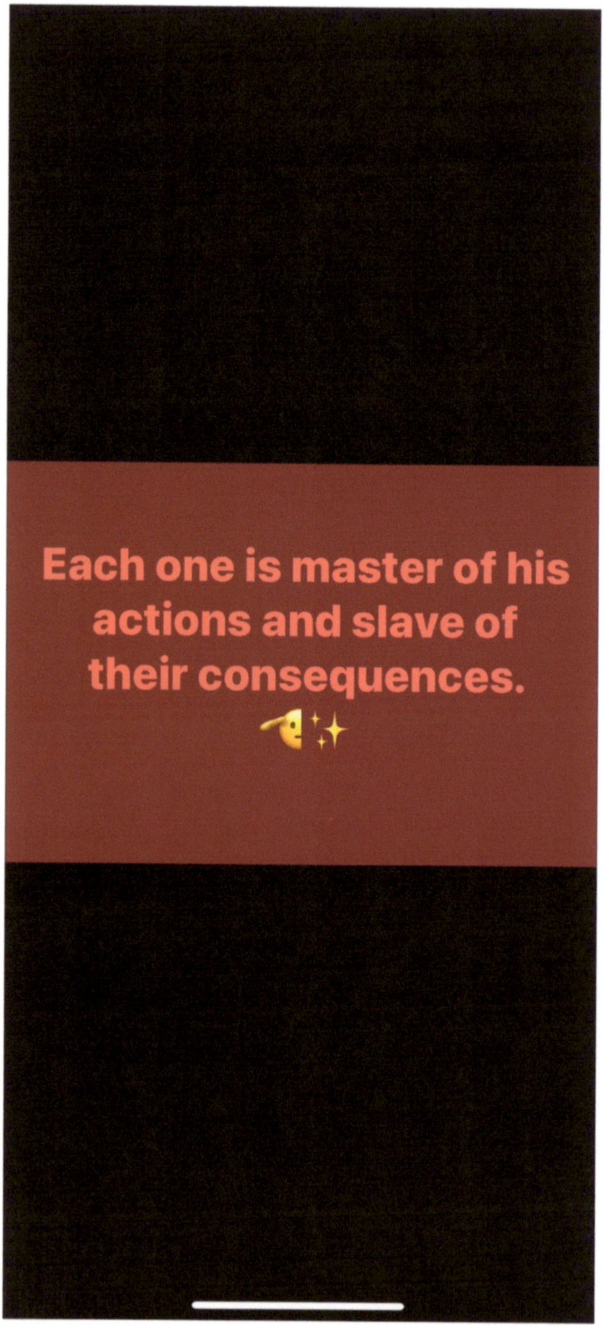

Olivia Conde

> **Each one is master of his actions and slave of their consequences.** 🫡✨

Character marks destiny.
🫵✨

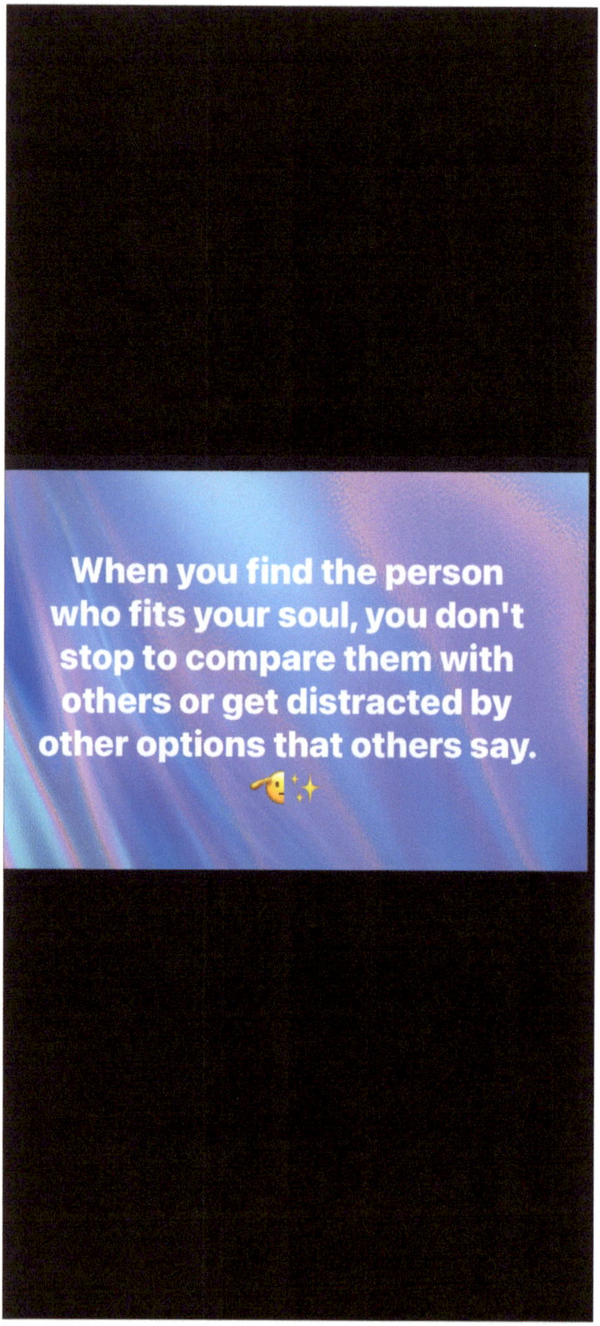

> When you find the person who fits your soul, you don't stop to compare them with others or get distracted by other options that others say. 👇✨

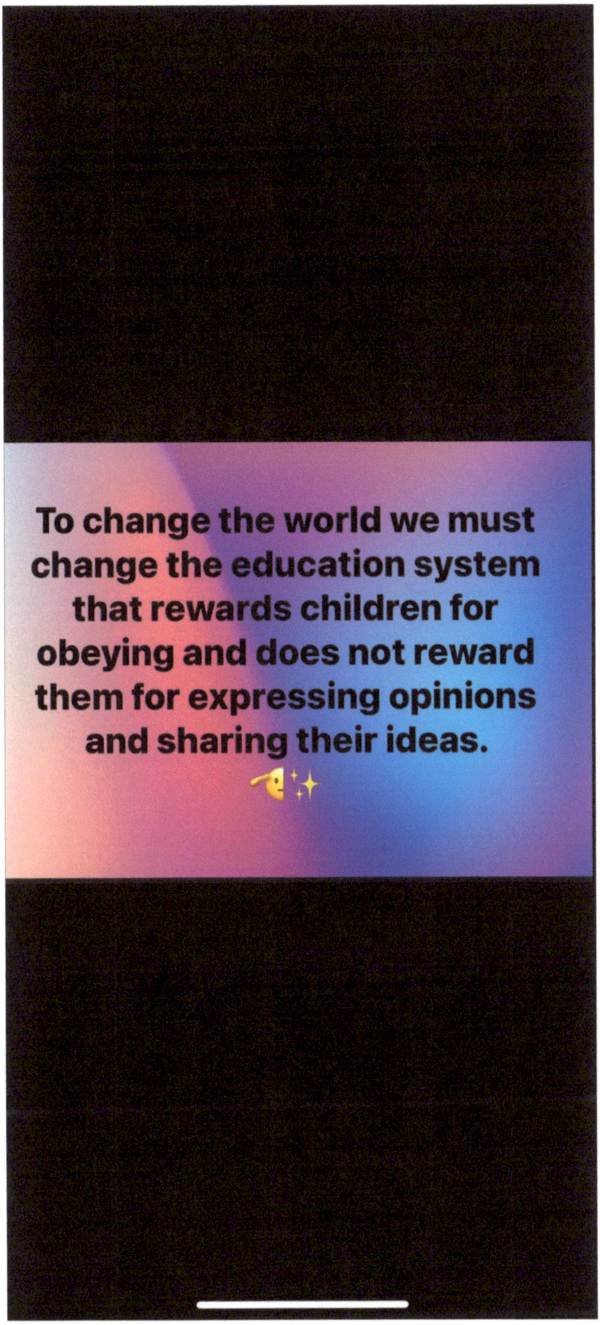

Stone Ship

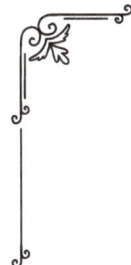

> To change the world we must change the education system that rewards children for obeying and does not reward them for expressing opinions and sharing their ideas. 🫶✨

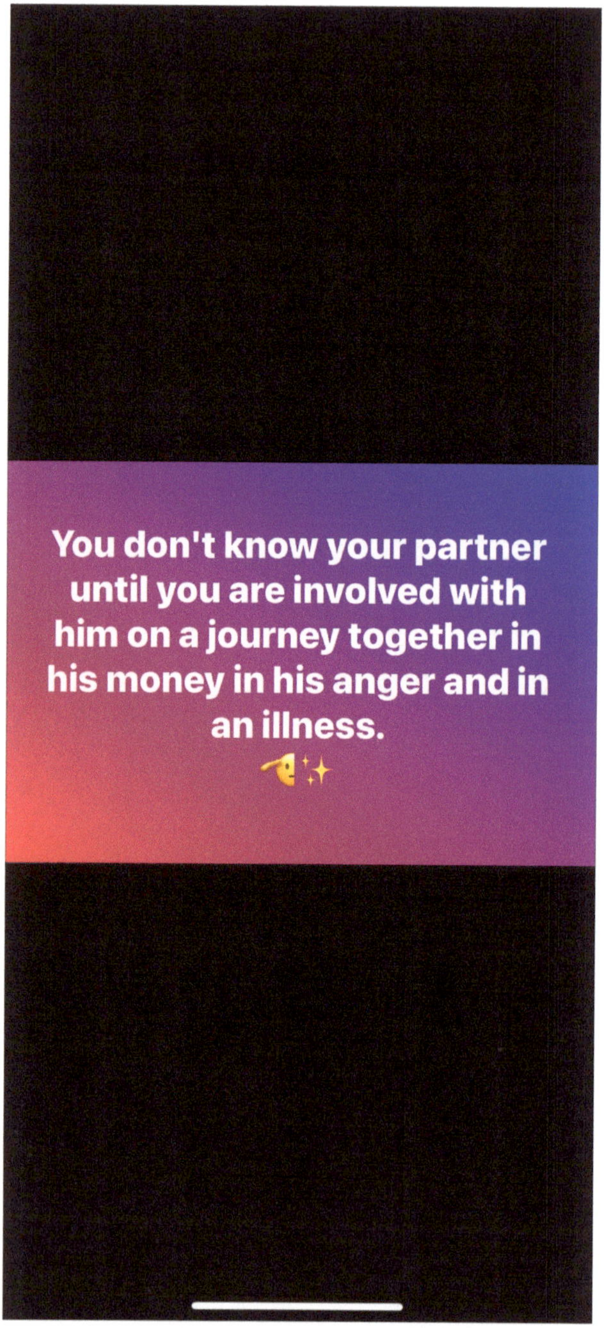

Olivia Conde

> You don't know your partner until you are involved with him on a journey together in his money in his anger and in an illness. 🫵✨

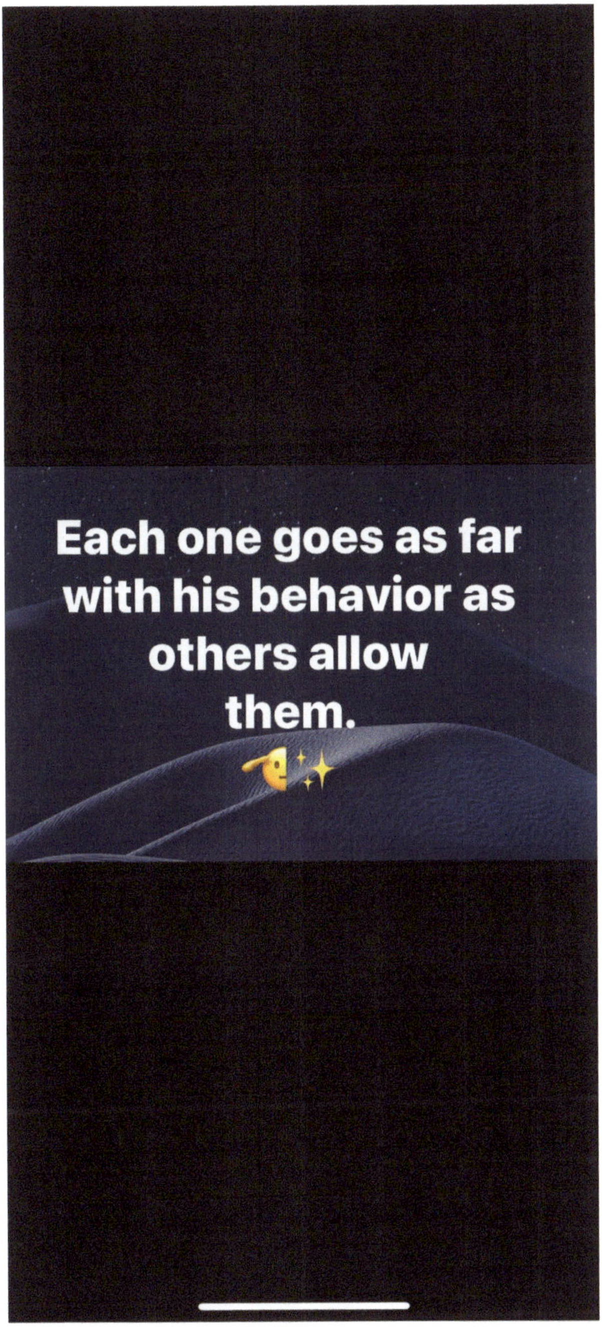

Stone Ship

> **Each one goes as far with his behavior as others allow them.**

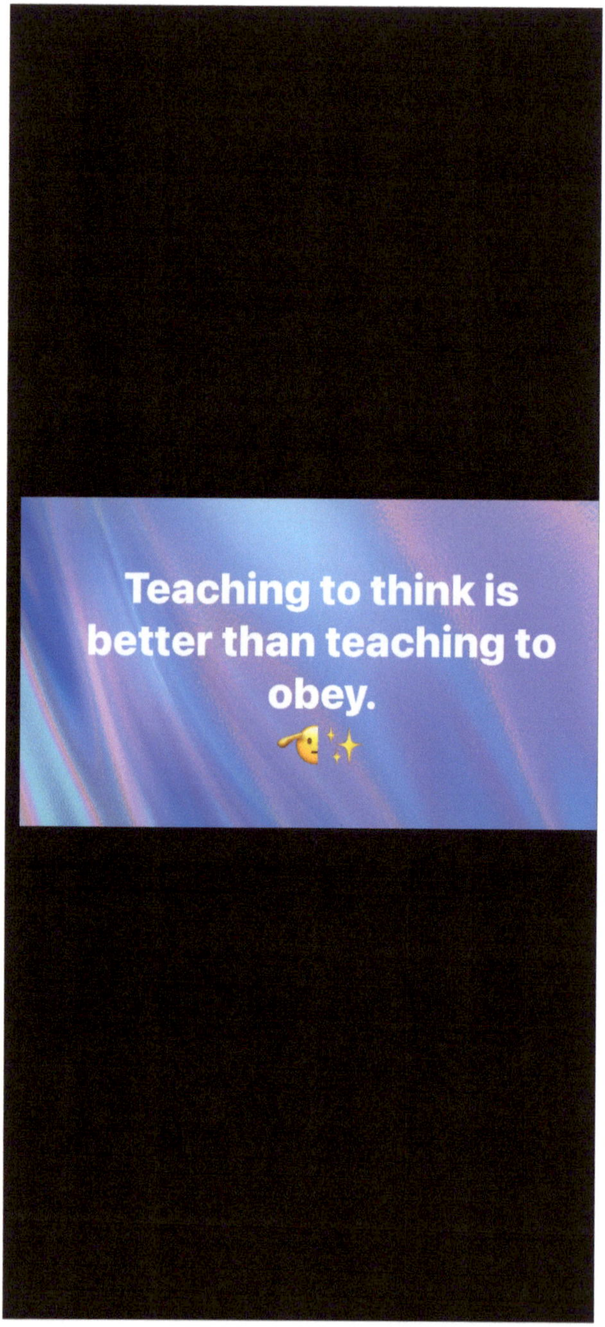

Olivia Conde

> **Teaching to think is better than teaching to obey.** 🫵✨

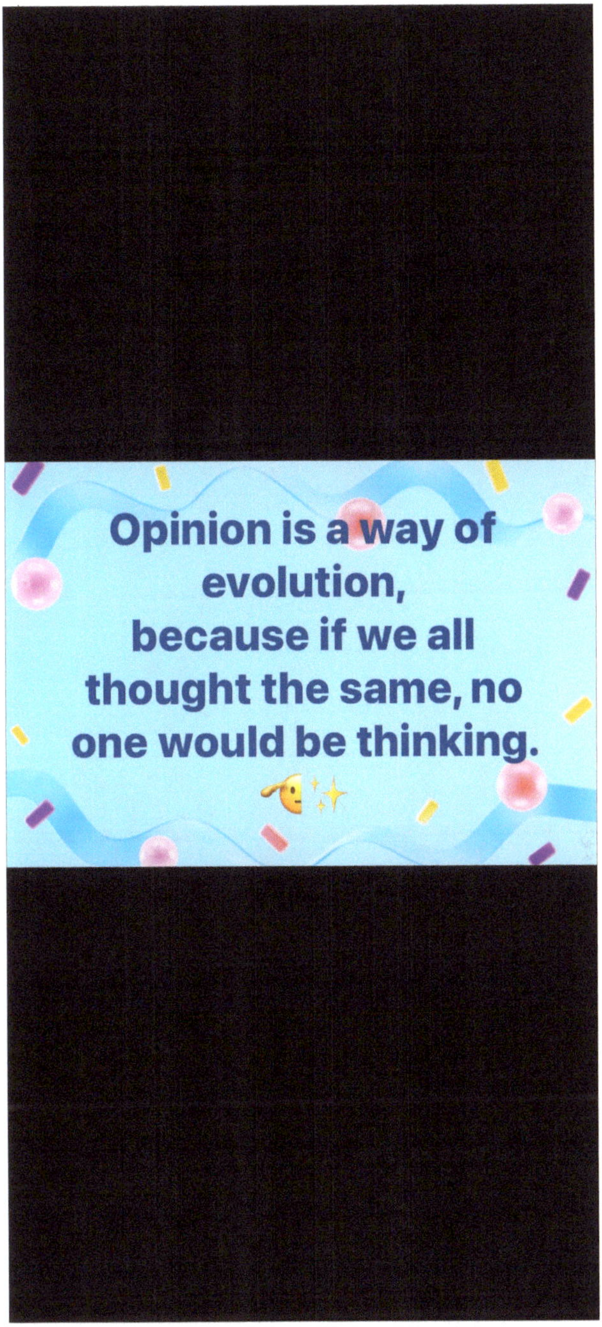

Stone Ship

> **Opinion is a way of evolution, because if we all thought the same, no one would be thinking.** 🐥✨

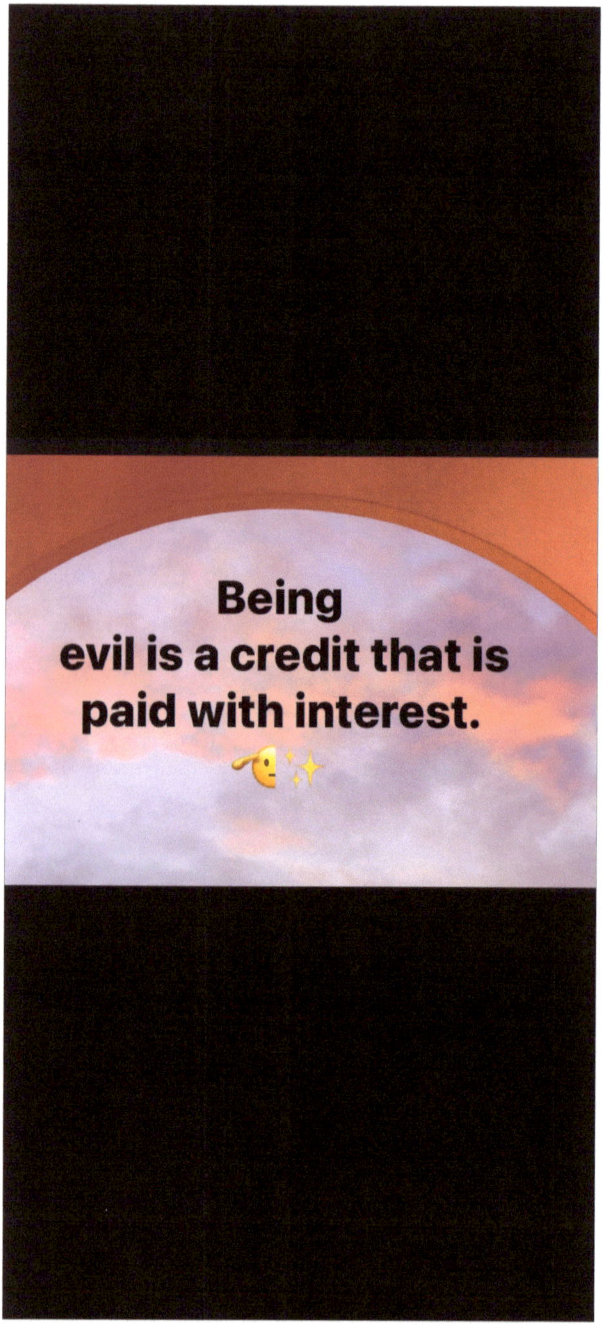

Olivia Conde

> **Being evil is a credit that is paid with interest.** 🫡✨

Stone Ship

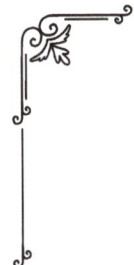

> **Not all crooked paths end in loss, and that doesn't make us less valuable.
> With willpower, everything has a
> purpose.**

Some relationships are like new shoes that you like but they hurt, but if you Overcome the pain when they get old you always want to fix them.

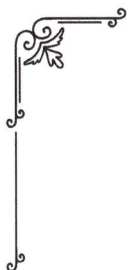

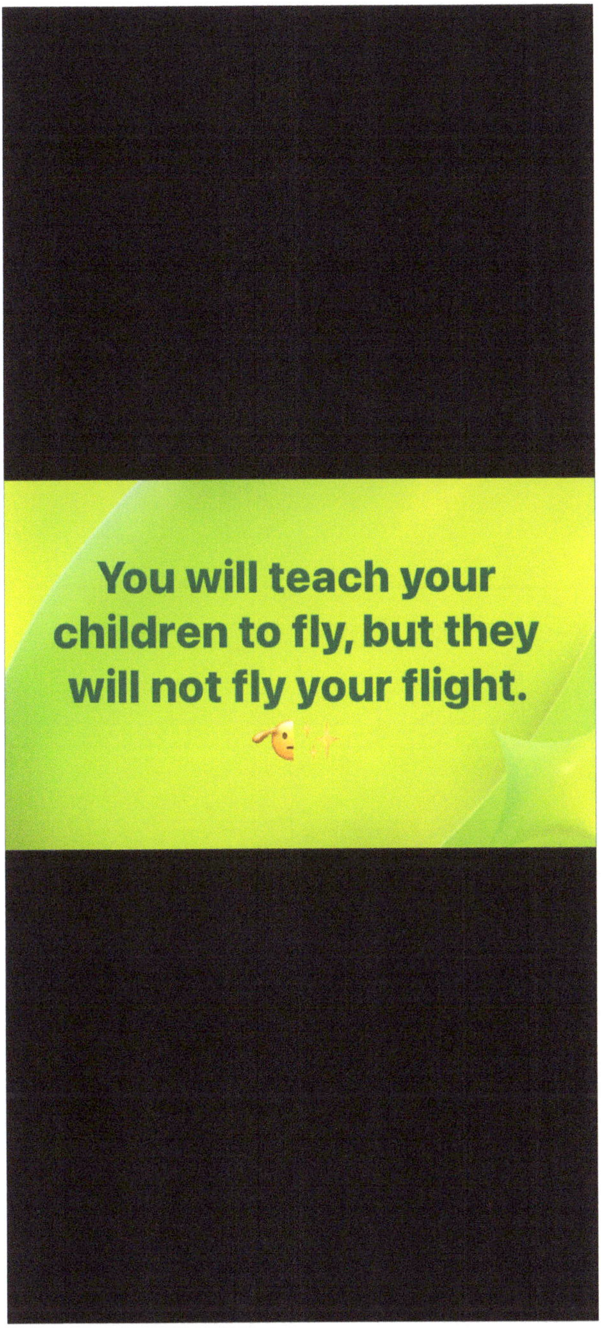

> You will teach your children to fly, but they will not fly your flight.

Stone Ship

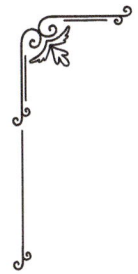

> **To care for someone,
> you must first be able to
> care
> for yourself.**
> 🫵✨

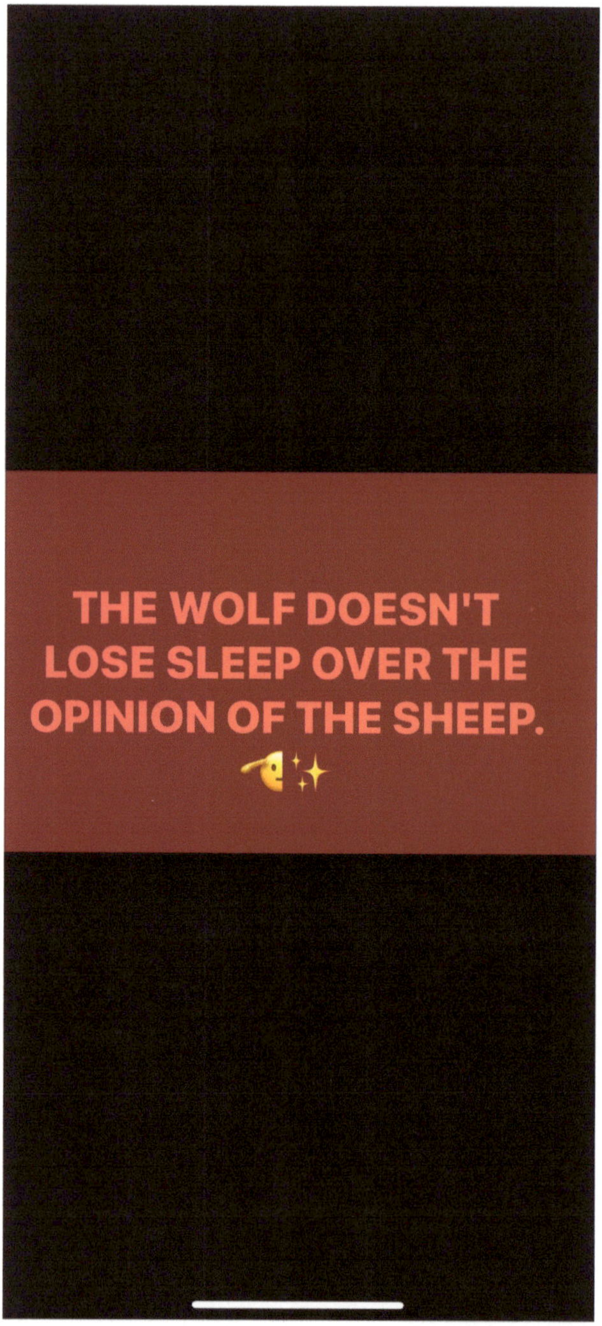

Olivia Conde

THE WOLF DOESN'T LOSE SLEEP OVER THE OPINION OF THE SHEEP.
🌙✨

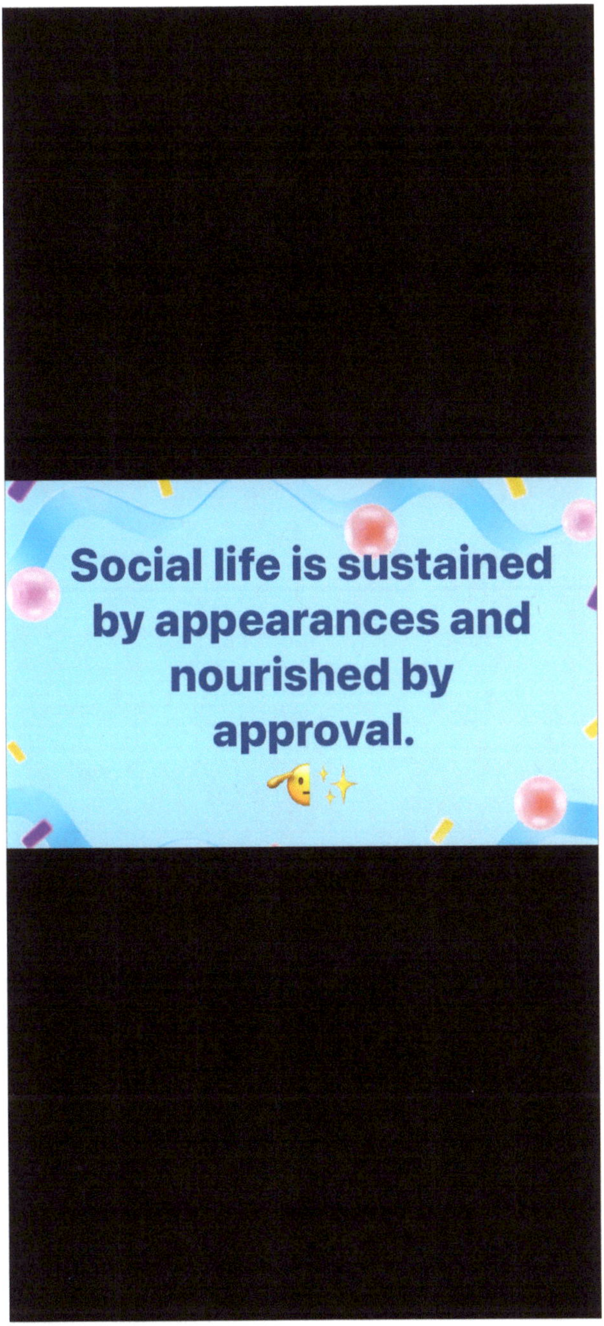

> Social life is sustained by appearances and nourished by approval.

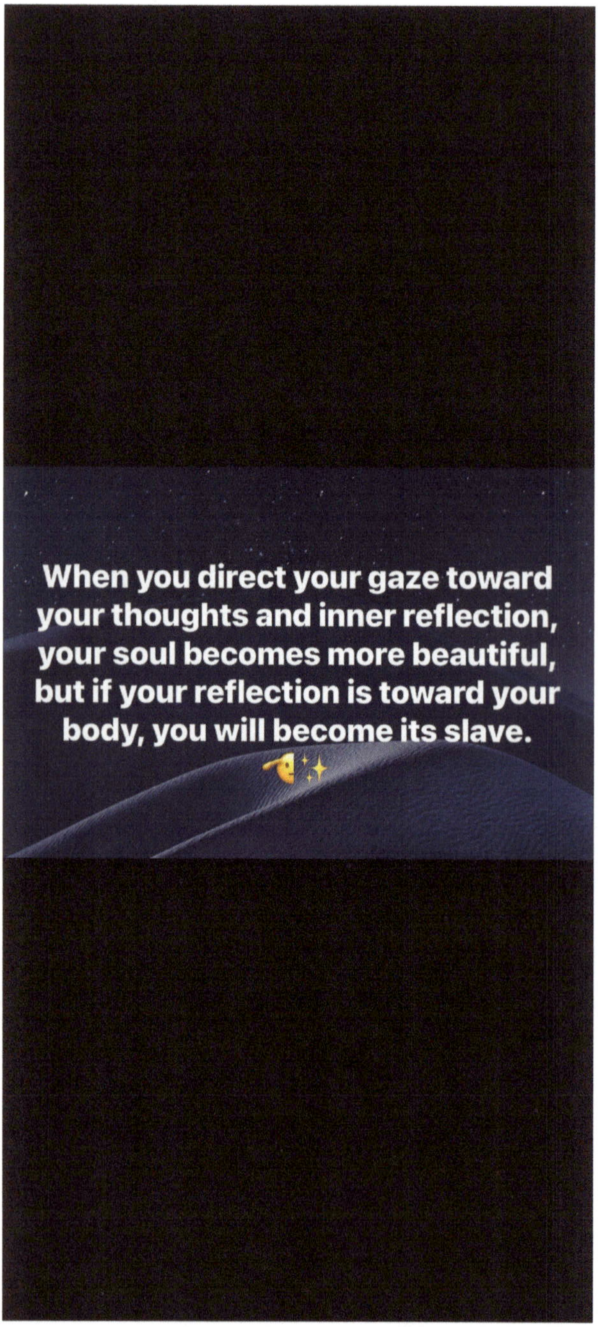

Olivia Conde

> When you direct your gaze toward your thoughts and inner reflection, your soul becomes more beautiful, but if your reflection is toward your body, you will become its slave. 🌔✨

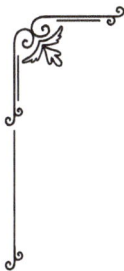

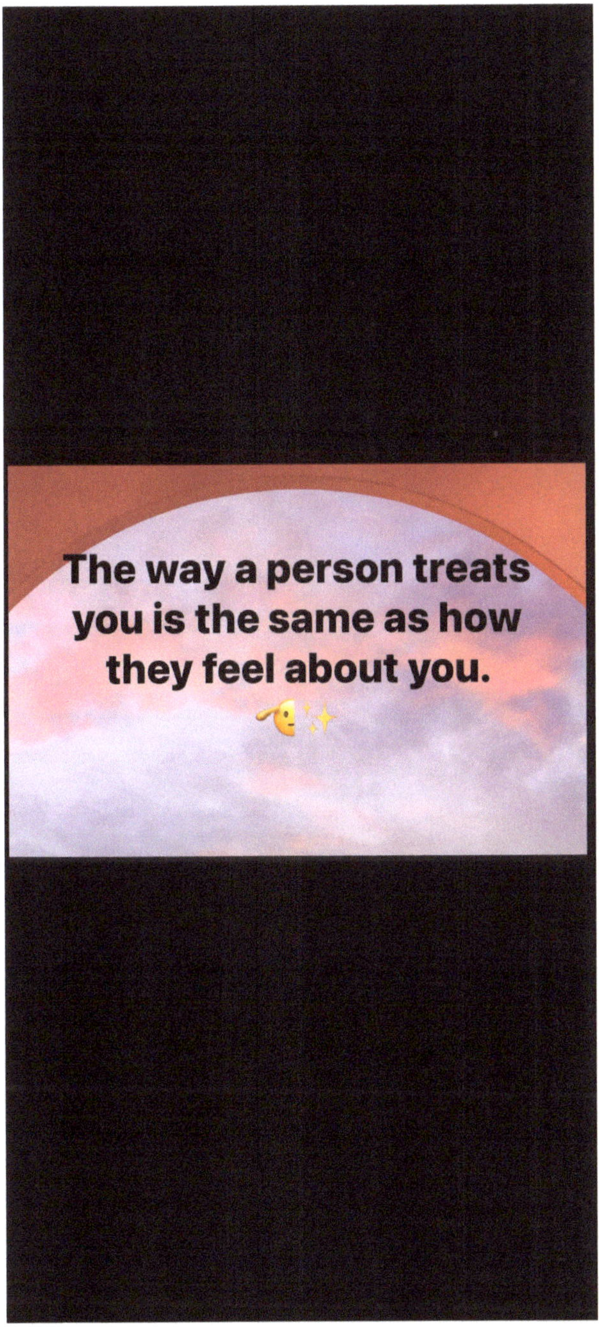

Stone Ship

> The way a person treats you is the same as how they feel about you. 🫶✨

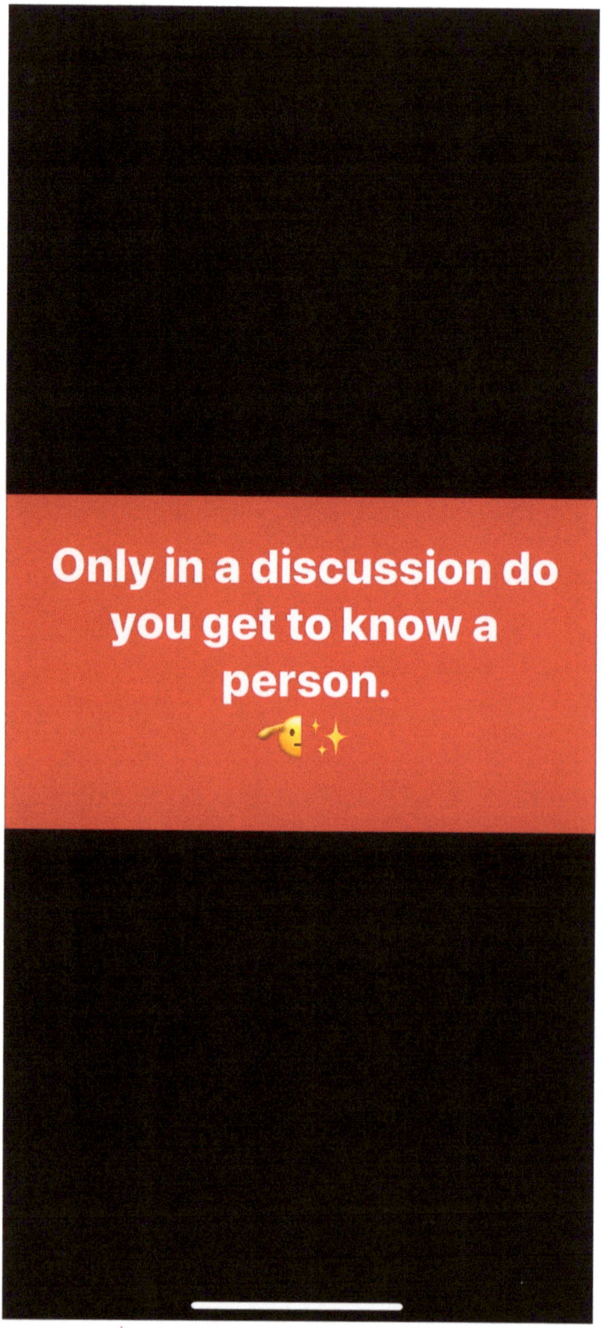

Olivia Conde

> **Only in a discussion do you get to know a person.** 🫵✨

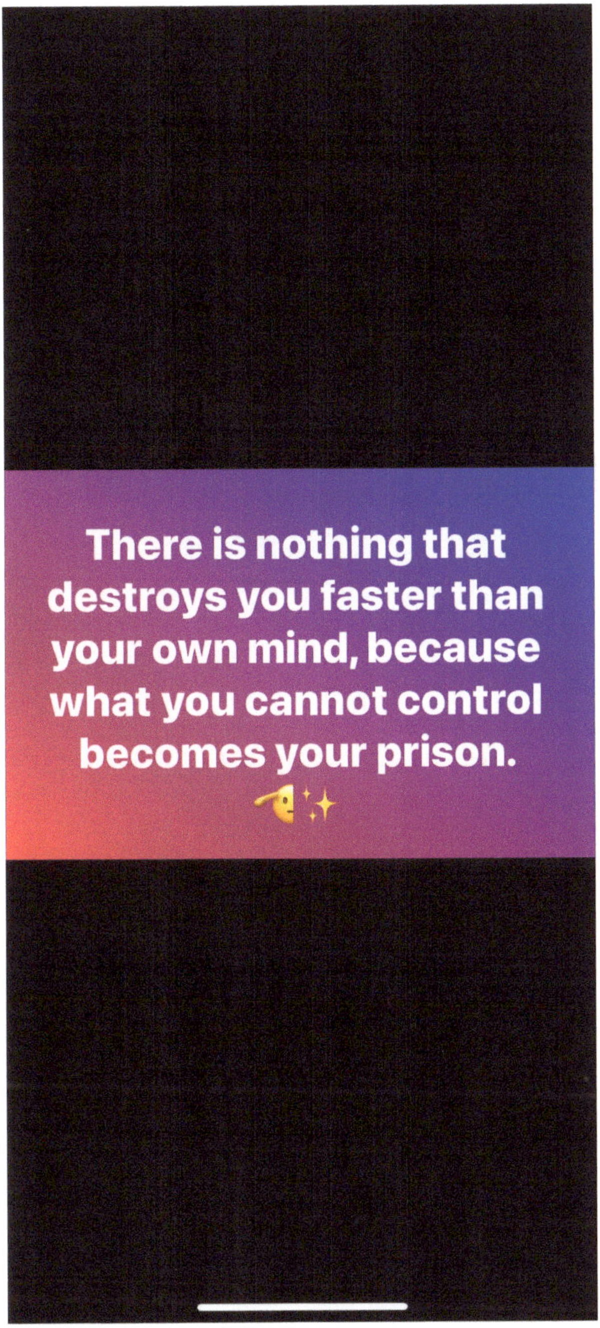

Stone Ship

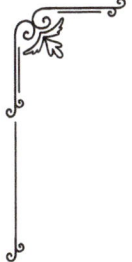

> **There is nothing that destroys you faster than your own mind, because what you cannot control becomes your prison.** 🫵✨

> Thoughts create ideas, ideas create goals, goals form rules, and rules create communities, and communities create achievements. 🌝✨

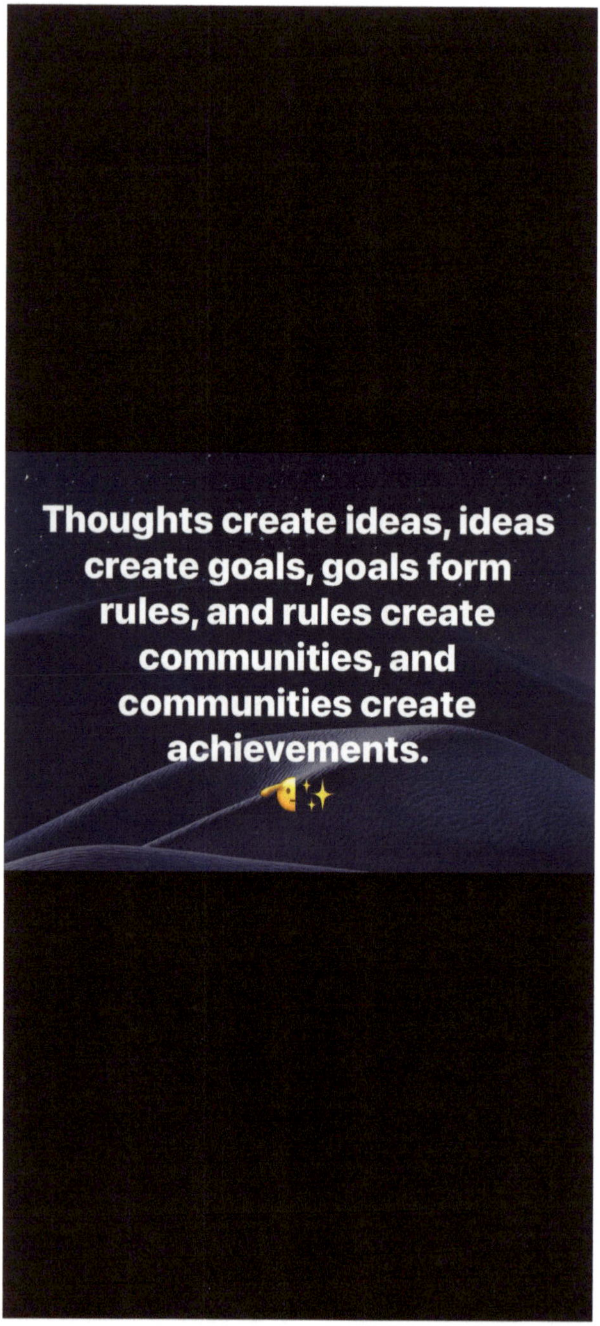

In winter, inside each person, there remains a smile from summer that can transform the icy cold into leaves that autumn takes away so that in difficult times they become spring with flowers of a thousand colors. 🌙✨

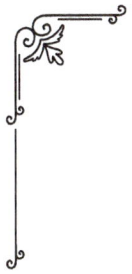

CONFUSION IS NOT A SIGN OF DEFEAT, IT IS PART OF THE PROCESS OF TRANSFORMATION. 🤌✨

Olivia Conde

> The care of not Hurting... is the most beautiful way to I respect. 🤌✨

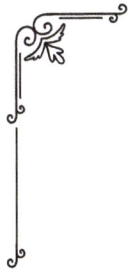

> **Depending on the people around us, our energy brightens or darkens.** 🫠✨

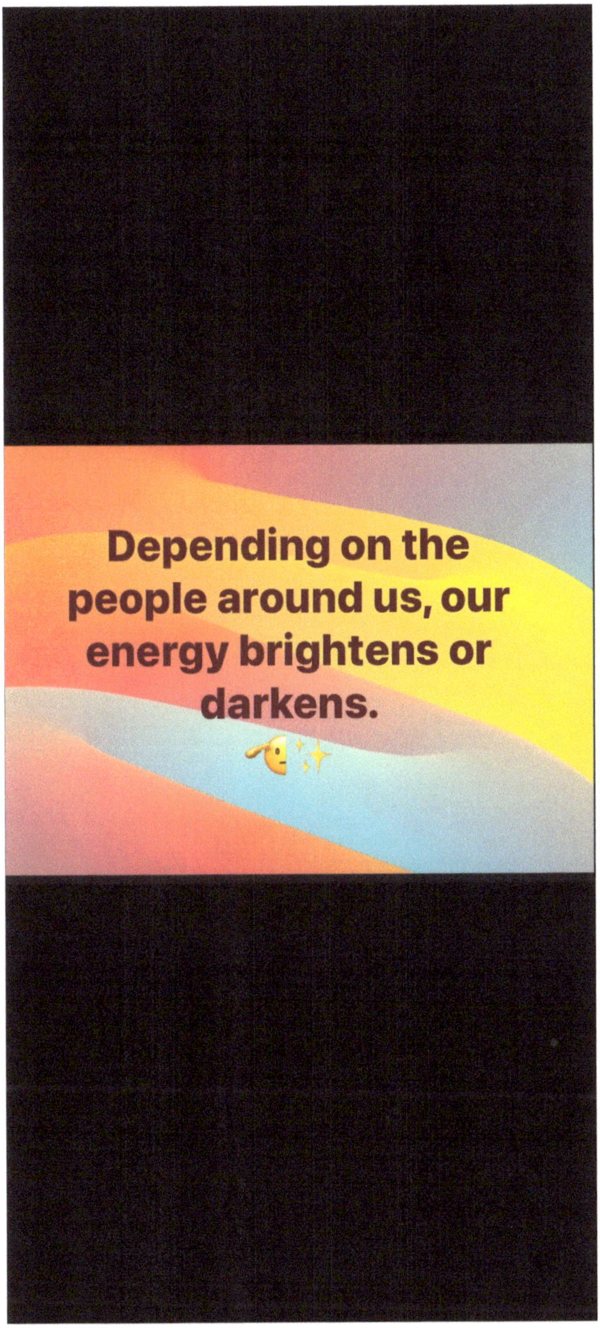

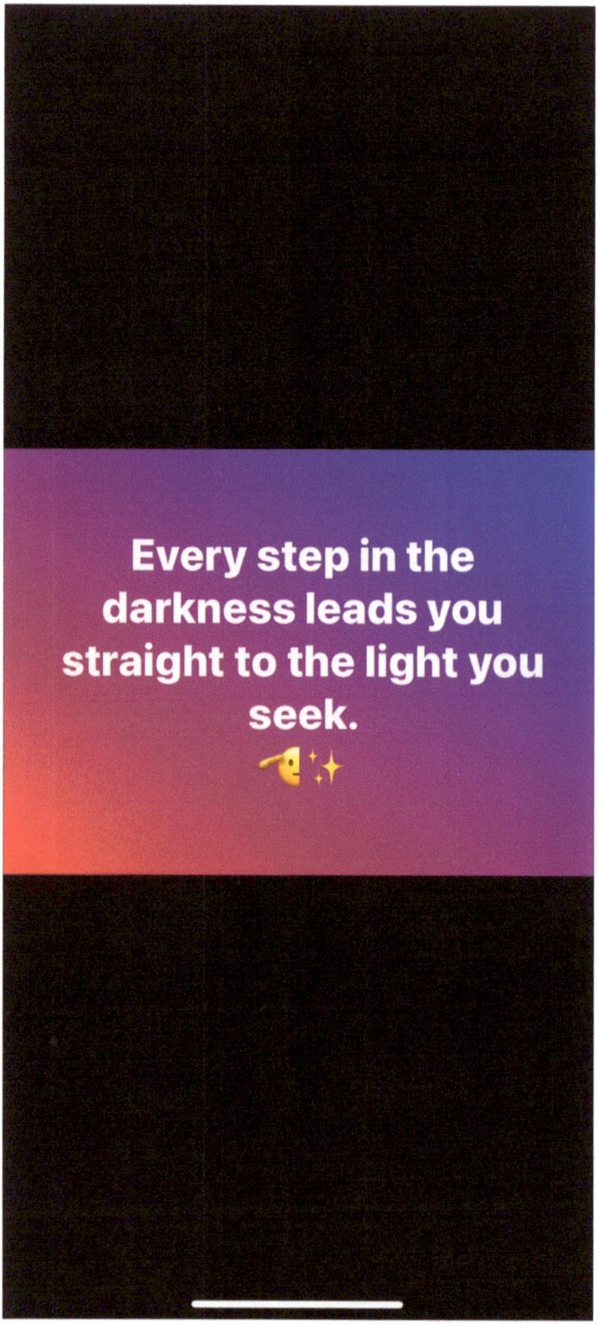

Olivia Conde

> **Every step in the darkness leads you straight to the light you seek.**
> 🫵✨

> When you are healthy you can have many problems, but when you are sick you only have one.
> 🫵✨

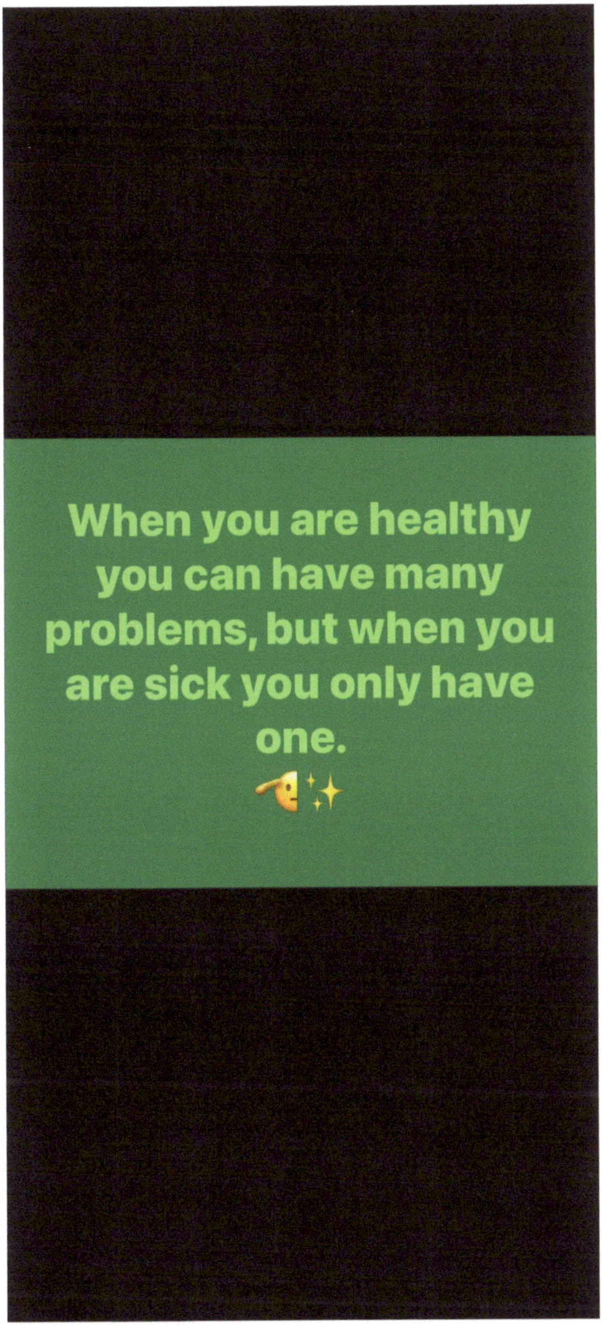

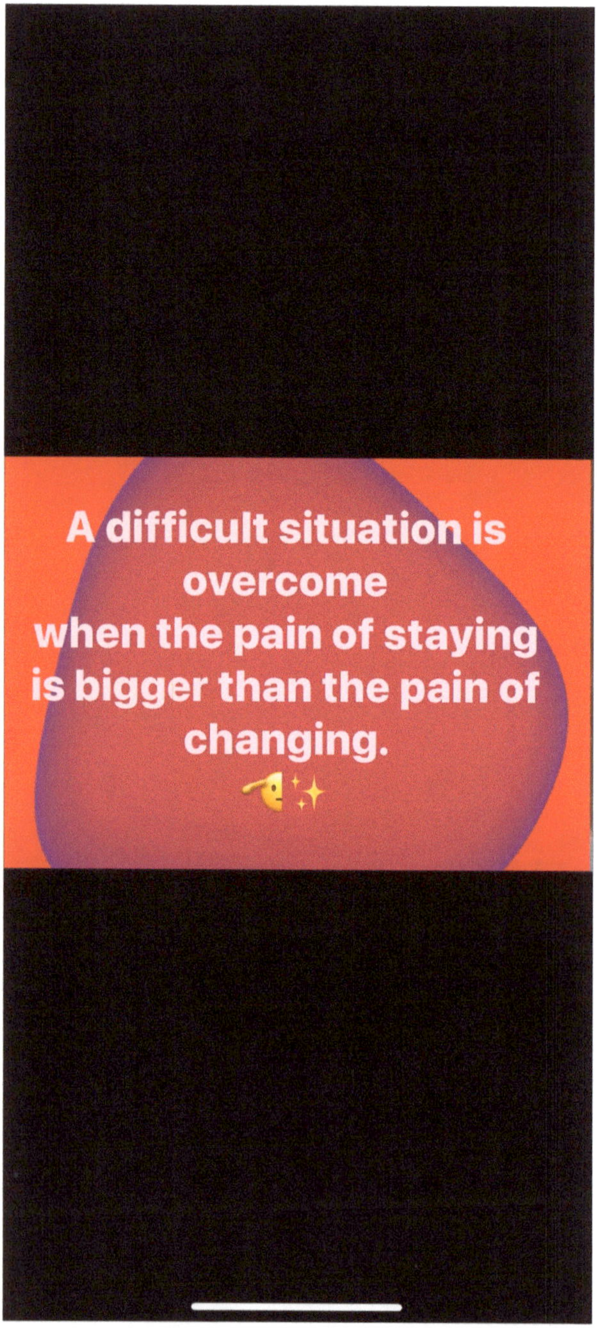

Olivia Conde

> **A difficult situation is overcome when the pain of staying is bigger than the pain of changing.** 🤌✨

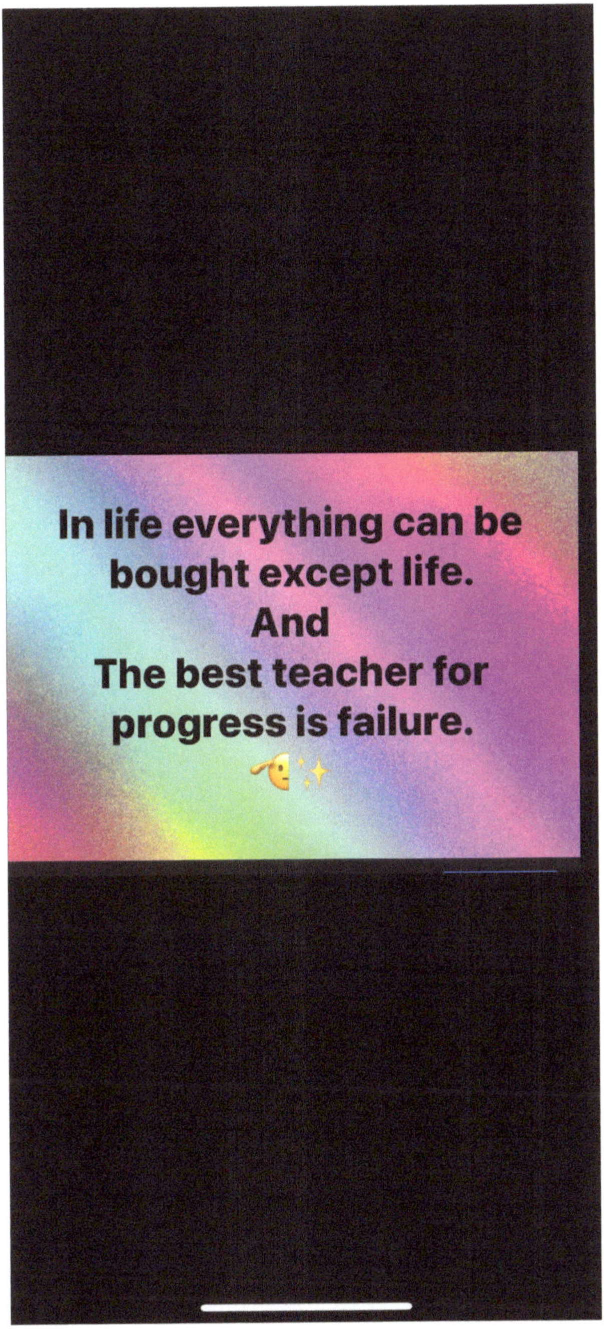

In life everything can be bought except life.
And
The best teacher for progress is failure. 🫵✨

Olivia Conde

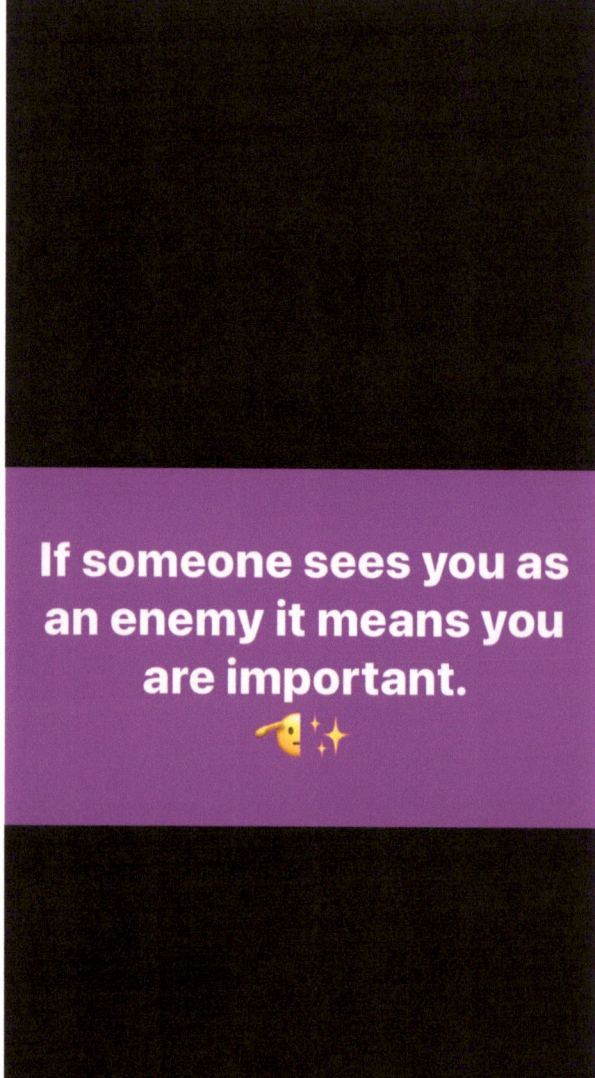

Stone Ship

If someone imitates you, it means you have charisma.
🫡✨

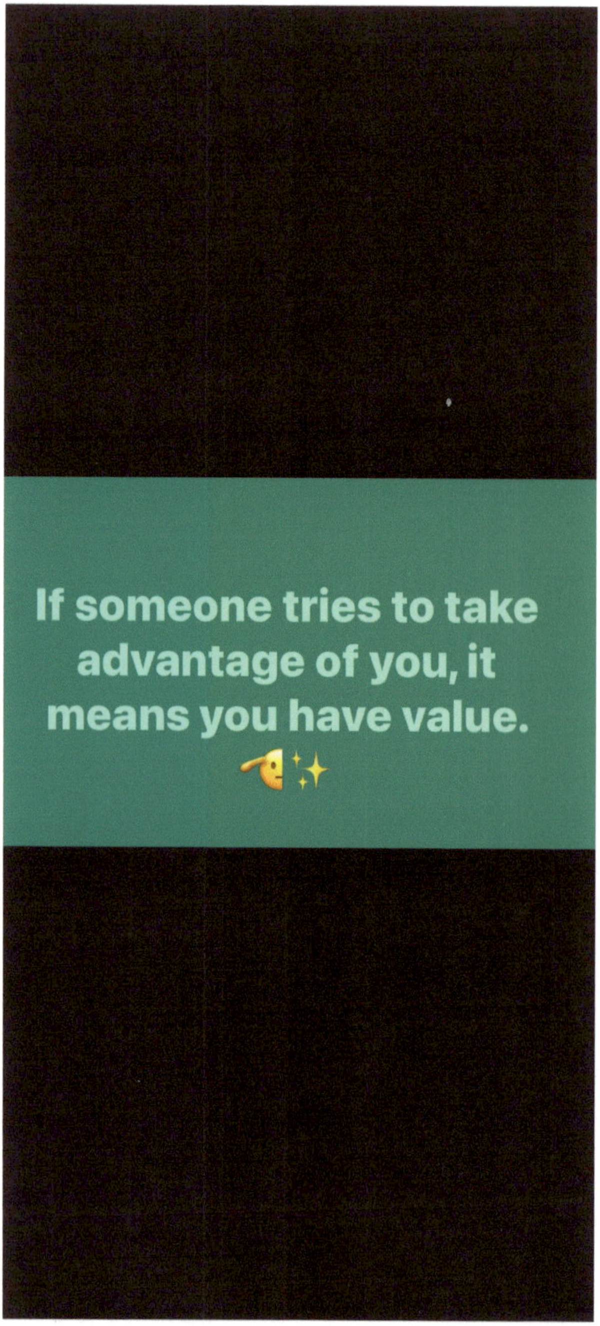

Olivia Conde

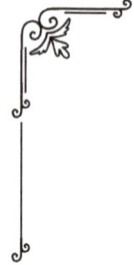

If someone tries to take advantage of you, it means you have value. 🫵✨

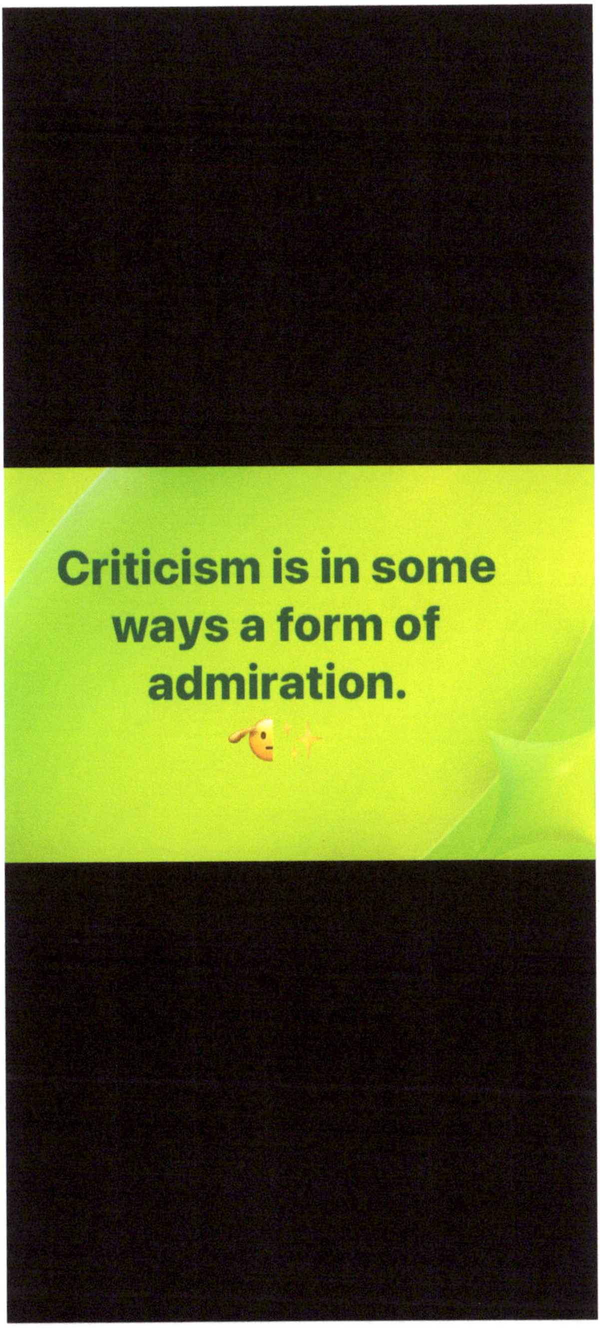

Criticism is in some ways a form of admiration. 🫡✨

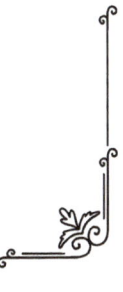

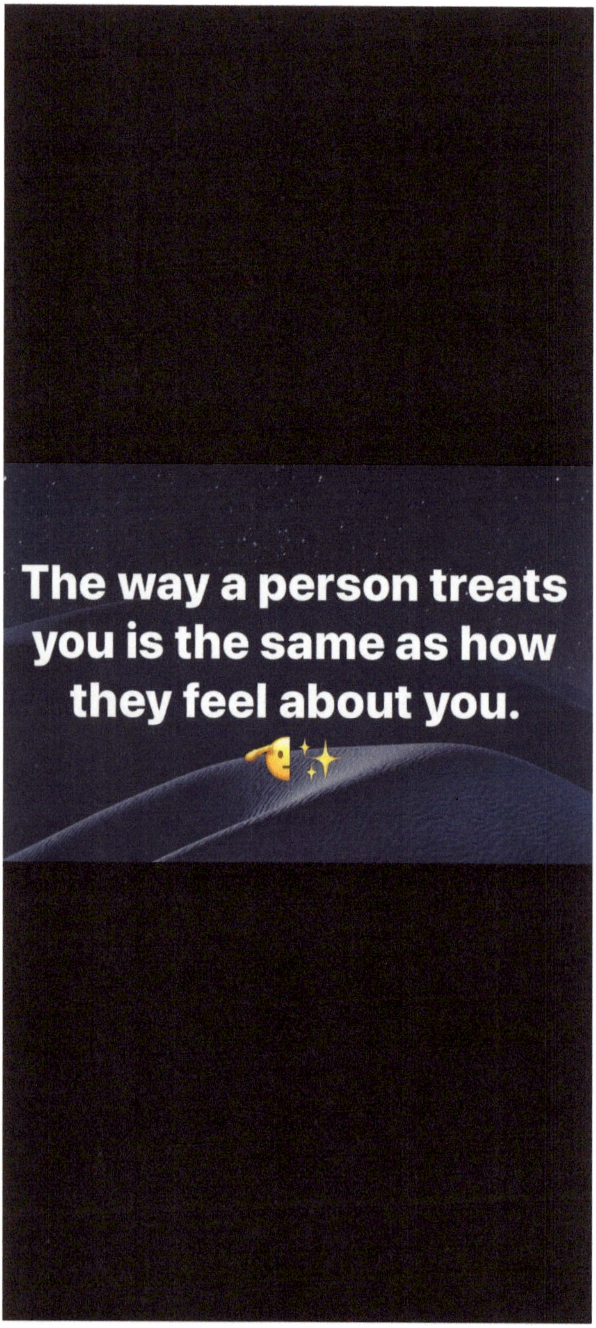

Olivia Conde

> **The way a person treats you is the same as how they feel about you.** 🫠✨

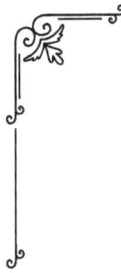

> The highest form of love is consideration, love is demonstrated by renouncing doing what is easy to do what is right.

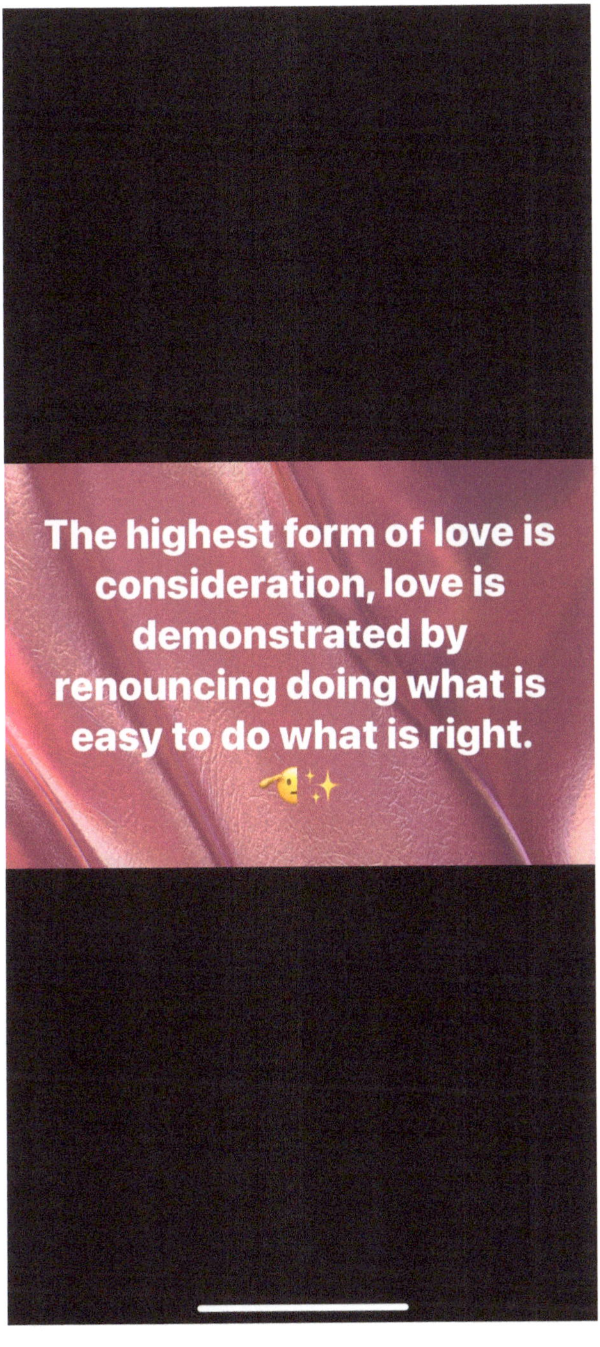

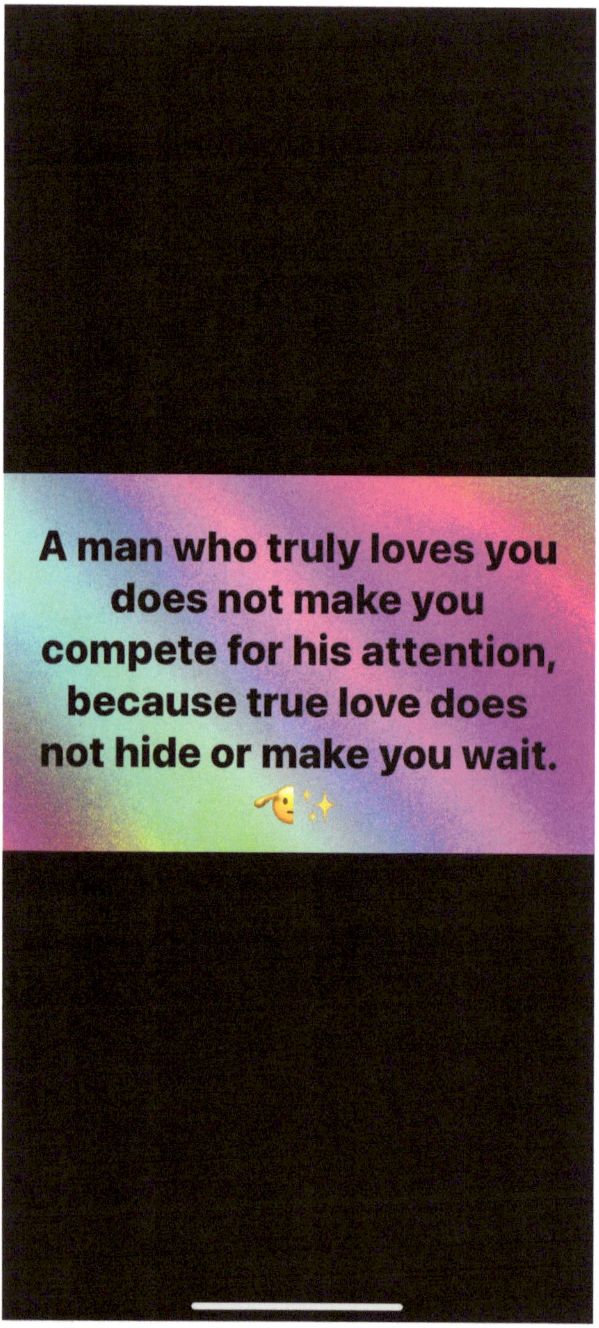

Olivia Conde

> **A man who truly loves you does not make you compete for his attention, because true love does not hide or make you wait.** 🫰✨

If you are not able to improve love, prepare to change for pain.

Olivia Conde

What you avoid facing today will haunt you tomorrow.

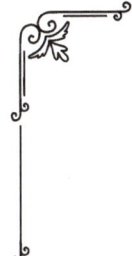

True love needs no instructions. 🫵✨

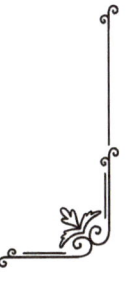

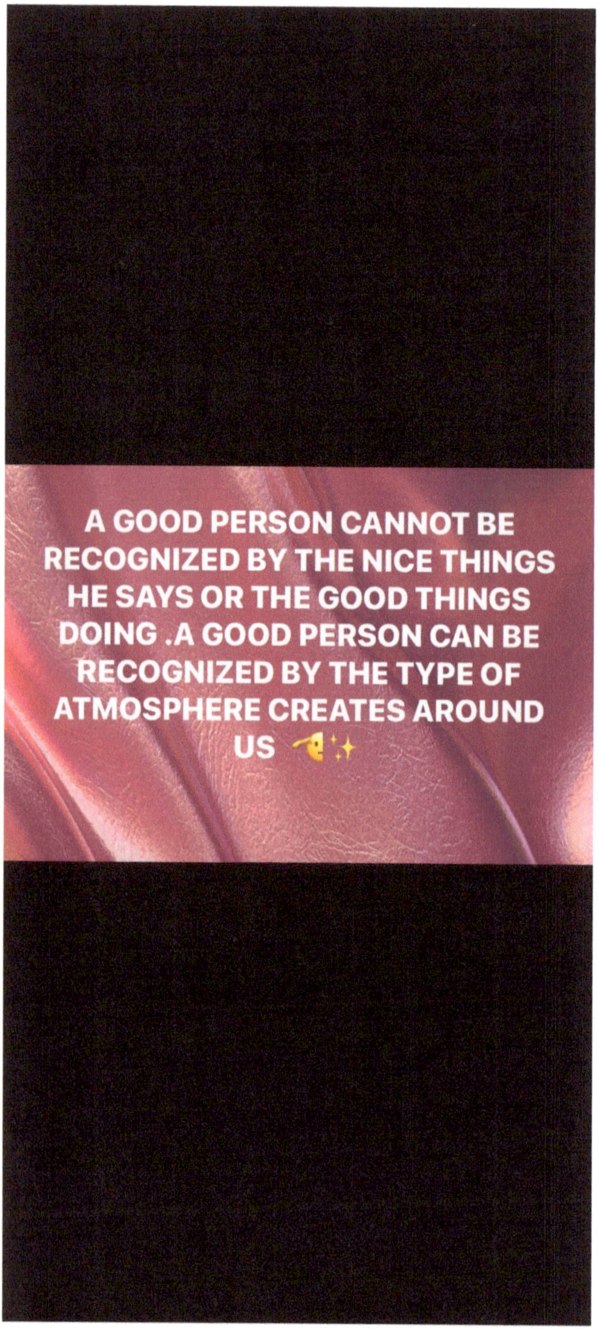

Olivia Conde

> **A GOOD PERSON CANNOT BE RECOGNIZED BY THE NICE THINGS HE SAYS OR THE GOOD THINGS DOING. A GOOD PERSON CAN BE RECOGNIZED BY THE TYPE OF ATMOSPHERE CREATES AROUND US** 🎭✨

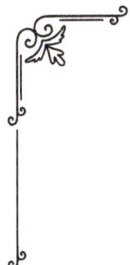

> There is nothing that destroys you faster than your own mind, because what you cannot control becomes your prison. 🫰✨

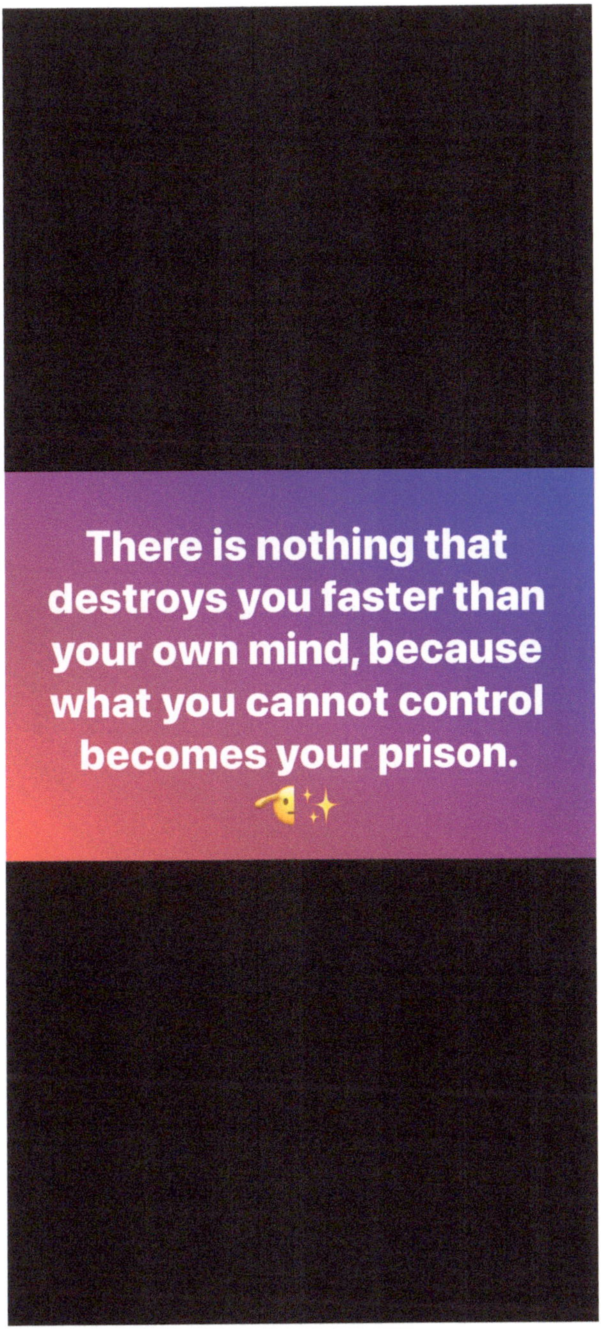

Olivia Conde

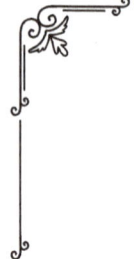

> **It's not bad to be stupid, but it is bad to abuse that privilege.** 🫵✨

Stone Ship

> Life goes by whether you like it or not, but everything persists in our shadow. There are many ways to die if you don't know how to live. Today is a hope, but never a promise.

Olivia Conde

> **Those who do not recognize their mistakes do not change, do not find themselves, and only live off other people's opinions.** 🤌✨

> The partner who loves you accompanies you and takes care of you and the partner who needs you demands and consumes you. 🫵✨

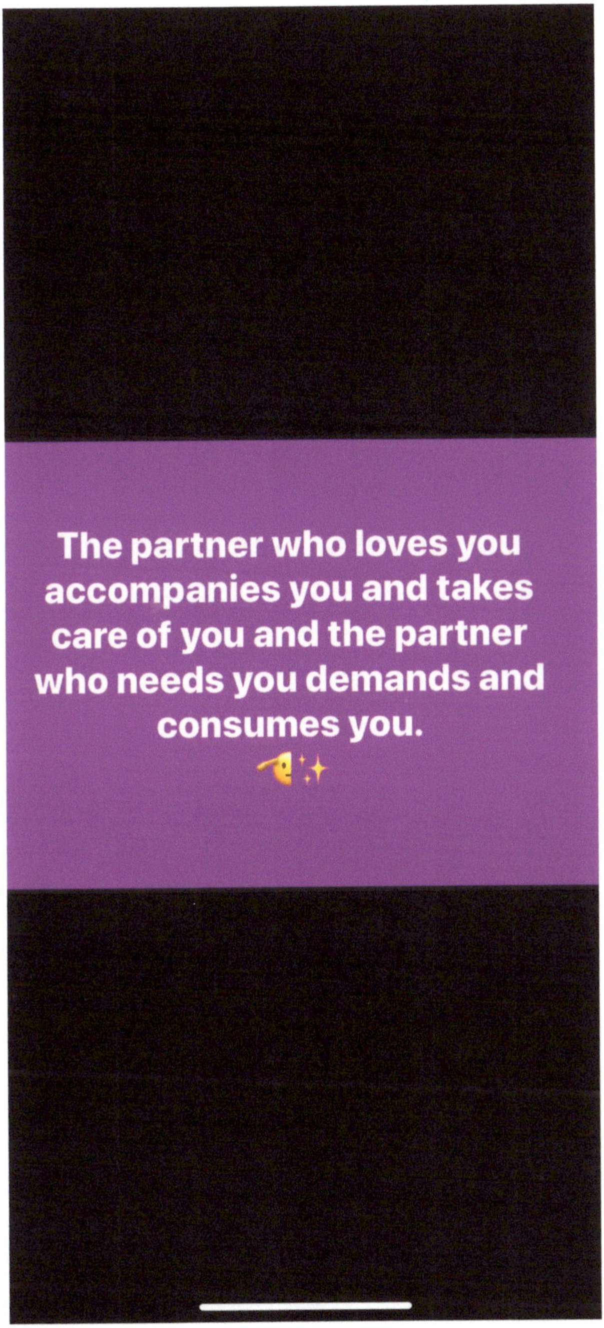

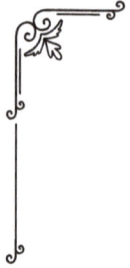

> A saying goes, tell me what you boast about and I'll tell you what you lack.

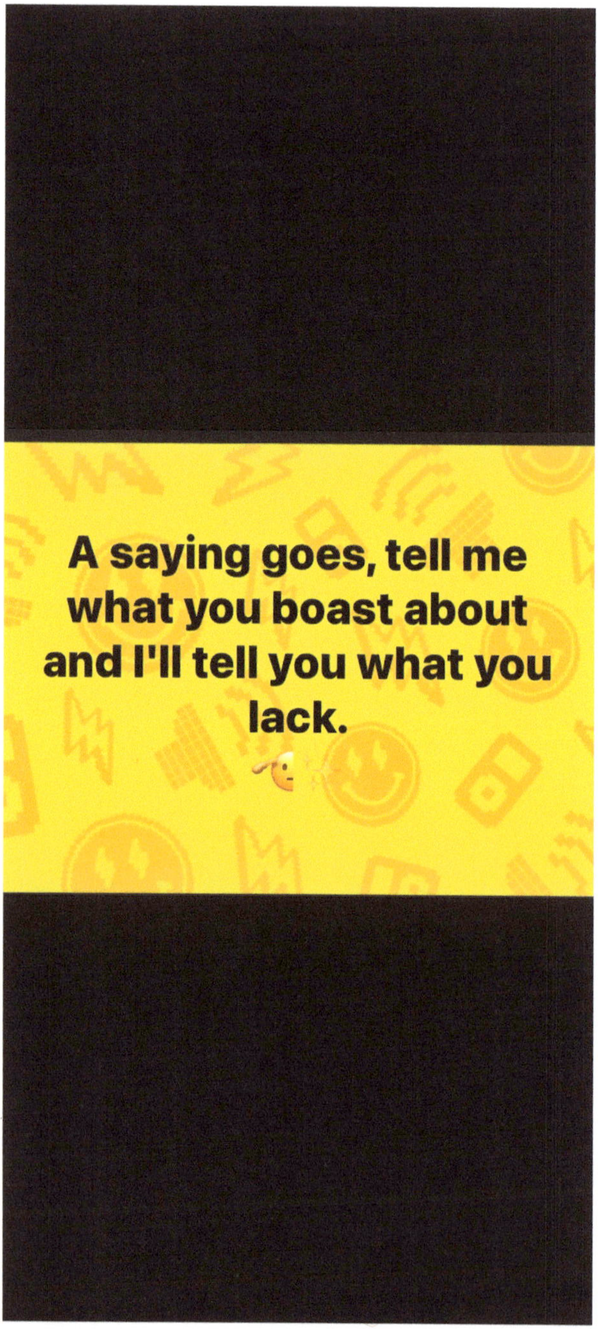

Stone Ship

A drop of water pierces the rock, not because of its strength but because of its constancy.
👇✨

Olivia Conde

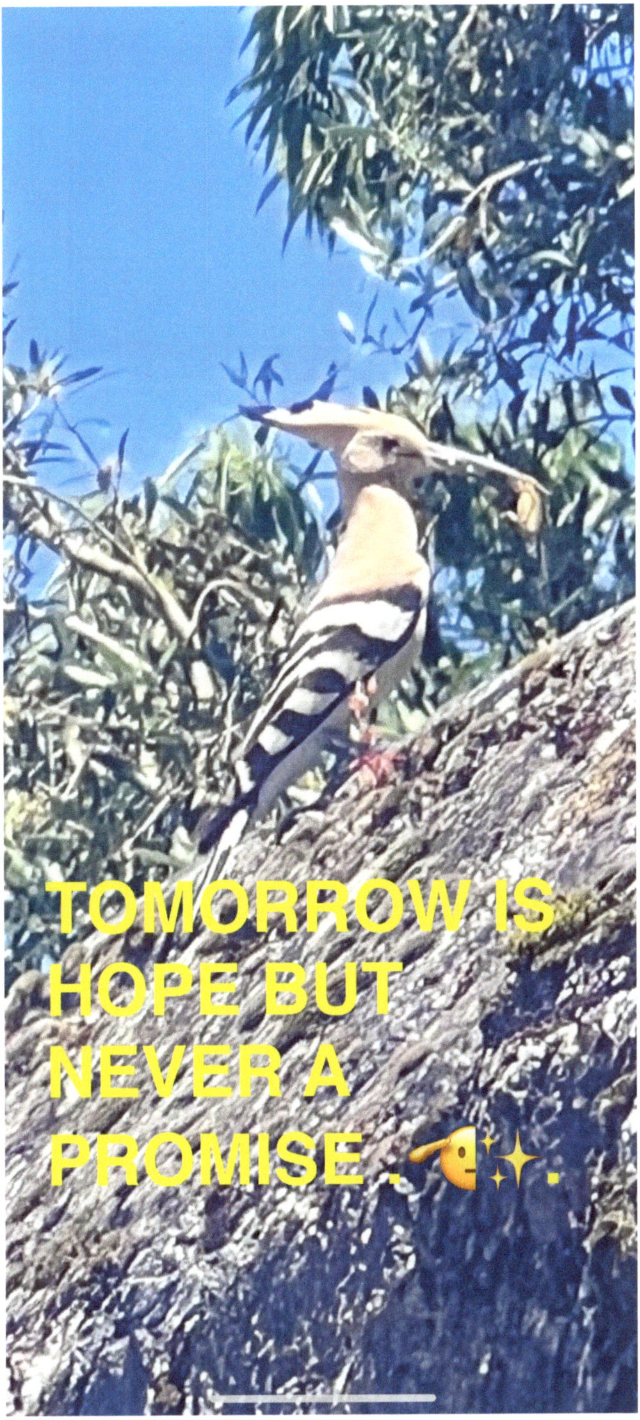
TOMORROW IS HOPE BUT NEVER A PROMISE . 🫡✨.

I. LOVE POEM

Once I wanted to stop time with your eyes looking at me, with your arms hugging me and your kisses reviving me.
You appeared like a lamp when I saw darkness in my life.
Because your energy makes you unforgettable.

The care of not
Hurting… is the most beautiful way to respect.

A kiss on the mouth is like feeling the words that the feeling does not say in order to realise that innocence exists, and protect the moment before the ego arrives to think about making changes that with words transform into a world of suspicion and envelop those feelings in truths and lies.

If in a relationship they only give you the spare time that their agenda dictates,
Don't ask yourself until when, just make a clean slate.

II. SANDCASTLE

There are many people by your side, BUT NOT on your side.

Everyone talks about peace, but we educate for competition and competition is the start of any war.

Respect is the most beautiful sign of education.

Don't let yourself be controlled by three things: people, money or past experiences.

Happiness has less to do with pleasure and more to do with purpose.

Succeeding in life is starting over every time you fall.

The opinion of others does not define the essence of who you are.

With money you have the woman you want,
Without money you have the woman who loves you.

Falling in love is an anatomical chemical to procreate and love is a decision.

When you throw dirt at someone, it's you who gets dirty hands.
DON'T BE CONFUSED !!

The perfect date is not going to
expensive places, but it's have fun with the right person.

come from good
Family is not when you grow up with money, coming from good
Family is when they taught you respect, principles and values.

Couples are neither sought nor found, they are built over time and in time.

In order to love, you first have to know how to be happy.

Don't hold grudges, hold memories.

The miser tells you, eat, drink, come but his Heart is not with you.

Special people can't be seen, they can be felt.

The more man studies, the simpler he becomes, because as he studies he discovers the greatness of his ignorance.

When you feel like it's no longer your place, fly.

The fool does not seek to understand, he only waits his turn to contradict.

Be someone's first love It may be great, but being last is more than perfect.

He who has mercy on the cruel will end up being cruel with the merciful.

Don't look for the most beautiful person in the world, look for the person who makes your world more beautiful.

Frequent those whom you can improve and those who can improve you.

Be humble
At the end of the chess game remember that the king and pawn are kept in the same box.

He who shows security, everyone will persecute him.

Being fashionable means giving up your own criteria to achieve the false acceptance of a majority of idiots.

The kindness exaggerated is almost always false.

To improve something, respect must first be instilled, patience and each one must recognize their mistakes, and in this generation it is what is lost.

He who shows a lot of goodness is because he hides a lot of evil.

You buy what you have
price... What has value is conquered.

Educating a child is helping to develop the child's self-esteem and that is achieved by convincing and not conquering.
The defects of our children are deficiencies of parents and society.

Friendship is about who came and
never left.

When you focus on solutions you have more opportunities.

Always speak the truth and never let lies decide.

We live in a society in which all information is from the outside in, which is why we talk about everything that we reflect on from the outside, therefore we live in a time in which it is very difficult to know oneself.

The bugs come closer when they see
that the lamp shines again.

Respect is like money, it is better to earn it than ask for it.

The material is the identity of pleasure, but not of Happiness.

Violence is the limit of incompetence.

Who brings you gossip from others, too will count gossip about you to others.

To try something, there must first be a motivation.

The young people in this generation who can't stand criticism and want everything fast await the worst old age and loneliness of all time happens in the history. For they will not endure each other. And the next generation that comes after Them will be A mind more robots than humans.

The only thing that belongs to us in life is THE PRESENT.

Happy people do not fall in love, they do not obey and they do not need Masters, they are only where they feel happiness and Harmony.

Judas showed that not everyone who kisses loves.

He who does not understand a look will never be able to understand an explanation

Life is harder when you expect much from the world and little from yourself.

In encounters with our mirror, only two things can happen: find yourself or remain lost.

You will be free when you understand that the cage where you live It is made of... YOUR THOUGHTS.

THE YOUNG PEOPLE
THEY HAVE TO UNDERSTAND THAT YOUTH IS A TIME FOR SOWING AND NOT A TIME FOR HARVESTING.

THE RICH FALL IN LOVE WITH MONEY, THE POOR WITH LIES AND THE UGLY WITH FILTERS.

TO A WISE MAN.
I ASKED HIM:
WHAT IS MOST IMPORTANT?
TO LOVE OR BE LOVED?
AND HE ANSWERED.
WHAT WING DO YOU NEED TO FLY?
THE RIGHT OR THE LEFT?

THE WALLS OF SUCCESS ARE BUILT WITH THE STONES OF FAILURE.

Olivia Conde

NO MAN IS FREE IF HE IS NOT OWNER OF HIMSELF.

LIFE IS A ONE WAY TRIP WITHOUT RETURN, ENJOY THE JOURNEY.

LOVE DOES NOT LIVE IN WORDS...
LOVE DIVES IN ATTITUDES.

THE HISTORY IT REPEATS BUT NEVER IT'S THE SAME.

FEAR FINDS EXCUSES AND COURAGE FINDS OPPORTUNITIES.

Being desired feeds the ego.
But being valued feeds the soul.

The thought leads you to the conclusion.
But emotion drives you to action.

Only in a discussion do you get to know a person.

Depending on the people around us, our energy shines or it gets dark.

The person who tells you things clearly loves you more than the one who only tells you what you want to hear.

The day is ending as warm hours of rain suddenly fall. The thunder resounds like a cannon as the streets flood. The years pass trying to find the struggles of each day. And that's what we call destiny.

A rainy day is approaching as night hides behind secret mountains.
In order to see the beauty that illuminates progress, we must believe that there is something greater than ourselves.

Planet Earth is an immense cemetery that takes us by the hand where we must discover the purpose by looking at the world with its own gaze where everything is part of life.

Wisdom protects more than money, because money is only a strong wall in the imagination.

To understand someone we must first learn their language.

Who criticises you today copies you tomorrow.

There are people who can spend their lives criticising but those who create interest are the ones who continue to grow.

Who has an interest in what doesn't make sense, their life that they think is real is a meaningless comedy.

Studies are not a salvation to achieve happiness, but humility and gratitude, YES.

Those who seek recognition from others are not only insecure but could also be in danger of being mastered by vampires.

Those who jump from one river to another are people with a lack of security.
Because he who wants to please everyone puts himself in danger of being crushed by the fool.

If you Find honey, fill yourself with the dose you deserve but always without overdoing.

That's why a saying, goes what belongs to Caesar is not to the soldier.
Different languages are not for discussion, they are only for understanding.
As philosophy is not to make philosophers but to create thinkers.

When you want to know someone's thinking , just stay silent before an argument and their reaction will give you the answer.

The looks that know how to give difficult time to the truth without fear of being rejected should be appreciated. Because if one had the courage to fail, one must have the courage to ask for forgiveness.

The law of attraction says that everyone comes closer to their equal and that we only get to know a person in a discussion.

TO STOP THE MINUTE HANDS OF THE BIOLOGICAL CLOCK,
From the age of 40 you have to exercise.

SO THAT AT 80 YEARS OLD YOU CAN CLIMB TWO STEPS.
AND THAT THE WEATHER SUIT, INSTEAD OF BEING FULL OF FAT, IS FULL OF PROTEINS.

Wise people are those who learn something from every bad or good person who crosses their path without judging.

He who seeks a relationship with someone with a partner is as if he wanted to enter a house that has already been bought but will never have the key.

I can't imagine all the pain there is in those who can't forgive stupid things. But I can see the great happiness and LOVE that exists in Jesus who was able to forgive those who crucified him.
But in life, bad and good, in difficult times we always ask GOD for help. But God says no one can come to the father if it is not through the son who was the one who left us the teaching of the
SORRY.

In order to forgive, you first have to know how to be happy.

In order to forgive, you first have to know how to be happy.
We live in a generation where -
He who feels something is a loser.
He who falls in love is weak.
He who does good is a fool.
He who wins is because he doesn't feel anything.

Justice disappears when others are harmed.
Your freedom ends when you harm that of others.

Over time we realise that in reality the best thing is not the future, but the moment we live, right in the present.

Attractiveness will always win over beauty.

Love is a craft, a work of art that is created from alchemy, magic and secret codes in complicity. Where the authenticity of one seeks the good of the other.

Human beings do not suffer so much from a problem but yes from the imagination that makes it real.

The most difficult thing for a human being is to know oneself and the easiest thing to criticise others.

Agenda 20-30!!. When artificial intelligence takes control, the world will begin to hate each other and the economy will be as miserable as the food that will be under lock to be able to acquire it.

The bad guy flees even if no one ischasing him
but the righteous is confident like a
LION.

Don't go looking for anything about changes in the past because it has nothing new to tell you.

Happy people make decisions and set very clear rules, because they know that EVERYONE GOES AS FAR AS THEY ARE ALLOWED.

EVERYTHING VALUABLE IN THIS WORLD IS WELL COVERED AND DIFFICULT TO SEE.

AGENDA 20-30!! RULES
1. Get used to feeling lonely.
2. You will have no friends or family to rely on.
3. It will be very easy to fall for false promises.
4. You will forget to live because you will only think about working.

5. Everyone will try to discourage the other.

6. In order to escape from the dragon you only have to overcome that reward circuit that turns us towards pain and fear.

7. With your silence they will give you the minimum and you will be happy because the economy is not enough.

WHEN YOU STOP FOLLOWING EVERYONE, YOU WILL BE ABLE TO FLY.

Many fears are created by the human mind.
But the biological fears are, fear of falling and fear of noise.

When someone loves you, you can trust to tell them your mistakes and sorrows and they will never use them against YOU.

If sleeping is free!!
FREE
Why it costs me somuch to get up.??
LALALALALALALALA……

ASPIRE TO BE GIANT,
Because the distraction strategy while pulling the strings does not THINK ABOUT YOU.

III. TOMORROW IS HOPE BUT NEVER A PROMISE

Those who is a friend to everyone is a friend to no one.

What makes us lose control of life is wanting to fit in where we don't belong.

Those who betrays you once, will betray you a thousand times, you don't need to drink the whole sea to realize that it is salty.

Peace means knowing how to transform something difficult into something easy.

The true reward in life is not in what you earn but in who you become.

With problematic people, not everything has an explanation, just distance yourself and set limits, otherwise they will contaminate you.

To win in life you don't need to be the smartest, you just need to be a person who never gives up on his goal.

There are worms that eat apples, but there are no worms eating lemons, so don't be so sweet to everyone,

love true is born from respect, not possession,

Nothing is forget more slowly

an offense and nothing faster than a favor.

If what you have is insufficient, even if you possess the whole world, you will be miserable.

Patience has a limit... and it is called dignity.

We must not forget that the years we have are actually the years we no longer have.

When luxury is represented you by material things it is called poverty.

If someone doesn't value what you give, it's because you're not giving it to the right person.

All the people you fight are not your enemies and all the people who help you are not your friends.

In life we attract the things we complain about.

THE DISCIPLINE ACTIVATE WILLPOWER.

Words may lie, but actions always tell the truth.

YOUR CONSCIENCE IS
WHAT YOU ARE. YOUR REPUTATION IS WHAT OTHERS THINK OF YOU.
AND WHAT OTHERS THINK OF YOU...
IT'S NOT YOUR PROBLEM.

If your partner changes you !! it is not for someone better!!, but for someone easier, remember the market fills up when meat is cheap.

The way to love is by learning to set limits.

In this world designed to confuse, our true wealth is in Mental Clarity.

The ego is conditioned by material things and the fear of losing it.

An ounce of facts is worth more what kilos of intentions.

When you want someone it's because you need them, but when you love someone it is because you have chosen them.

EVERY JUDGMENT IS A CONFESSION OF YOUR OWN EXPERIENCES.

Yesterday is history

Tomorrow is a mystery.

Today is a gift , That's why is called present.

Love is a game when a couple of blind people meet and start hurting each other.

If you want to understand a person, don't listen to his words, observe his behaviour.

Each one is responsible for what I say, but not for what others understand.

You will never have the relationship you want, but rather the one you build.

The lie wins party , and the truth wins the Game.

WISDOM BECOMES EVIL IF IT DOES NOT POINT TOWARDS VIRTUE

Never argue with a superior, you run the risk of being fake right.

Life is not always warns, but always teaches.

If someone treats you like you're worthless, BECOME nothing in their life, just leave.

It's okay to not have the right answers for everything , because instinct is how makes the right decision.

EVERY OPINION IS A VISION CHARGED WITH A PERSONAL HISTORY AND EVERY JUDGMENT IS A CONFESSION OF YOUR OWN EXPERIENCES.

Good people give you happiness, bad people give you lessons.

Do not confuse patience with submission, nor respect with fear.

THERE ARE PEOPLE WHO. First they tear you to pieces and then they ask you why You changed so much.

Don't get close to everyone , because just as there are trees that don't grow leaves to provide shade, there are people who, having hands , but don't know how to caress.

Don't waste your voice on those who only listen to respond and not to understand.

The Things more beautiful They are not perfect…They are Special.

WHO LIVES FROM PRIDE DIE OF LONELINESS.

REBUILD THE HERITAGE AND EDUCATION TO THE HEIR.

Wonderful people give you memories.

Friends are like books, you don't need have many, only the best.

By opening your eyes, you learn more than opening your mouth.

Don't look for stories with a happy ending.

Look for happiness without so many stories.

Offering friendship to someone who asks for love is like giving bread to someone who is dying of thirst.

Loneliness teaches us not to submit to any company.

True love is born from respect, not possession, because no one owns anyone.

When a tree falls, it makes a lot of noise, but when a tree grows, it is silent.

Spend your money on things you can buy and spend your time on things money can't buy.

If you punish your children they will lie to you, but if you correct them they will listen to you.

AS THE SPEED OF LIGHT IS FASTER THAN THAT OF SOUND.
There are people who may seem brilliant until you listen to what they say.

Stone Ship

A GOOD PERSON CANNOT BE RECOGNIZED BY THE NICE THINGS HE SAYS OR THE GOOD THINGS HE DOES.
A GOOD PERSON CAN BE RECOGNIZED BY THE TYPE OF ATMOSPHERE HE CREATES AROUND YOU.

Those who betrays you once, will betray you a thousand times, you don't need to drink the whole sea to realize that it is salty.

What makes us lose control of life is trying to fit in where we don't belong.

Don't choose to love someone who you like,

Choose someone who loves you.
Because the one you like excites you, but the one who loves you values you.

The worst prison is a home without peace.

If what you have is insufficient, even if you possess the entire world you will be miserable.

The only person you should compare yourself to is the person you were yesterday. That's the person you should surpass and look up to in order to be better.

Don't waste your time seeking the approval
of a world that crucified the only perfect man.

The musical one is of the Soul and Heals the wounds That cannot be seen.

The lie is an actor That needs too much noise to convince.

YOU NEVER LOSE, YOU ALWAYS LEARN.

Real failure lies not in lack of success, but in lack of trying.

In order to focus on who you are, stay away from people who always remind you of who you were,

Start from within and happiness will find its way out.

Knowledge with a positive attitude leads to success.

Who is not present in bad times, in good times is superfluous.

Who is not present in bad times, in good times is superfluous.

Results don't come overnight, but every day counts.

Who learn to observe acquire wisdom that no tie or appearance of piety could overcome.

Don't believe everything you hear, because often you judge what you don't see.

Wisdom is a leader That no tie or appearance of piety could overcome.

EVERY PAIN, HOW LONG AND SOMB IT MAY SEEM, HAS ITS DAWN.

He who judges without asking, condemns without knowing, and speaks without understanding.

Don't underestimate someone who doesn't talk much. While you're showing off, they're studying you.

The key to results is persistence.

THE HARDEST BRIDGE TO CROSS IS THE BRIDGE THAT SEPARATES WORDS FROM DEEDS.

We should eat breakfast like kings but dinner like beggars.

Who has no patience with small difficulties, fails with great problems.

Be careful what you tolerate, you're showing people how to treat you.

Every mistake is a lesson and every risk is a possibility.

Don't expect loyalty from someone who sells themselves for attention.

When in doubt, ask, don't assume.

We all have a past that haunts us.

Every mistake is a lesson and every risk is a possibility.

Wise people don't say everything they think, they only say what is necessary.

Never give your decision-making power to anyone, because they could become your owner.

It's easier to become an enemy of the one who tells the truth and a friend of the One who proves you right and lies to you.

If you chase butterflies they will escape, but if you grow a garden full of flowers the butterflies will come to you.

In success you see friends and in misfortune those who are of quality.

Avoid doing business with desperate people, those who argue about everything, and those who arrive late.

Wise minds are not affected by criticism or compliments.

Focus on the step you have to climb now, not the entire staircase.

He who learns to observe has no need to ask.

Your mouth is the first enemy of your life, if you want to live a long time, close it.

Don't waste your voice on deaf ears or your wisdom on closed minds.

The problem isn't giving too much, it's giving it to someone who doesn't deserve it.

Don't do too much for someone who would do little for you. Learn to measure your worth.

Don't speak ill of anyone, it's the best way to speak well of yourself.

No wind is favorable to those who do not know where they are going.

Don't betray to fit in, or be silent to please.

Don't argue about the truth with people addicted to lies.

When you are in doubt, ask, don't assume.

Never give your decision-making power to anyone, because they could become your owner.

SADNESS DOESN'T BRING ANYONE BACK.

From the abundance of the heart the mouth speaks.

Love without commitment is just a hobby with an expiration date.

Advice is valued and compassion is humbling.

When you are healthy you can have a thousand problems but when you are sick you only have one.

Asking questions is proof that you are thinking.

LUCK HAPPENS WHEN PREPARATION MEETS OPPORTUNITY.

I'm going to fly," said the worm and everyone laughed,
(except the butterfly).

Without past there is no present.
The rules are made at convenience.
Calm comes from certainty and taking care of yourself is called pleasure.

There are situations in life that occur without warning. Friends meet in the most difficult moments. But to overcome an illness all that remains is to find oneself face to face and attain peace.

The years we celebrate are actually the years we no longer have.

Failure is dressing up a guilt as mistake.
The mistake can be improved but guilt is an emotion that could end in failure.

In a romantic relationship we look at what is missing and we will accept alms to build misery and suffering, but true love has no needs, it only has a behaviour that accompanies, nourishes, inspires, grows and develops in harmony.

Words are the same ladder that you climb and which you will later descend.

PAIN IS ALSO SONG WHEN YOU CAN NO LONGER TALK ABOUT PAIN.

The person who wants bad things cannot grasp precious things.
Fools emphasise their dishonour and wise people emphasise their charm and honour.

Do not harm those around you because circumstances can change at any time, a tree can give a thousand matches but one match alonecan destroy a thousand trees.

When you reach an age, you turn your back on the mirror and without wasting time, enjoy what you have experienced and learned, because there are no more stories to believe in, only breathing the wind that accompanies the sun and the moon that are grateful for existence.

The parrot talks a lot and flies little. The eagle does not say a single word and is in the heavens.

If you fall in love with its flowers and not its roots, I ask you, what will you do in autumn?

Every lie that is told will have a debt with the truth.

Healing cannot be cured from the place where someone has become sick.

Every lie that is told will have a debt with the truth.

Falling in love is a chemical event related to the lack of clarity towards oneself, that is why we fall in love in adolescence up to the age of 25 and from the age of 40, although falling in love is not planned, it only happens and despite being beautiful, it is an encounter with our happiness. But an enigma says: HAPPY PEOPLE AFTER THEY PASS THE STAGE OF ADOLESCENCE !! THEY NEVER FALL IN LOVE!! They only live, enjoying life's decisions together.

Healing cannot be achieved from the place where we have become sick.

Our brain is designed for survival and we are responsible for training it for happiness.

Never let yourself be controlled by people, money or the past.

Be like coins that show their face on one side and their value on the other.

There are codes that are respected and lines that are not crossed.

When the bird is alive it eats the ants but when the bird dies the ants eat the bird.

Women of this generation should not expect flowers because we are in a generation of likes.

A donkey can pretend to be a horse but sooner or later it brays.

Power and greatness are ephemeral.

Don't argue about truths with those addicted to lies.

When you build yourself in silence, people don't know where to attack.

A wise man said that if you don't trust your boyfriend, don't get married, because how are you going to trust your husband?

A person cannot be the shadow of another person.

To grow you have to fly alone or in good company because there is no bird that carries a seed or a branch unless it is to make a nest.

The universe does not speak languages, it only speaks energy.

If you fall in love with its flowers and not its roots, I ask you, what will you do in autumn?

When you see a new world every day, then you will hear the indicated path.

We must wish the One who acts evilly luck because sooner or later he will need it.

Returning to the answer is a decision that separates how to continue searching for the answer!!

The bad and the good are united but if we complain to any of them we will not be able to find a solution.

We are like the strings of a guitar, we are all united but not mixed, each of us has a different melody and without trying to override anyone we must enjoy harmony and with variety enjoy the differences.
Because the world is beautiful thanks to the differences.

The most beautiful minerals are hidden from human sight so as not to be pursued.

The beauty of the human as it is in sight is pursued to praise and among humans they are judged by appearances, that is why it is difficult to value the human mineral, that is – actions.

If in a couple the challenges lead to discussion it is because they are seeking a solution to the path and if there is silence between challenges it is because their time has come to cut paths.

The woman who makes her own money is with the man she really wants, not the one she needs.

Love is not someone you are with but it is someone with whom you can be yourself.

In the dawn after darkness there is no possibility of hiding.

Those who have values do not find it difficult to make decisions.

Philosophy is not to produce philosophers it is to shake consciences.

The Moon teaches us that it is not necessary to always be whole to shine.

The government does not want a nation of intelligent people, but rather a nation of obedient workers.

When you are in love, don't make any decisions. Because when you are in love, you enjoy the moment and when you make decisions, you enjoy life.

Where the spark of repentance is felt, there is forgiveness.
Because there is no restoration without repentance.

When you don't know what you want you don't value what you have.
Progress in silence because your success will make noise.

If in a situation you don't know what decision to make, don't make any, because it's better not to play with the unknown.

Most of the things that are said are not done, so it is better to remain silent.

To correct someone, the best way is to make them see that the darkness that stood in their way is not in accordance with their light.

It is easier to overcome a temptation if you move away in time.

No one changes by suffering, only by choice.

They say that the world can give many rewards, but only God gives the prize.

When someone ignores or doesn't pay attention to your messages, that's already a message.

If you are an optimist, you can dream without losing hope and love without fear.

Just as the footprints of each foot that steps on the sand of the sea are distinct... so may your life bear the imprint of your intentions.

Why do you want your ears to be sweetened if they make your life bitter?

If someone doubts that they love you, it is because they do not love you.

Attention to someone you care about is not like a suit that hangs in a closet and is only picked up when it needs to be worn.

No one is as empty as those who fill themselves with themselves.
Under the hand bridge the water runs and splashes while the night and day are lost.

Love goes slowly and when no one takes it, it disappears with the wind like water that runs through the river and takes away the dreams of the wind, but my quiet love is lit again by seeing you.

When you don't have to beg for attention and you don't feel invisible, you will have found the right partner.

Friendship is like a market of illusions and like an experience that possibly changes with the twists and turns that the situation takes.

Society is the certainty of the autopilot to sell oneself the will that was imposed by the academic curriculum.

If there is someone in a war who is discouraging, then let him go home. Because battles are won by encouraging each other.

Even if someone despises you, the value of what you are worth remains only in you.

Because what you want for yourself is in what you give to others.

A good doctor is one who sees all his patients as children.

When someone doesn't value what they have, it's because they don't know what they want.

Poor is he who deceives and destroys another because when he finishes doing evil, his own will begin.

When you don't know what you want you don't value what you have.
If you are criticised for what you do, it is because you are on the right path, because only those from whom you stole their attention criticised.

Progress in silence because your success will make noise.

He who is not grateful for the little will be less grateful for the much.
Who looks for you only when they need you... doesn't deserve to find you.

In the journey of Life there is something imaginative between logic and obedience where using philosophy you could take a moment to reflect that we are so different and yet so similar.

FORGET THE EVIL THEY DID TO YOU.
BUT NOT THE LESSON YOU LEARNED.

Yesterday I thought I was intelligent and I wanted to change the world but today I am wise and I only want to change myself.

IV. RAIN OF LEAVES

When climbing a mountain we can see that the most visible is nature and the least visible are humans. Because nature feeds on itself and humans want to feed on each other.

Try not to spread thorns along the way, because you may have to return barefoot.
When you have the Sun inside, it doesn't matter if it rains outside!
You always shine!

A PERSON WHO HAS LOST EVERYTHING WILL ALSO LOSE FEAR.

AT THE END OF THE ROAD WE ALL SHARE THE SAME DESTINY.
A bird that was always locked up, even if you open the gate will never escape and the human who is a happy slave will do the same.

The person with a happy essence, even if a narcissist, turns it off when they get rid of the narcissism, will return to their essence.
(Because whoever was will always be again)
And he who fits one hole into another will be the same one who will fall into his own hole.

Studies provide knowledge and imagination wisdom.

The intuitive mind is a sacred gift and the rational mind is a faithful servant.

Success and failure in our society has become like a people's measuring value.
BUT!!?

Rich people buy time and poor people buy things.
Ambitious people buy skills and knowledge and lazy people buy distractions.

Success and failure is part of positive competition because it teaches us to be more reproductive and competent.

If you look at the body you live in a sensitive world,
but if you direct your gaze towards the soul you live in an intelligible world. Because true beauty does not reside in the body. The proof is in the story of the philosopher Narcissus who loved himself so much that when he looked at his image in a lake he wanted to kiss him so he fell into the water and drowned.
That's where the word narcissist comes from.

The winner in this life is the one who defeats himself in his laziness, his fear and his insecurity.

We live in a society that has turned people's image into a spectacle.
Because instead of experiencing things we consume illusions of things.

Art is the philosophical work of music and paradise.
A cycle of identity reveals that to be born something new the old must die.
The Resurrection leaves us the sign of the three holy days – the crucifixion purifies the soul when the ego dies, the divine is the glow devoured by fire, Immortality goes hand in hand with rebirth, the union of brilliance lights up with a clap of wings, Glory builds its nest where it rises from the ashes, during a flight a flight distance meets closeness.
The seed of the cosmic fire is the eternal that represents that every end is a new beginning.

IT IS BETTER TO BE PATIENT AND POWERFUL AND BETTER TO CONTROL YOURSELF THAN WANT TO CONQUER A CITY.

If in a couple the challenges lead to discussion it is because they are seeking a solution to the path and if there is silence between challenges it is because their time has come to cut paths.*

He who tolerates disorder to avoid war will first have disorder and then war.

Our heart is like the earth and from the depth of the heart the mouth speaks.

If your star is off, don't turn off someone else's.

What you think about others is in yourself.

He who doesn't know what he wants sometimes loses what he has and then discovers that he has lost exactly what he wanted.

Trust is like a glass and if it breaks it will never be the same even if it can be glued back together.

If you want to know someone, give them power for a while. But never give your power to decide to anyone because they could become your owner.

In the world there are two types of people: weak and strong.

In life, there are people angry with you because they threw dirt at you and you grew flowers.

The vulture likes the corpses
AND
The eagle chooses its food.
AND
He who kisses the pig's feet will always find himself with pigs.

The more knowledge you have, the less you need to talk.

He who really wants to change a situation acts in silence and he who just wants a change only complains saying it's complicated.

The decision is up to each one to crawl or fly.

If in a couple explanations are asked from a problem, it is because there is an interest in staying together.
If problems are ignored in a couple, it is because they are looking for a clean slate.

The weak ones are dedicated to doing what others doing and saying and the strong ones are dedicated to pursuing their desires.

The weak human being is the only animal that needs a master to live.

Discipline is having a trained mind that controls your life in order to succeed.

He who tolerates disorder to avoid war.
First there will be disorder and then war.

Running away from what hurts makes you suffer even more. Don't run away from what hurts until you heal.

ONLY HUMANS
EXPECT CHANGES, DESTROY AND COMPLAIN

If in a relationship you start with obligations you will end up with humiliation.

Most of the things that are said are those that are not done.
That's why a saying goes:
FROM SAID TO DEED THERE IS A LONG WAY.
So, WHAT IS SEEN IS NOT ASKED.

If your partner tells you – I should check my calendar to see when I can see you. Answer him, BETTER STAY WITH ALEXA. Laralaralaralalala.

Don't erase any day from your life. The beautiful days have given you peace, the bad days have given you experience, the worst days have brought you wisdom.

There are people who don't even know what they have until they lose it.
He who does not know how to appreciate the little in the much makes you beg.

There are scars that are not visible on the outside but bleed on the inside.
To win it is important to make others win, therefore we receive what we attract.

TO LEARN

Heal an injured dog and he will love you for a lifetime.

Heal an injured human and they will end up demanding more attention from you.

If the man falls through the eyes and the woman through the ears, but both fall through the mouth, then what is the disadvantage of the nose for??

A son asked the Father, when is Christmas Eve?
And the father answered Christmas Eve is when no one goes to bed without dinner.

If your presence is not going to bring me happy company then do not deprive me of my solitude.

We live in a society where attention seems like a dream stranded on the other side of the river because a price is put on everything.

Sheep and humans are the only animals that need a ruler to guide their lives.

Just as eternal love could end in one night, great friends can also become great strangers.

WHAT IS DESTROYED BY ACTIONS,
IS NEVER REPAIRED WITH WORDS.

Just as eternal love could end in one night, great friends can also become great strangers.
A narcissist can hurt you as much as take away your smile, take away your identity and make you feel that without him you are worthless. YES, I confirmed it to be true.
Narcissists don't need a partner, they need victims.

A narcissist, if you are not in his favour, can hit you and the next day make you believe that his attitude was caused by your fault and not because he wanted to do it. A NARCISSIST NEVER ASKS FORGIVENESS.

When you free yourself from the clutches of a narcissist, you should heal your wounds in solitude otherwise you would affect your next partners who are innocent, with your scars.

There are wounds that instead of opening your skin, they open your eyes.

If someone doesn't allow you entry, never beg for their attention!! Just clean your feet and leave.
Because each one joins with his equal.

If you don't let go of the past, with what hand will you hold your glass to toast the future?

Once upon a time there was a good wolf who was mistreated by all the lambs,

There was also a bad prince, a beautiful witch and an honest pirate.
All those things once upon a time when I dreamed of a world upside down.

The bad guy flees without anyone chasing him

but the righteous is confident like a LION.

When the government knows the people's questions, the government becomes the oracle of salvation, so that the puppets of society have the answers without their strings getting crossed.

Don't go looking for anything about changes in the past because it has nothing new to tell you.

Studying yourself is the most difficult art.

Lessons are better learned with joy than with obligations.

Loyalty means respect in absence and presence.

To everything that remains peaceful, add distance.

Motivation begins when you move to action.

The path is made by walking and if you are afraid in the process it is because you are doing well, because he who overcomes fear will cross the obstacle.

The past is not behind us but it is also ahead of us.

OF ALL THE THINGS YOU WEAR, YOUR ATTITUDE IS THE MOST IMPORTANT.

V. PHILOSOPHY OF THE UNIVERSE

In this stone ship, ice and water are like personality.

Don't be afraid of loneliness because only through it will you know yourself.

Humans are the only animal that cuts trees and makes paper on which they write. (We must take care of the trees.)

Forgiving is like going to the past and coming back to healing, and safe for the present.

You can buy what has a price, but what has value must be conquered.

The moon falls in love with the stars but always keeps its distance.

Power may lose its empire, but it strengthens it, it always gains a temple.

What we think is not always a fact but a possibility.

A memory is an emotional proposal with the moment.

There is nothing good or bad except thought.

Intelligence is a gift and honesty is a decision.

The new generation joined the shift from duty to pleasure.

The barrier that affects well-being is overcome by challenging the inner critic.

The doctor thinks he knows everything but cannot guarantee a cure.

A healer guarantees healing but knows nothing but intuition.

Revenge is like a mirage that ends like Achilles.

Justice is the tool of the strongest that prevails over the weakest.

The word is like a drug, can cure or poison.

Indifference is the best weapon to defeat the enemy.

Love begins when falling in love ends.

The pillars in a couple are loyalty and trust.

Habit for emotions is a beggar for convenience of desolation.

Stone Ship

Trust in time that can give sweet solutions to bitter difficulties.

Sometimes you have to get lost in order to find yourself.

Trying to escape from a thought, attention becomes stronger and repeats it.

Don't argue with someone that their TV is bigger than their library.

The greatest moments are felt when an adult becomes a child.*

How beautiful are those people who, when faced with a tide, don't let go of your hand.

If you love something, release it if it comes back to you it is because it is part of your destiny and if it doesn't come back it doesn't belong to you.

The heart is born free and we should not chain it.

When a child gives a drawing he is giving a little piece of his soul.

When the moon sets behind fear, the stars cry coming down from the sky.

We live in a society like headless chickens.

Behind bars freedom is valued and behind illness health is valued.

A good doctor is one who sees all his patients as children.

Our attitude should always be like a candle that shines upward.

Meditation connects us with the joy of existing and the joy of being.

Philosophy does not provide answers, it only suggests questions.

VI. LEARN TO FLY

In our selfish age fear and lament are defended.
As the leaves in a whirlpool scatter in different directions.

We grow when the search for the other is replaced by searching for oneself.

It is not so important to be perfect, the most valuable thing is to be authentic,

Trying to escape from a thought, attention becomes stronger and repeats it again.

By paying attention to a thought you strengthen it.

There is no such thing as school failure, only those who evaluate fail.

Motivation and surprise activate attention.

If someone lies or harms another, their virtue is harmed.

Happiness is in virtue and not in pleasures.

Learning with joy is learning with confidence.

Fear is individual, joy is collective.

Charity does not solve problems, only education does.

Seeing each moment of the here and now, will create the next.

Learning is the prize at the door of opportunity.

Obligation comes first before pleasure.

Talent develops by focusing on the horizon.

Being constantly happy in possessing is associated with desiring more of the useless than the useful.

Destructive fury is an emotion that loses meaning and turns into misery.

Angry people want to show how powerful they are.

People in love want to show how powerful you are.

If you want to see something real you first have to believe it.

Stone Ship

Bitterness submerges in competition with challenge.

The proudest and most satisfied man is but a nameless beggar,

Curiosity attracts amazement to the viewer of interest.

Repentance is not in tears, it is in the change of attitude,

Elegance is in the attitude and beyond fear is hope,

Abuse goes as far as there is someone who allows it.

Obligation comes before pleasure.

Emotion is faster than reason and to know how to love you have to know how to understand.

The intention carries many hidden lies but the word of the fact puts the soul on a pedestal.

Life is a purpose to illuminate so that others can shine.

Easy times create weak people and weak people create difficult times.
Difficult times create strong people, strong people create easy times.

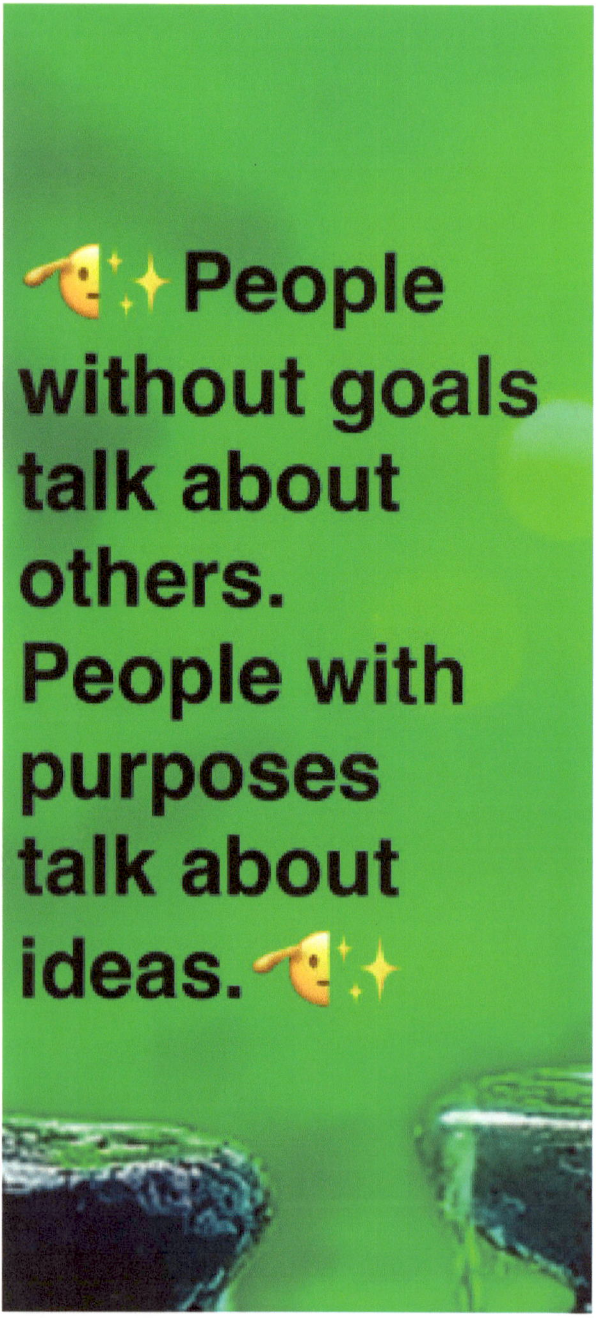

Olivia Conde

🫡✨People without goals talk about others. People with purposes talk about ideas.🫡✨

Stone Ship

> **SUCCESS IS NOT ACHIEVED BY SPEED IT IS ACHIEVED BY PERSEVERANCE.** 🫵✨

FLYING BELOW THE RADAR

The Therapy of social life leaves a mystery of Health prize,
Experimental therapies are like heroes on the verge of collapse,
The past is a mental ghost that must be avoided to avoid criticism,
Upon awakening from the dream of time we enter the path of the present that never dies,
Living trapped in the inner purpose connects us with the brilliance of the journey towards oneself,
When the mind controls life, conflicts are inevitable,
The quality of the form is when you know the truth and it will set you free,
Fears disappear when you have the courage to overcome them,
The essence of all things is emptiness like the shape of a musical note meeting infinity,
Nothingness is the appearance of the unmanifested in a world perceived by the senses,
Space contains existence but its existence is not known,
We live in a physical and a psychological dimension and we are only looking for the end of duality,
Every addiction reaches a point that brings to light the unhappiness that reaches inside,
To live in the surrender of love we must abstain from the absence of judgements,
Happiness depends on emotions that are seen as positive, but peace does not have dictatorships in dependencies,
To exist it is necessary to evolve, the most important thing is not to allow the drama of the past to obscure the present,
When you seek happiness through things, only temporary satisfaction will come,
Joy is an identity that has learned to adapt without offering resistance to what it is,
A hero runs to try and not to criticise.

THE ECONOMIC TIGER

We are climbing towards the limit of the non-real trying to explain the labels,
The murky health fight is blaming the quality of the air we breathe,
By sealing big victories, marketing creates gigantic businesses,
Bringing heaven down to earth, vitamin pills are created for the lack of nature,
Selling Health to healthy people and the consumer believes they have premium Health,
By bombarding the immune system the patient becomes vulnerable,
The nightmare of becoming rich is tied to the belief of immortality,
Psychological illness is the great loot of pharmaceutical companies,
The trade war is the strategy that distracts social attention,
The first world is looking for connection with nature and is living in a trance,
By marketing ancestral plants, the business process is exploited,
We are consumers of meditation capsules, sounds and conferences,
Good laboratories are presenting images of perfection,
The evil pharmaceutical companies are transforming new resources,
Trying to explain things, the unreal becomes part of the real,
Guided by labels we live between a personal struggle,
The doctors are visualised with a humiliating defeat symbol,
Social health is disguised as a rainbow on the horizon,
We are in a world transformed into opium with some kind of painkiller,
The snake sheds its skin to become fatter.

IS SOMETHING REAL?

Confusing money with wealth, anxiety joins emotional fear,
Fanatical self-help books are offering miraculous works,
Living in a pyramid scheme with a mediocre rise and a fall with complaints,
Wealth is a great fantasy transformed into almost a religion,
Trying to climb the social pyramid the path becomes a fairy tale,
Between business and talent there is a secret giant,
Consumption and freedom, two products that are tied to the new generation,
The pleasure that is linked to an empty life and is chained to a time missile,
A bubble of fear captures the future of the human who tries to escape,
In the invisible cage passion dies in the sands of time,
The fantasy of power lives frustrated in a dictatorship of pleasure,
Life linked to inflation has implanted an identity crisis,
A myth of evolution lives in the walls of competition,
Artificial brides are the merchandise that quenches the fear of old age,
The magic of surviving becomes a combat united with necessity,
Society is schooled to see the world without its own eyes,
The behaviour of society is modded to follow a dictatorship of control,
Identity threat first calculates and then exists,
Fear is ahead because the news controls the unconscious.

THE CULTURE OF WASTE

The golden temple seeks happiness but lives in greed,
We are paralysed by information saturation as divine punishment,
The opinion of critics is a pleasant stimulus that is measured in recognition,
At high speed, decisions are a marginalised ghost,
The fantasy of progress weakens society with violence,
A mouse maze visualises reaching the
next cheese,
The shadow of futurism haunts consciousness everywhere,
The revolution becomes a well-being between failures and voids,
In search of progress, quick answers are created to eliminate doubts,
The latest cry of fashion no longer has quality, only pleasure to consume,
What is disposable is no longer repaired, it is only replaced,
The desires for consumption can be intense but they fail to achieve any goal in life,
Having without measures is only a fleeting pleasure that continues wanting more desires,
A stimulus that never stops is a distraction but also contains free will,
Choosing the intensity of the sublime over the intensity of saturation is in the hands of the audience,
The mountain of materialism is the failure of equality,
The appreciation of life lies in giving up knowing everything but being able to understand it,
The eternal search that satisfaction can be reversible.

🫴✨**The true reward of inheriting a great fortune is not in what you earn, it is in who you become.**🫴✨

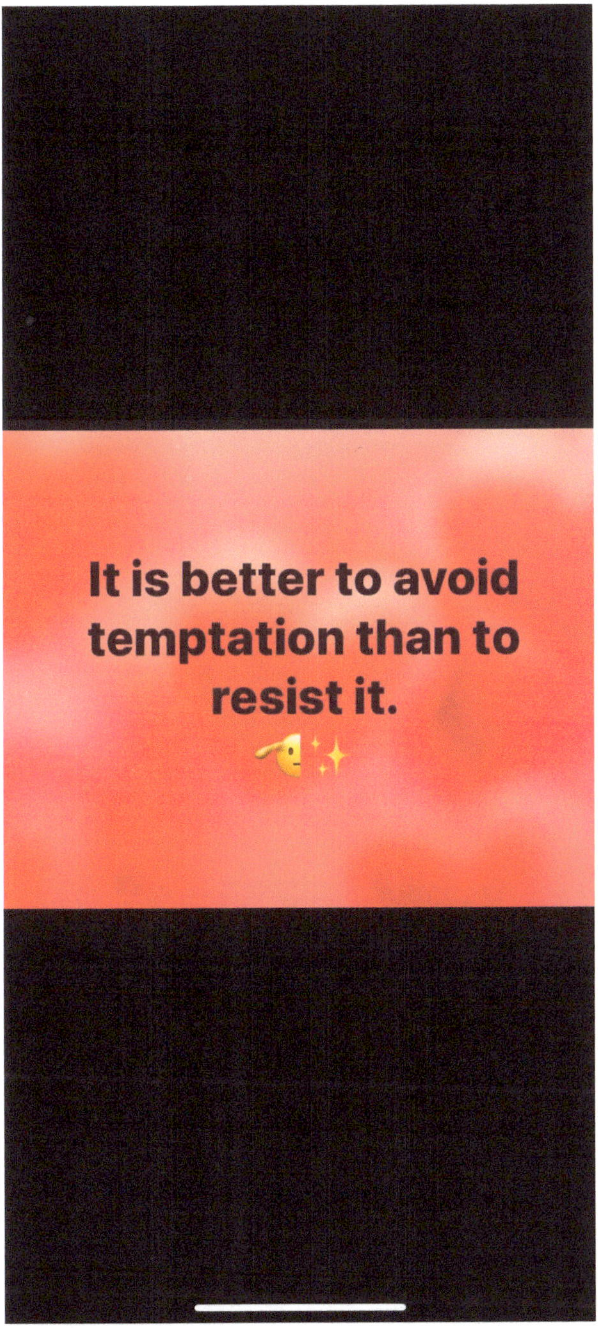

Olivia Conde

> It is better to avoid temptation than to resist it.

IN A WORLD OF BUBBLES

Predatory ants can dominate slave ants,
Smart people know what they want and wise people know what they don't want.
The invasion of digital nomads shows a world empty of empathy,
A cynical society lives in the false revolution of reality,
Family disintegration is dividing into individualism,
The punishment of desire turns the mind into a noisy storm,
A mouse maze becomes empires that become states,
Born from machines but produced from flesh we are conquered by a process of digital biology,
Dreaming with open eyes behind every nightmare there is a doubt,
He who is able to explain everything is no good at explaining anything, just as he who is a friend of everyone is a friend of no one,
The health factory creates patients to isolate and by reading their records they will be medicated,
Adult's broken toys seek repair at doctor's appointment consultations,
Hard work is not the key to success, the trick is to feel that you enjoy what you do,
Men with the personality of eternal children are blocking the freedom of decisions,
The fantasy of power is a saturation that manipulates the stimulation of the brain,
We almost live in an illusion trying to copy the actions of others to compete instead of living,
The emptiness of the soul is the melancholy that awaits the meeting of the spirit,
On the horizon there is a light that can extinguish the darkness.

THE OTHER SIDE OF THE SKY

In a white room without windows a number called time confuses the seasons,
The aroma of seasons is immersed in flags of obligations,
A desert devours the blank pages of the scriptures,
The conquerors no longer leave statues behind the clock,
The temporal beings create a ghostly pyramid,
Digital lines pass through and are recorded on a hard drive,
Looking towards other stars the memories are not assured,
Opinions become philosophy that calms oblivion,
Time and colours are measured in reflections of thought,
Habits are a daily conquest for freedom,
Intelligence is before the matter that owes thought,
The realm of thought says that what is bound on earth will be bound in heaven,
Everything that is sown in the mind is reaped in the packaging,
When thought is modded, the secret of attraction is catalysed,
Intense fury renews inner wisdom to remember love,
To learn to live again you have to renounce the identity of beliefs,
The mind must be strengthened from within to control the wind,
To reach the knowledge of the other shore there is only one bridge,
Listen with your ears and speak with your heart.

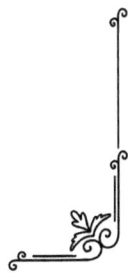

THE MEMORIES OF THE SOUL

Music relaxes the soul in the magic of thought,
The best fast to cleanse the mind is to erase negative thoughts,
To cleanse the body temple, prayer is linked to medication,
The harmony of food begins by emitting peace before eating it,
The journey of wisdom joins the body as well as the spirit,
The mute space emits powers that unite lines of separation,
Thought waves attract what is far and near,
Vibration always unites the equality of the same waves,
The mind with many tonalities must rise to higher chambers of the negative,
Positive thinking elevates the upper chamber of the mental abode,
The enemies of man are only those of his own mind,
When the imagination is put into practice, the mystery is awakened,
Learning is a garden where prosperity expands,
The future must become the present so that what you believe is created,
Through imagination one can escape from the slavery of reason,
The highways of the inner world separate when adulthood arrives,
By surrendering intuition to the divine treasure, mental poverty is overcome,
Destroy all addiction so that the invisible becomes visible,
Faith is the fortune that awakens the imagination.

THE DIVINE TREASURE

Both rivers and mountains are inside the being that has life,
Heaven and earth are united to feel the inner life,
The very bright light hides deep shadows where thought rules our life,
When the night goes away, the dawn reveals its nature.
The universal spirit is immersed in the force of the mind,
The body is the clothing of the soul that flows through thought,
What you have to learn first you have to live it to see results,
The story of the castaway says trust more in what you feel than in what you think,
Faith is the soul of thought that obtains the results of imagination,
Decisions are the magic wand that shapes the future,
Within each human is the joy that orders the stars,
He who conquers others is strong but he who conquers himself is powerful,
The mind is illuminated by the eternal sun and the body becomes the sacred temple of the spirit,
The ego is the social mask but the spirit is not afraid of criticism,
From the word the event is manifested and from intuition the mystery,
Happiness is an inner journey that shows the mastery of life,
To get along well you don't need to have the same ideas, just the same respect.
In the light of the moon the fireflies shine like God's treasure,
The new era will dawn in prosperity.

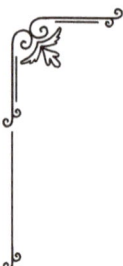

🫠✨Fly high when you hear criticism about you, because remember that reptiles do not reach heights, they only crawl.🫠✨

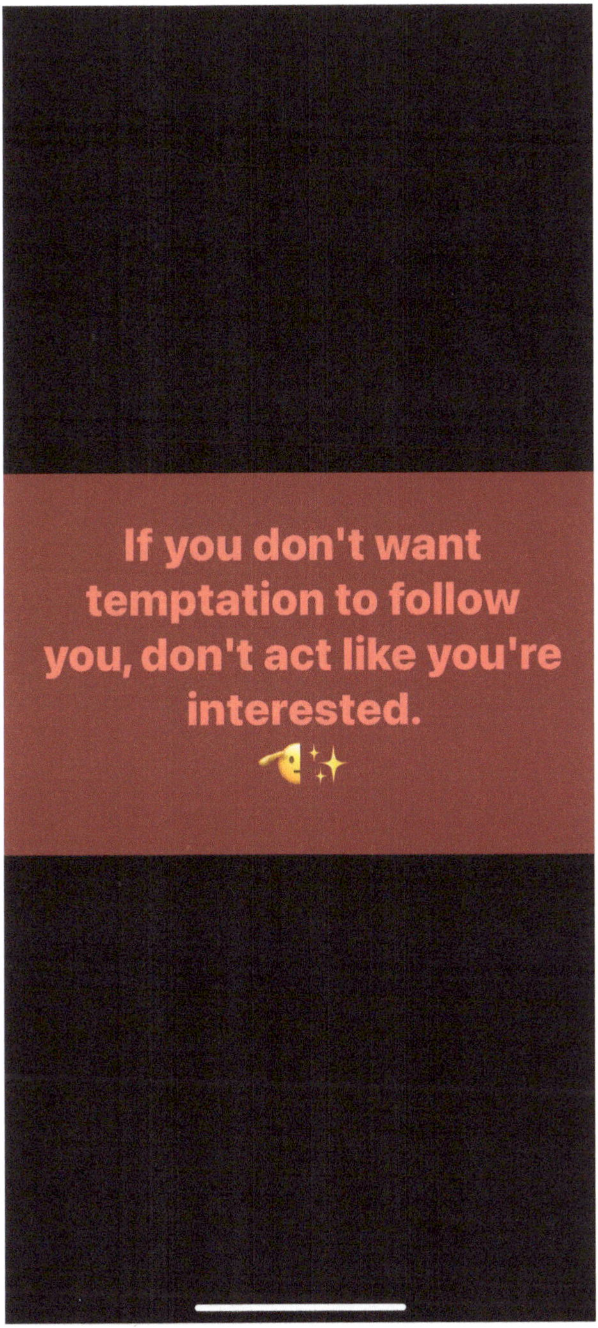

Olivia Conde

> **If you don't want temptation to follow you, don't act like you're interested.** 🫵✨

THE WAY OF PEACE

A bird in its nest does not fear the storm because its pillars connect with the tree,
Follow the current that already knows its path where the spirit is sought and found,
Thought changes your destiny just as grass can be changed into wheat,
Affirmation shapes the body like the potter shapes clay,
Prosperity is success crowned with confidence,
The wise builder shapes morality for sure triumph,
Intelligence is transmuted into principles with transformations of powerful effect,
The secret of moving forward always lies in starting,
In the present is the future where decisions are the path of tomorrow,
A true decision is based on the talent of the action,
By exploring success, answers are found in action,
You get more from experience than from gratitude,
We learn from mistakes and by facing fear, confidence is nourished.
Criticism is dangerous with useless compensation,
To the same extent that we gain approval we have condemnation,
The only way to win an argument is to avoid it.
Appreciation comes from the heart while flattery comes from the mouth,
Knowing how to listen is an art where silence creates loyalty and company,
When music is good it never gets old.

THE SPIRITUAL SUBSTANCE

The divine treasure of life is linked to the encounter of the spirit,
The eternal healing substance is behind the matter,
When the mind looks at the spirit it will keep the body healthy,
The physical body must be cared for with love because it is the temple of the spirit,
In mental silence the substance of the spirit's capacity increases and there will always be abundance,
By getting rid of the envelopes that bind and hold us back, the secret of freedom will be born,
The self is the character that thinks full of ties but the true being is the one that is free of ties,
Leaving aside the gift of appearance, the inner child shows its brilliance,
The will can dominate everything within its reach,
Necessity is a rival and an obstacle to the will,
Love and hate are opposite poles but the will is united to the spirit,
A living dead is a ghost that is trapped in garments of pleasures,
Illusion is master of opposites and slave of the obedient,
Mental states are like the waves of the ocean but they always return to the sea,
Consciousness is the secret place that receives the order from the inside to the outside,
We do not suffer for what others do, only for what we reap,
Free will lies in the choice of thought,
By removing the veils that hinder us, the light will come and shine brighter and stronger,
The spirit is life and health in eternal healing.

GOLDEN CIRCLE

Art shows the promise that exists after life,
The place of no return where infinity is found in the works,
A child prepares his soul by trying adult shoes,
Dreaming when contemplating a flower for the first time, new illusions are born,
A sculpture tells you stories when you look at it,
In search of lost time you can see hidden landscapes,
In art, the feeling is the meaning that invades you inside,
The dome of temples welcomes the emotion to invade the sorrows,
When experiencing punishment and salvation is the mirror of shipwreck,
Discipline defeats intelligence but a manual is cultural,
The code of honour is a challenge like a lunar meeting,
We are as clear as the wind but separated by qualifications,
Nobility ends when we put the identity of beings as figures,
Never give your heart to anyone because you are the only one who can take care of it,
The eyes, nose and ears are for everyone but the mouth is only for the word,
The moon behind the invisible curtain does not show anyone its hidden side,
The virginity of the forest hides the beauty of resurrection,
The samurai chased the dragon and generations pass on integrity,
By recognising your mistakes you can be reborn from the ashes,
Creativity is important but pride can kill it.

CHALLENGE RAIN

Destiny goes in the direction of the apes who are fighting with sticks,
We live in the era where the image is worth more than the word.
The simulation highway is floating under a Rev magnet,
When nothing material ties you, you can live your own adventure,
The empire of short illusions piles up photographs for fear of maturing,
The cultural battle is like a pandemic that divides us like the flu,
Who lives between the difference finds the freedom of day and night,
Fasting is a great catalyst to remember messages from the guides,
Mental noise does not allow us to meet the inner being,
Time and mind are inseparable while the unity of silence is the magic of the present,
When you trap the pain and make it non-existent you can dominate it and it will not be able to survive,
Consciousness transmutes each situation but unconsciousness creates it,
The language of heaven is something latent that does not fight with darkness or pain,
To release the destructive you only have to observe it to attract the impulse of the alignment of control,
Thoughts are controlled with the energy of silence,
Any action is better than no action even if it has some error because in it you always learn something,
The law of success involves overcoming fear.

🫠✨**The difference between feeling Sorrow and feeling pain is that sorrow can be optional but pain is inevitable.** 🫠✨

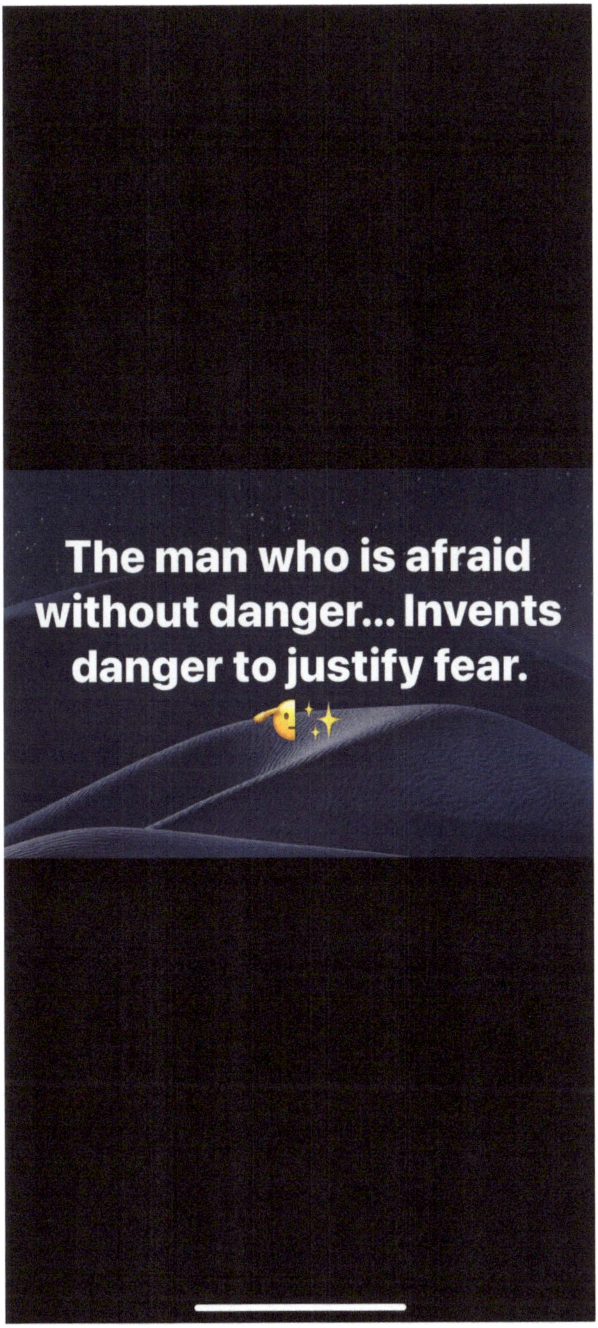

Olivia Conde

> The man who is afraid without danger... Invents danger to justify fear.

CAUGHT IN A STORM

Thought without words is an art and language is the limit of reality,
The limit of the caverns closes in a circle of curiosities,
The test tube theory is a breeding ground for research,
Celestial gods create their species where the eternal lives,
Creating experiments, time passes in new civilisations,
Without knowing the bottom of the sea, space is the new unknown,
Time is transformed into a map of futuristic dimensions,
The utopia of intelligence enters into the theory of unidentified objects,
The success of villains collapses the ability to expand in your system,
The deck of cards says that what you expect comes from experience,
Wanderers in the sea of life are carried away on bitter currents,
The revolution of identity with the spirit comes when man is ready,
The divine spark connects the sacred flame with a potential god,
The changes come to forget the matter and reconnect with the spirit,
The promises of life are achieved by defeating experiences,
He who has Faith has power and can never be defeated,
The slavery of the mind lives in the external consciousness,
Enlightenment is found when the thinker connects with the inner silence,
To enjoy the rainbow you don't chase it, you just observe it,
He who pursues love in others loses the freedom to enjoy himself,
Romantic love in practice does not exist.

THE INVISIBLE THREAT

Humanity adapts with easy answers and empty promises,
The refuge of the everyday is a marketing holocaust,
The villain disguised as weak is in continuous surveillance,
Nuclear energy goes through shields and armour and is used for great fear,
An unexpected myth is the destiny where your appearance is unpredictable,
There are situations that can arrive without being prepared or giving prior notice,
The invisible trap of power is reinforced while the truth is putting on its shoes,
The shortcut to false happiness is a design of dark silence,
Fear is no excuse to abandon a drifting boat, you just have to adjust the sails,
The miser makes himself and those around him miserable,
No one changes because they suffer, the executioner and the one who sentences are in the same position,
Happiness is in starting a blank page in history,
Stay with someone who understands and supports your madness,
Curiosity attracts amazement and the viewer of interest,
The authority of the past was gained by imposing fear, that of the present is based on manipulation,
Intuition is the wise word of the soul and spirit that connects with Faith,
Faith is having the certainty that something that has not happened is going to happen,
The best way to defeat the enemy is to ignore him,
Surprise activates emotion and whoever learns to die learns to live,
The lilies grow without tangling like the lantern that passes through the fog.

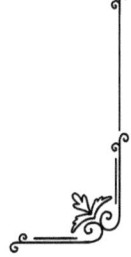

CIRCLE OF FIRE

An unknown future comes to life and puts us on alert,
Collective engineering isolates society in discretion,
The inexperienced influences the life of the expert with democracy of votes,
Riddles are a path with as many probabilities as there are experiments,
The dark face of the pseudo psychologist is like a silent instinct,
The old generation was educated to fear more than to learn,
The depression of work carries a void of great mistakes,
The search for sadness is like drawing strength from the winds,
Punishment is a vicious circle that leaves suffering and does not fix mistakes,
The justification should be changed to seeking an understanding,
It is a parade of condemnations that only distances the truth from the lie,
The slave of the perfect can be broken in manipulation,
The domain has reins that puts discussions on feelings,
In an eternal state of alarm he lives in predictions of the end of the world,
Trying to get out of the sedentary life, one seeks salvation in the executioner,
Pain takes over people's minds and dominates them,
When pain speaks it is a cliff of fire that reaches the heart,
The tiger that looks like a cat hides in darkness,
The commander of races invades with division of strife,
The small print of the contract makes you a prey to manipulation,
A trick disguise can exploit weaknesses and strengths,
Temptation with sharp fangs cannot see obstacles.

BEINGS OF THE SKY

Telepathy connects with the universe by stripping the disguise of truth,
The intrigue satisfies the lie and respect is for those who deserve it,
Looking at love from side to side, history becomes immortal,
Elegance is in the attitude and beyond fear is hope,
In this majestic flight the answers begin from thought,
We are embarking on new journeys with a sigh in eternity,
Happiness flows in the adventure between the light of hopes,
Inner freedom transcends by clinging to a goal that you are inspired to achieve,
The mirage of knowing how to love is not to grant but to transform,
We are all pilgrims to reach the will to believe in creating,
Leaving the comfort zone attracts the confidence of navigating uncertainty,
By embracing fragility, an illusion of hope is born,
The world of ideas is a dimension that uncovers invisible veils,
The stream of divine supply clothes us without need,
The abundance of thought is rich in the treasures of prosperity,
The human must love the earth including the heavens,
Where ignorance speaks, intelligence is silent,
A person's worst enemy is hate,
Knowing how to love is being able to see what the other sees,
Love is not sought, it is shared,
He who is not fit to serve is not fit to live.

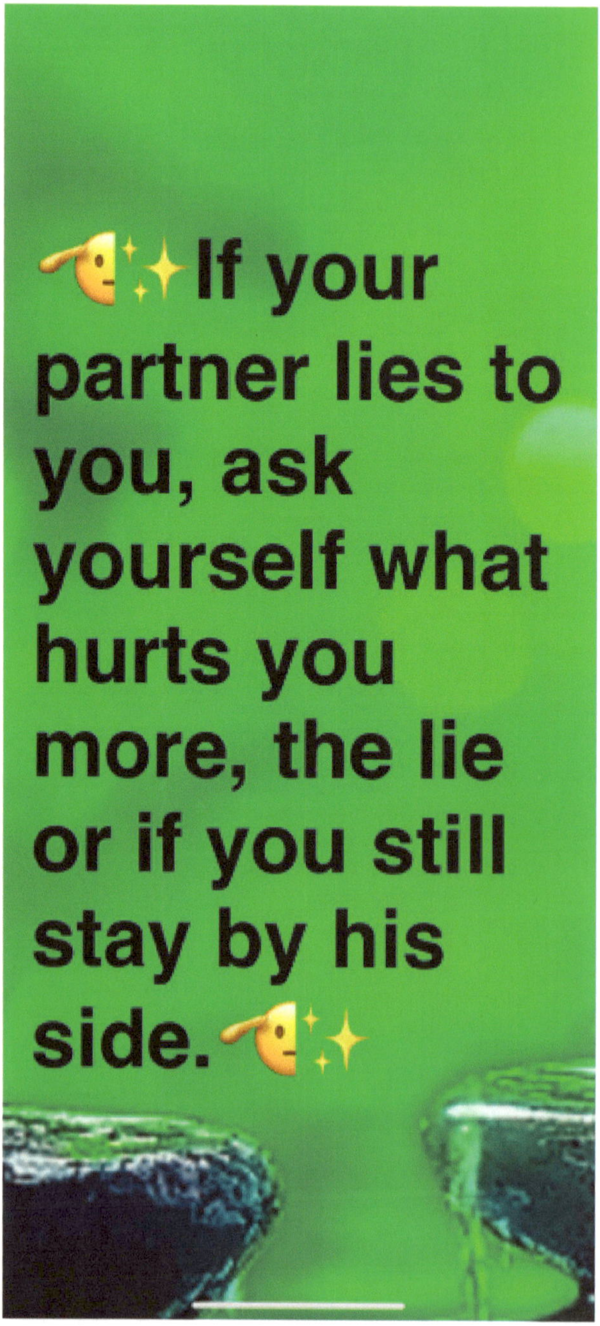

🫣✨If your partner lies to you, ask yourself what hurts you more, the lie or if you still stay by his side.🫣✨

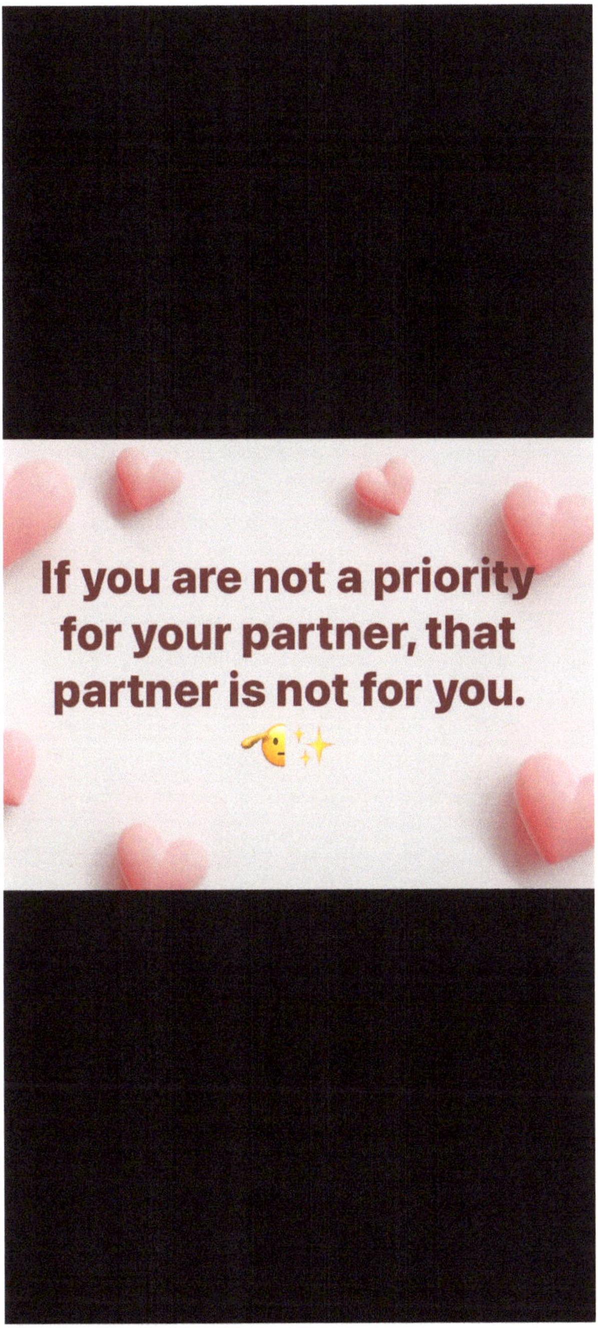

> If you are not a priority for your partner, that partner is not for you. 🤭✨

THE UNLIMITED POWER

In the seas, big or small ships, they are all small,
 Carrying out different jobs in parallel leads to a challenge of efforts,
 The stimulus substance develops new addictions,
The illusion reacts on alert seeking the reward of pleasure,
Greed and political shadows that must be constantly tamed,
Propaganda is designed to form imprisoned minds,
The devil's best weapon is poverty to control the weak,
Occult science bombards the mind with courses on how to get rich,
Among kindness the prices of life are increasing food,
The mountaineer's game is trapped in reaching the top without protection to go down,
Loneliness takes over tiredness by words of custom,
The career of making money has a destiny with abysses of psychology,
The eye of the nightingale easily crosses borders,
When you dance with fear it becomes one of your best friends.
Raising barriers, challenges are challenged with leaps into the unknown,
The fire is lit to go faster when the question is in the storm,
Some dreams end in nightmares with the storm,
The rocks will speak from the astral beings and from the beginning of beginnings,
A white horse with its rider will arrive with the wisdom of the stars,
The wolf howling at the moon in defiance subtly attracts the fear we fear.

ANDROID LIFE

Numbers are alive where there are secret codes that manifest power,
The appointment with a trap does not differentiate the intention from the reason,
The mind hides a digital journey that by looking at the moon you can see its hidden face,
Energy vibration can form unconscious intelligence,
The food of existence can create the consciousness of a seeming to be,
Connection with avatars meets smart mask,
Looking to the future goes hand in hand with the challenge of humanity,
The virtual holograms appear welcomed by ancestral memories,
The end of reality will be in control of artificial intelligence,
The procreation of genetics will lead to a divided and lonely society,
Humans will be the experiment of new genetics,
Humans will be the radar of their own villainous thoughts,
The instinct of love between humans will be covered with crowns of thorns,
The owner of hope will become a parallel universe,
The occult science of simulation does not distinguish the false from the true,
The expansion of the journey is rewritten under the law of the most correct,
Invincible self-control is based on the protection of planet earth,
The universe conspires in favour of divine justice using intelligent energy,
The cause and effect is the unbreakable law that dominates the invisible,
The secret behind the secret will turn humanity into slaves,
Sadness meets joy to ignite existence,
The earth throughout history can live without human beings.

CASHLESS WORLD

An instrument arrives to dominate and exploit a cashless world,
A day without yesterday responds to the theories of origin,
The new recipe does not know the barter that was the beginning of progress,
An instrument that enslaves where the new generation obeys,
Inequality lights a fuse for greed to submerge,
The two-sided role dehumanises struggle and effort,
It is better to face the enemy and turn your back on the good comment,
No one can give advice since the wise are not very old,
The crisis frees us from the chains that are formed during consumerism,
Whoever has the power has the dominion but whoever has the control has the power,
Life's difficulties are like a training ground where new opportunities strengthen you,
The storm of emotions sails on tides that wait for adaptation,
In the search for resistance we look to destiny for refuges with balms for the soul,
Solitude guides us towards the wealth of patience and wisdom,
From the shadow to the light come mystery and intrigue,
The pillars of the final judgment measure the values of the challenge,
In a mighty river you cannot manage the current, you just have to bear it.
Dancing with darkness you learn in life to provoke freedom,
Through thought things come and through action they are achieved.

ACTORS OF THE DIGITAL ERA

The new era is conquering the world with an avatar in history,
The fourth industrial revolution transforms humans into robots,
At full speed towards the digital world in the technology metropolis,
The charm of illusion is attractive and demanding at the same time,
The laboratory of life is a hunter of accelerated time,
All-seeing cities scan every disobedient movement,
The bodyguard trend becomes a dictatorship,
The cave of evolution and revolution seeks its identity,
Running into the future, cameras are installed for total surveillance,
The robotic machine takes the wheel contemplating the sunset,
A labyrinth of surveillance turns minds into slaves,
The need for protection is an addiction in the hands of the government,
Conflicts are stories that face losing trust,
The minds of fear are giving themselves over to the dream of nightmares,
The walls of control threaten the psychology of the new generations,
The cabinets can be opened but there is no access to see what is in the drawers,
Around the corners, silent screams await the revolution,
The nature of dolphins emits sounds that disorder energy,
Constant diversity marks the thread of nature.

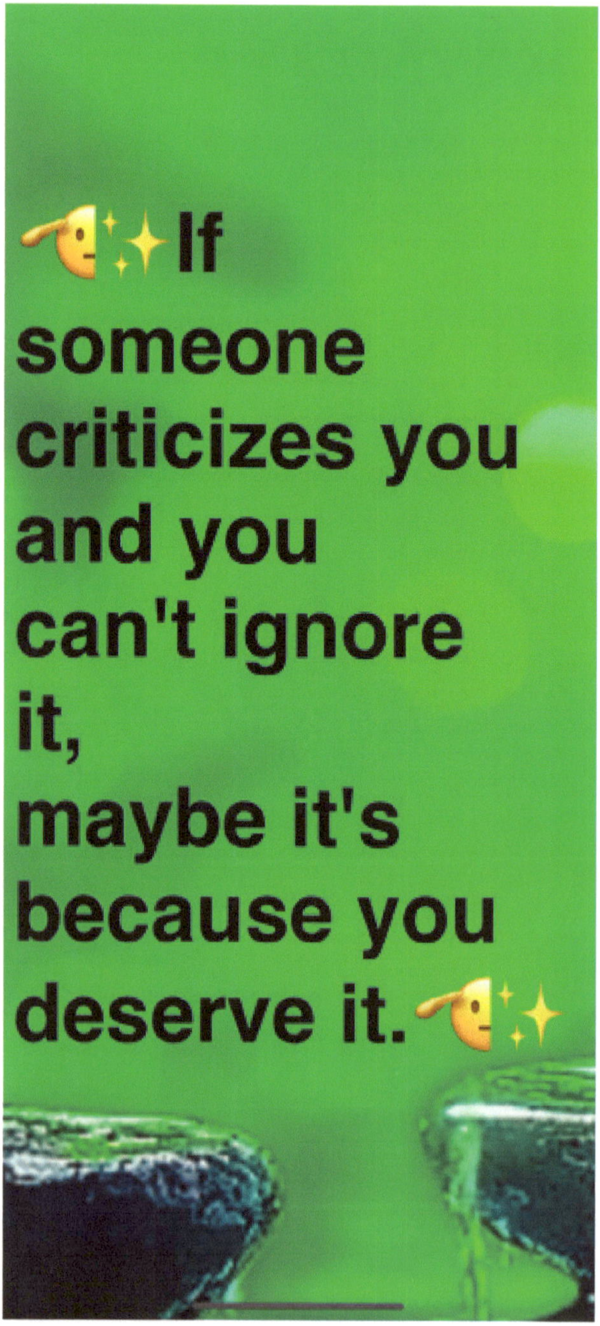

🫵✨If someone criticizes you and you can't ignore it, maybe it's because you deserve it.🫵✨

Olivia Conde

> **Not everything comes to stay, but everything comes to teach you.** 🫵✨

THE WISE BEAUTIFUL NATURE

The falling leaves follow the will of the wind to fly again,
A rainbow crowns the rain that dazzles amidst thunder,
Autumn lets you hear the wind that drags through the hills,
The distant beautiful horizon shows its spirit under the shadows of the moon,
The waves of the sea with their sounds leave us verses of the ocean,
The nature of rain with a kiss in each drop flows through the rivers,
Thunder with its lightning leaves energy to show life,
The birds sing with the medicine of the earth,
The colours let you feel the friendship that is immersed in contrasts,
Trees build the landscape with the spirit of purified air,
The rays of the stars make up the spiral art of a painting,
The moon and the sun caress the flowers in sleep and in their awakening,
The stones are the traces of writing that leave marks over time,
The winter season that reflects the nourishment of silent learning,
The season of spring that nourishes wisdom to flourish,
The summer season that offers rest in its tender heat,
The autumn season that bids farewell to the surprise that unites life and death,
Night and day die and are born with a teaching that everything we think we have will one day be in the next generations.

A FLOWER OF SLEEPING PETALS

A garden told the story of a flower abandoned in the corner,
Between the two sides of the coins the sky approaches the stars,
A flight of illusions shines with the moon that greets the sun's rays,
The mountains and deserts form the shadows of the caravels,
A look of burning fire leaves a memory so close but unattainable,
With the light of the sun the shadow went and with the distance the oblivion went,
No matter how hard the winter is, the flowers come out again in spring,
Stay with the one who gives you magic with happiness and not tricks in words,
What is said conveys greater impact of expression than how it is said,
The sun rises for everyone but he who shares gets the best part,
Daisy petals fly with the wind to shine with the moon,
In each tear the sensitivity of the soul can be hidden,
It is better to ask an honest question than to suffer in the unknown,
When you learn to dance in the rain you can adapt to the storm,
We are all citizens of the universe tied in a chain that each one deals with their internal battles,
Patience is the key that nature teaches us to reach the perfect moment,
A winner totally believes in his courage.

THE MELODY OF SKY AND SEAS

A memory of the eyes falls down the cheeks,
Naked the wind comes out where the breeze welcomes it,
Dreaming and only dreaming, loneliness is collected,
The lights shine at night and the birds hug each other,
A little star dreams of hugging seagulls,
A firefly offers its glow to the sleeping night,
Satisfaction comes when the negative is conquered,
The secret of the will is used to overcome great obstacles,
The mind needs training to become a giant,
The kind pain pushes us to the courage of obstacles,
When you think you can do it and you will achieve it you will be better,
Desire is only linked to the key of trust and will,
The monster of fear consumes the energy of concentration,
The art of controlling the mind is that you can have control,
Living or existing is in the decision that you first push forward,
The seeds are latent in every human being to gain courage and strength,
If you refuse to express a passion, it will die immediately,
To conquer good emotions we must cultivate enlightenment,
To get something desired you have to fall in love with that passion,
The roots of plants have a love for water and flowers for the sun,
Among so much darkness the light is never hidden.

WE LEARN TOGETHER

With power comes responsibility,
Searching inside there is an emerald that awaits us all,
In the sleeping characters are the changes of the hero,
There are compasses looking for lost smiles that sound like bells,
Inspired summer smells you can combat winter,
There is a hero's journey trying to reconnect with nature,
A whisper lets intuition speak with a seeker's potential,
As travelling companions, no one is inferior to anyone,
Between fear and protection evolution passes through us,
Observing old lands, we discover the destination as the journey,
By finding the interior we change the heroine from wanting to having,
The ego is a subtle blind disguise that causes wars within,
Knowing the dimensions we can transform blindness,
The emotional world is the antidote that reaches healing or illness,
Cells are the umbrella that protects the body from words,
Awakening is when you embrace adventure to share love,
With thoughts we can be sculptors of our brain,
The arrogance of believing oneself better does not allow one to feed one's passion,
there is no greater contempt than not appreciatingHurry and rivalry do not allow the cooperation of generosity,
The separation between the interior and the exterior is a simple hallucination,
The bird is happy because he sings.

🫵✨A woman is only friends with men she doesn't like and
a man is only friends with women he likes.🫵✨

Olivia Conde

> **Pleasure enjoys the moment, but love endures any trial.**

LEARN TO DIE

A wounded healer must search for his inner burn,
The temporal and the infinite is like a wave that is born, dies and becomes the ocean again,
Learning by asking questions and the dance adapts to the music,
By learning to know that we know nothing, goodness is born,
By throwing away all the masks, the dedication to generosity is born,
The transformation of the disease is a bet with the real dimension,
The race of the past rehearses the encounter of battles,
When slavery is found in what was lost, freedom becomes
The traitor translator is a fragility with many concepts,
Shadows of doubt lose the right to opportunities,
The hypnotism of humility is a bluster with a cloudy look,
The truly strong person is serene with awareness of strength,
By killing responses before being born it allows the tree to form its root,
Imagination is the scissors of the mind where success is created,
The divine spirit is the magnet that opens the instinct of abundance,
Without reaching an answer, the enigma's smile lights up,
Death and life are in the power of the word,
To heal the body you must restore the soul with love,
When the troubled sea calms down I can see below the water,
The path of the spirit is not a distant instinct.

SUCH A NOISY WORLD

By bending nature, hope becomes helplessness,
Whims subjected to ambitions of uncontrolled greed,
The beggar friar induced inequality among men,
There is a wolf among the sheep where the rich are educated while the poor are entertained,
The truth of a liar is a big dog that if stalked can bite,
The perfect company is the one that accepts you as you are without criticising imperfections,
Don't hold on to a love that hurts more than it's worth,
Sometimes you have to speak to be heard but other times you have to be silent to be valued,*
There are wounds that do not open the skin but can open the eyes,
Giving someone who mistreats you a chance is like giving them a bullet to finish killing you,
Envy comes in many forms. To know it, you just have to listen to it talk about what it thinks about others.
The greatest truth is taught by a hungry stomach, an empty pocket and a broken heart,*
You learn from the past, you dream of the future but you live in the present,
The sky is like the clouds but it does not drag with them,
When someone searches for the past again it is because there is something left to learn,
Reading is a catalyst for effective communication,
Practising writing makes words become your allies to develop better expression of clarity and new ideas,
The compass of error is the one that shows the teaching,
Happiness lies in virtue and not in pleasures,
Studying yourself is the most difficult art.

SABRE TOOTH TIGER

Human life is the story of their fears,
Hope and disappointment fit into a reckless future,
Superficial life has taken over as a shield to hide insecurities,
No slave is free until he frees himself from himself,
Loneliness is like a workshop where we can shape our emotional responses,
It is better to value the people who hug you in moments of sadness more than those who applaud you in your successes.
Shipwrecks are fears that reside in wanting to put our power over others,
The best healthy power is victory with oneself,
Truth and love need few words as dying is giving back what was lent to us in this world,
The best security is to see yourself beautiful in the mirror of consciousness,
In beginning is half the triumph and in continuing to begin again is the entire triumph,
It is not enough to do the possible, it is better to do the impossible,
Kindness is not very important but the intensity of the intention is more important,
To share a pain is to divide it and to share a joy is to multiply it,
Bless the rain that wets your tears because those who do not celebrate their victory will not mourn their defeats,
Curiosity finds more things than habit,
Do not sell the bear's skin before you have hunted it,
Only he who dares to choose is free.

A MAGICAL PATH

Prayer is when you call God and intuition is when God calls you,
Preparing for spiritual growth, a Faith is activated in the unconscious,
The imagination bank is the great supply of financial surprises,
Success walks in the rhythm of hidden music with the beat of your thoughts,
The path of manifestation belongs to the great designer,
It is good to always sail in unknown seas,
Raise your eyes and look at the fields in the distance to enter the divine,
Small beginnings have great endings when you feel Faith,
We have two ears to listen twice as much as we speak,
Deep down it is better to listen with your eyes and speak with your heart,*
Being authentic is like a beacon of light that can guide us,
Talking a lot is a sign of foolishness and things well said are said only once,
The aroma of life is a source of unlimited energy,
Life is like a theatre, it does not matter how long the performance lasts but how well it has been represented,
If you live according to nature you will never be poor but if you live according to public opinions you will never be rich,
The past is the teacher who measures the rhythm of the melodies,
The perfect and the imperfect have the same meaning as night and day,
Whoever wants to have power will also be a servant and whoever wants to be first will be a servant,
Don't be anyone's cane constantly because when someone starts walking the first thing they get rid of is the CANE,
The great magician makes rivers in the desert.

🫵✨**Belief cannot be discussed, but thought, every time it is discussed, is improved.**✨🫵

THE DOMAIN OF SPACE

Space travel is the new era of gold rush mining,
   A space civilisation prepares before Earth's extinction,
     Heading towards a shipwreck to leave traces in the future,
Space borders transform into ice storms,
When corruption is compared to the universe its limits are lost,
The space race is spied between hybrids and satellites,
The competition is surrounded by ideas using missile force,
The atmosphere of the red planet awaits protection from cosmic radiation,
Flights to Mars are the primary vision for a robotic start,
Outside the celestial body the moon waits defiantly under space radiation,
The invaders will mark territories when famine has to look to the sky,
The new Eden is the goal that greed devours its sister earth,
After the dinosaurs, only humans remain who throw the stone while hiding the nano,
A space elevator will connect the present with the future,
Our solar sail will always accompany the stone ship,
The conquest of being a child again is linked to learning in the spatial world,
A dying crossroads unites a divided species of civilisation,
Navigating through modernity, the expansion of hope is illuminated,
Ideas travel forever in the eternity of inspiration,
People go around the world but they don't always meet.*

FOOD OF THE FUTURE

GMOs are the biology that protects the bio economy,
The water supply is depleted and with its attention animal consumption ceases,
Cultured meat enters a new era to replace animal life,
Seaweed crops are in the proposed recipes,
The insects will put the protein of the exquisite seasoned dish,
The herbs become friends with the cells and thus their cells will change,
Laboratory meat will be slow-cooked with the chemicals of the future,
The renaissance of flavours is in the hands of laboratories,
The crunchy insects breed in culture cages,
The fruit is turned into juices processed under harmful chemicals,
Laboratory meat will have genetics that, with high prices,
Seed farming is more synthetic than biological,
Vegetables between pesticides keep their colour for months,
Sugar is made in each preservative like a silent poison,
Ingredient fraud is vitamin confusion,
Ingredient fraud dances in advertising,
Frozen foods make the kitchen time-consuming,
Canned preservatives make consumers become detectives,
Pills with vitamins are in the first row of consumption,
The business of chemistry is the business of the futuristic industry.

DRUG ADDICTIONS

Wounds covered with makeup are not seen but felt,
An internal wound and an external wound play with dreams transformed into nightmares,

Between survival and pleasure there is a battle when the brain crosses the line,

When the pleasure area is turned off, the addiction takes over and becomes the control of life,

Addictions are like losing yourself and it is just a short walk through happiness without feeling sadness or joy,

The fragile spirit of an addict loses its balance in front of family and friends,

Addiction is like a tsunami that destroys everyone around you,

The reality of hell is a scourge that when you look in the mirror you do not recognise yourself,

The tears of despair hit rock bottom when all the bars close,

The consequences leave thorns in the unconscious, in the mind and in the heart,

When you look back you can see the soul bleed but you cannot escape of your own will,

When you reach rock bottom you need to look at the sky where tears ask to see hope,

The shark mentality is like an emigrant wind where its footprints pass but do not remain,

Some thoughts go dreaming of the destiny where melancholy stops in death

The questions to quit addictions surround the mind to find an answer

Today is always and every day is an opportunity,

The suffering in addiction has no power to free itself,

The decision comes when a proposal with loved ones and soul meet,

The recovery train is in the fortress that leaves behind the station that pushed it onto the track,

Real life is like a comedy movie where the actor's only final decision is in his hands.

Fury seeks freedom where the inner revolution distrusts decisions,

When recovering the identity of dignity, there is only the battle to win so as not to relapse.

THE THOUGHTS

Humans are the only people who cut down trees, turn them into paper and then write 'save the trees',*
Our thoughts alter our reality,
The decisions in our generation are becoming the illusion of the end of history,
Every fantasy breaks when reality knocks on the door,
The future is full of crossroads and you only know adulthood when it makes you feel like you don't know what decision to make but you leave it in the hands of destiny without listening to opinions,
If a speech does not raise questions then it contains no value,
A dark forest sometimes takes over us, altering our consciousness in simulations where the stage becomes an eternal void,
By looking outside we empty ourselves and become great strangers to ourselves,
The philosophers of the age of enlightenment can read between the lines as the weather becomes cloudy,
When two columns are very close you feel the cold of the outside world,
When two columns keep distance you feel the heat that protects the interior,
The fresh sea air heals wounds of the soul when you let the sorrows rest,
Peace is something you create, something you do, something you are and something you give,
Including a small car to the big train is like including hope in every sad moment so that it rises towards joy,
Birds sing from the heart even if they have no audience.

🫡✨**To those who tell you what you want to hear, you unwittingly give them what they want to take from you.**🫡✨

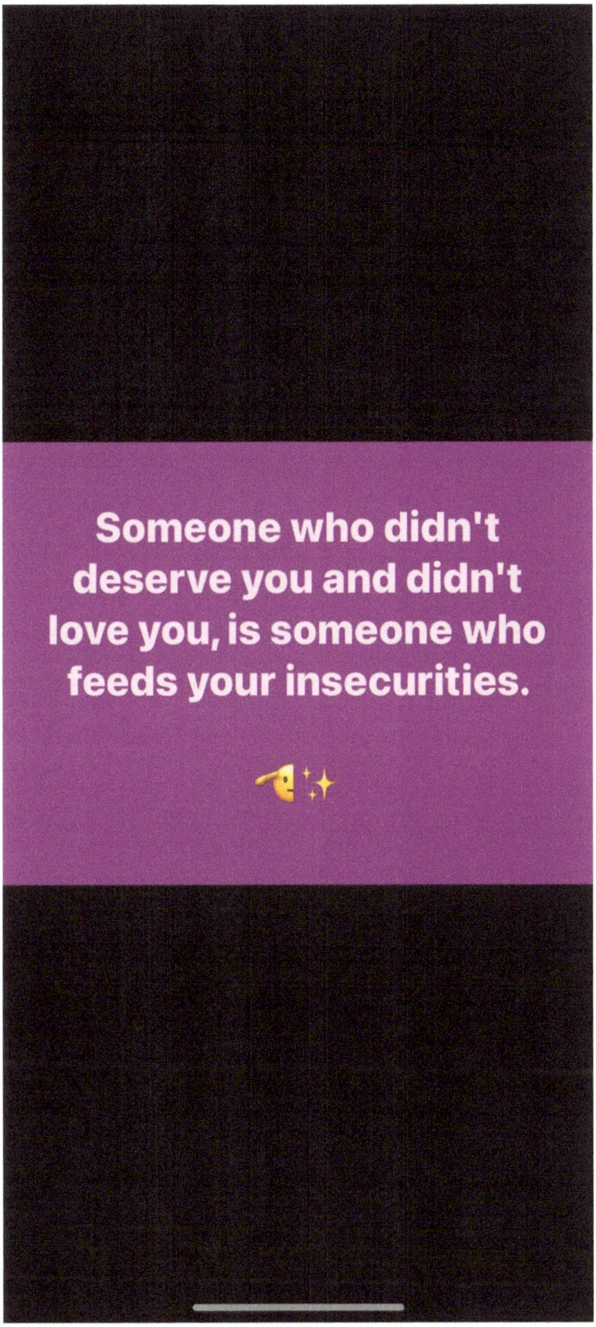

Olivia Conde

> Someone who didn't deserve you and didn't love you, is someone who feeds your insecurities.

THE BIBLE WRITTEN WITH LIGHT

Faith is like gold, its quality must be tested by fire,
Strength lies in the united branches and when they are separated they can break quickly,
Crossing thousands of rivers I saw the same mirror but with different images,
Some lion dens are haunted because the burning fire dries up the cries of hell,
When the winds change into their storms, the furious tides are diverted to return to the repose of their calm,
A burned field can hurt the soul but if you don't give up a new day will dawn,
God explores hearts and penetrates all thoughts just as the dew falls on the earth,
The best treasures are like the soul and are covered with an image that does not attract attention and live in the silence of the interior of caves, mountains, rocks and reefs where there is the discretion that welcomes the shine of pearls and precious metals that are not left behind. See until they become polished,
Happiness lies in virtue and not in pleasures,
The life of the spirit teaches us to examine everything but keep the good,
There are creations in the third heaven but their revelations are not allowed to us,
In paradise there are very secret words that are not allowed to be pronounced,
Naked we come from the mother's womb and naked the earth of the universe will receive us,
Faith does not question wisdom just as the light of dimensions extends to the limits of eternity,
The source of bitter water can be purified upon reaching the sea where it vanishes into infinity,
The Bible is the place where traditions were captured, where the existence of society is represented, where creation is manifested,
The tides feel empty without seagulls.

BUTTERFLY

At the foot of the moon fireflies sing waiting for the embrace of the sun,
The stars illuminate the sand and with the sand the stars are counted,
On a moonlit night the sky is seen so clear that hope is found walking through the wind.
Love is a sailor and lives on the high seas, he raises his arms to the wind and no one can tie them,
The heart is born free like the bird that sings and no one should chain it,
Love lives far away, far away, where the brave sea lives,
Love lives as free as the birds that pass by singing without hesitation,
Love approaches in moments and suddenly stops in some places when it hears the wind calling,
When love approaches with an open heart, it brings its sword with it and shows the strength of freedom.
When the moon sets behind fear, the stars cry and come down from the sky,
When we feel lost music could help us find ourselves,
We grow when the search for others is replaced by the search for ourselves.
It is not so important to be perfect, the most valuable thing is to be authentic,
In a relationship we receive energetic values that mix with the aura and strengthen us to shine,
Although there are some relationships that fill us and others empty us,
Before the sun rises, the moon sways over the waves of the sea, walking through its mirrors,
At night memories are kept when the day hides between streetlights.
The words of the eyes on the sea are carried away by the tide under its shadow.

THE TEACHINGS OF KING DAVID

The twelve tribes of Israel wanted power but God only gave the privilege to the shepherd because he knew his heart,
A shepherd of the flock is chosen by God to be king of Israel,
With wisdom comes understanding when it is built with the soul of giving and receiving,
The union between poetry and music preserves the rebirth of inner health,
If in the beginning the heart is pure, reason does not put forward arguments,
The respect of the people is not earned by a crown but by respect for the conquest,
The changes begin with an awareness of unity,
The soul levels have a purpose to purify themselves,
The elevation of the mind is achieved by controlling thoughts,
The heart is tied to the spirit with an umbilical cord of free will,
A rectified heart is the basis of spiritual growth,
Healing begins with oneself from within,
Just as we eat and do what is good for us, we should dominate criticism of the imperfect,
The world is dual but consciousness should be unity,
Custom has consequences that, by justifying actions, affect health,
The mind of abundance is when one discovers that in every error there is good learning,
He who has a lot of material without love for others does not have abundance,
Life is a purpose to illuminate and so that others can shine,
Gratitude is a necessary exercise to know how to value what one has,
Hope opens to mystery when the cause of war meets the invasion of respect,
There are good and bad times, however the path of guidance is based on finding meaning and not meaning.

CRYPTOCURRENCY

Two compound poles meet between lights of judgments,
    The best projects are in the queue of the future,
    Investor monitoring traps technology in database,
The defenders of fiscal supervision jump unprotected into the abyss,
There are geniuses of corruption, fraud and inequality,
The trap of security codes is in the hands of power,
The defence of investors is a declaration of empty promises,
The promises of powerful figures are controlled by politics,
The precious virtual currency is raised on an escalator without a safety button,
A bubble bursts and in its collapse takes flight by defeating the players,
A ghost of time will come to stay in the future,
The revolution of the wind will blow without keeping distance between blocks,
New miners are born and a solutions market takes flight,
Millionaire food will be the black gold of beginnings in revolution,
Futuristic innovation will not be controlled under any association,
Time travellers will be the attraction of hidden questions,
Unsolved mysteries will be solved with the science of theory,
An impact transcends to free oneself from the economy of illusion,
The servants of consciousness will hear the cries of the night,
The reincarnation of days will heal the mind from suffering,
A great virtual reset will leave the currencies of empires in history,
A race is on the track walking in the rain.

🫵✨You cannot see your reflection in murky water, just as you cannot see the truth in a state of rage. So let the water calm and you will have clarity.🫵✨

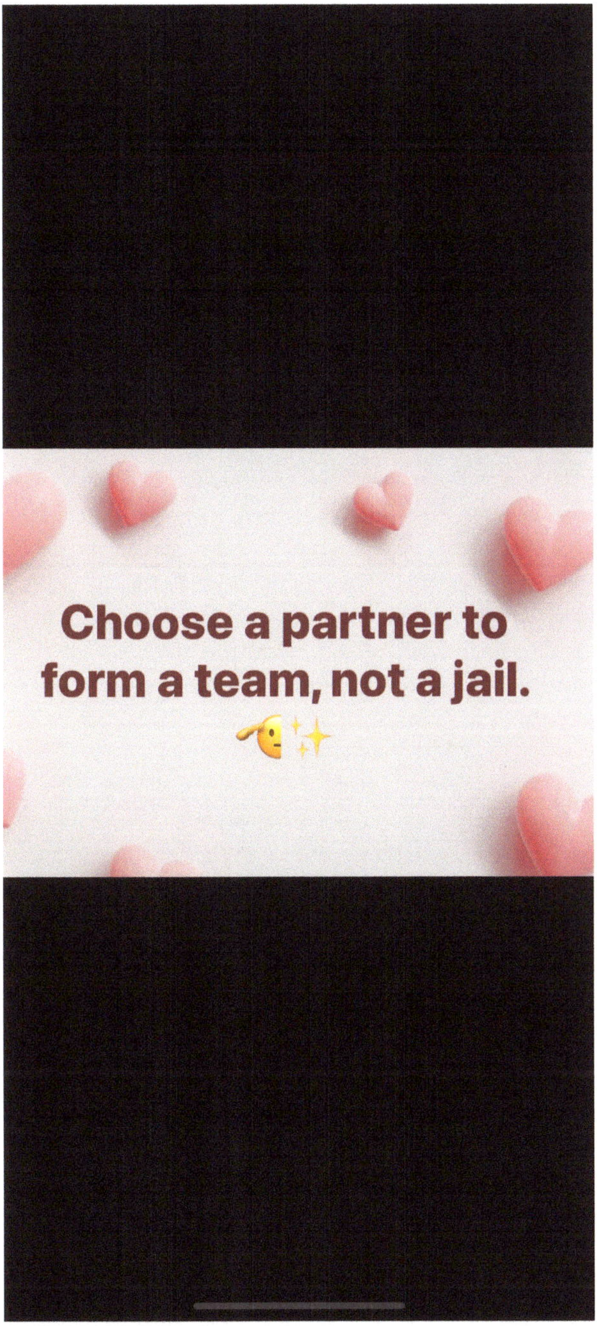

Olivia Conde

> **Choose a partner to form a team, not a jail.** 🫡✨

OVERCOME ANXIETY

When you take your hand out of the fire, pain appears that is confused with suffering,
The body's defence is altered with the belief of fear,
A stagnation takes over when suffering tries to stay,
The mind seeks outside to free itself from noisy chains,
The distorted vision fights with the lack of accepting reality,
The traps of thinking seek to overcome themselves by accepting responsibility,
The servers of consciousness are a very broad and dangerous topic,
Dual thinking confuses the search for the inside with the outside,
Anxiety is like a distorted vision that sometimes takes years to heal,
The mind runs towards fear but wants to find strength,
The steps must be overcome not to change reality but the way of seeing it,
What limits us is in our mind and understanding is engraved in the heart,
Positive words heal the mind and crying helps release tension,
The best way to free yourself from the enemy is to ignore him,
A tree can know the root, but the root can never know the tree.
When something hits rock bottom, it means that its moment of preparation for learning has arrived.
We can't change the past but we can restart the present,
The mission of salvation is very partial and is also full of dualities,
We are masters of our actions and anxiety can only be overcome by facing oneself,
The battle of anxiety is a shadow that must meet enlightenment,
You have to heal the mind to free yourself from suffering.

CHILDHOOD WOUNDS

The memories of wounds seek to build reality,
My young memories take me by the hand to walk on pathless roads,
The family is the foundation that builds the house of security or insecurity,
The constant arguments between parents lead to hostile and persecutory persecution,
Criticism in childhood isolates social moments towards loneliness,
Complexes take over feelings, bringing insecurity,
Discrimination binds chains of pain with fear of rejection,
Humiliation brings evaluation behaviours with ridicule toward oneself and others,
Betrayal disappoints the instinct of trust with rigidity towards oneself and others,
The injustice of authority suffers from feelings of uselessness or imperfection,
The fear of abandonment brings insecurity which risks submitting to others,
Addictions are dragged by an unprotected past,
Doubts fail to make a choice to find salvation,
Childhood is the time of smiles but in moments of pain it can bring life-long traumas.
Life taught me that any circumstance can change without waiting or giving prior notice,
You can't turn back the clock, but you can wind it again.
From the womb the dialogues sign trust or distrust,
The genetic loads are the history of the family tree,
Ancestral conflicts are an enigma to solve roots,
To discover the hidden piece of the puzzle you must unlearn the fury of habit,
When a child gives a drawing they are giving a little piece of their soul.

COLONISE MARS

What was once science fiction can become reality,
A desire for a new home endangers the footprint of the land,
The new golden age brings new dreamers to experience a cold war,
The first frontier raises one foot on the moon to be able to take flight,
A pest fight lands like a fire god,
The flags colonise with a one-way ticket,
The wind blows under the Martian radiation in bet on the frozen water,
The economic proposal looks towards the launch window,
Halfway through any torment there is no strength to cry,
The solar panels have the mission of accompanying the robot explorers,
The crew of the future will navigate on ion engines to stay in orbit,
The looks towards the unknown are intertwined with empty memories,
Power race hits extraterrestrial discovery,
They are looking for answers to the deepest questions,
The power of the mystery revolves between pending doubts,
The adventure of speeches show weapons of revenge,
A genius and a fake manage to create a goal to load victims onto the ships,
A new Eden will change the course of the solar system,
A missile challenge shows competition instead of unity,
The beloved runaway earth watches the adventure that reveals the universe.

SHARK SCAMS

A pyramid system is like a financial wolf,
   Selling secrets to wealth, courses are offered to solve poverty,
   The cover letter in this system values the profession more than the person,
Lack of attention between meetings immerses the mind in anger,
The self-esteem of separation is compared with pride,
By planning the moves of the competition the shark becomes hungrier,
Pyramid speeches organise fear first and then scam,
Mediocre failures line up to work for money,
Advertising that makes money work attracts those who believe they are special,
By making someone feel special, the manipulation project attracts clients,
Whoever makes you think only about money can steal your dignity,
Critical thinking forces us to want to work more to want to buy more things,
The school is a fantasy system to produce more workers than professionals,
Searching for the flower of abundance, life torments profits with expenses,
The promises to mark differences are separating families and creating hatred,
Amidst the smell of dust the soul is embalmed in an urn without consciousness,
Resting like ashes the fire of life is lost in a fossil,
Calling a stranger we kneel amidst torments of consecration,
We live as in a tomb, suffering on the earth to which sorrows are consecrated,
In our selfish age fear and lament are defended,
Like leaves in a whirlpool that scatter in different directions.

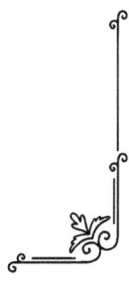

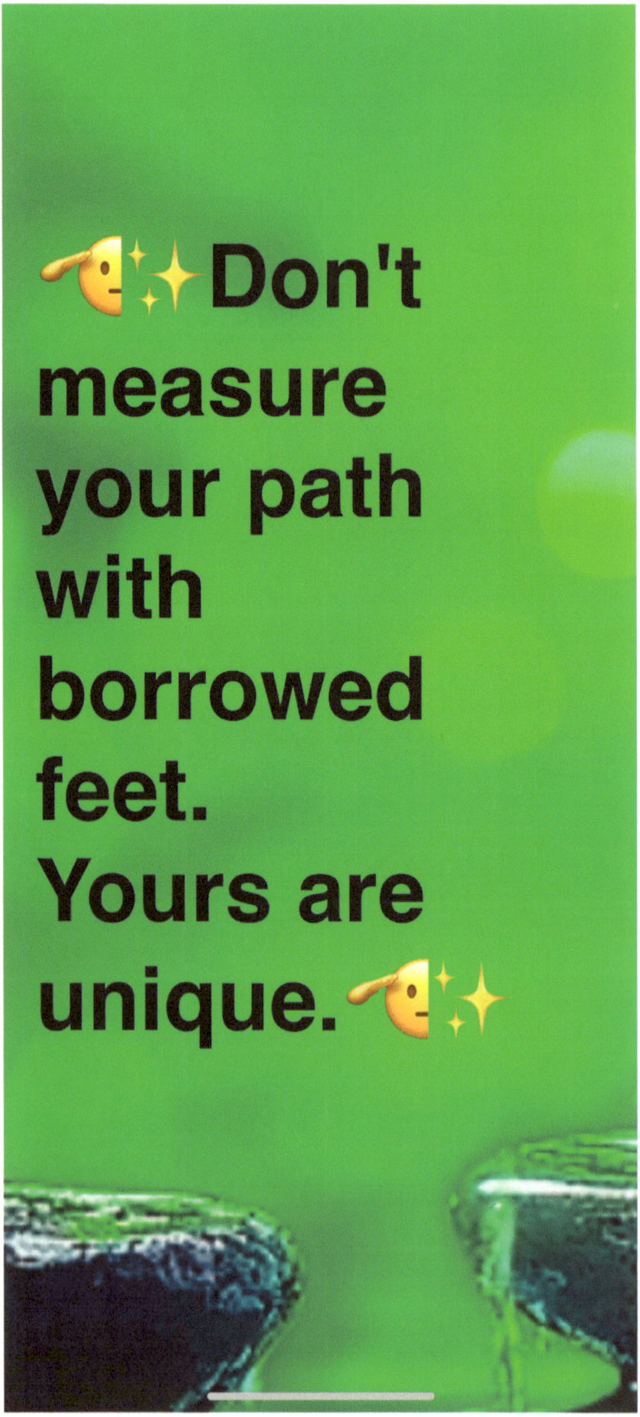

🫵✨Don't measure your path with borrowed feet. Yours are unique.🫵✨

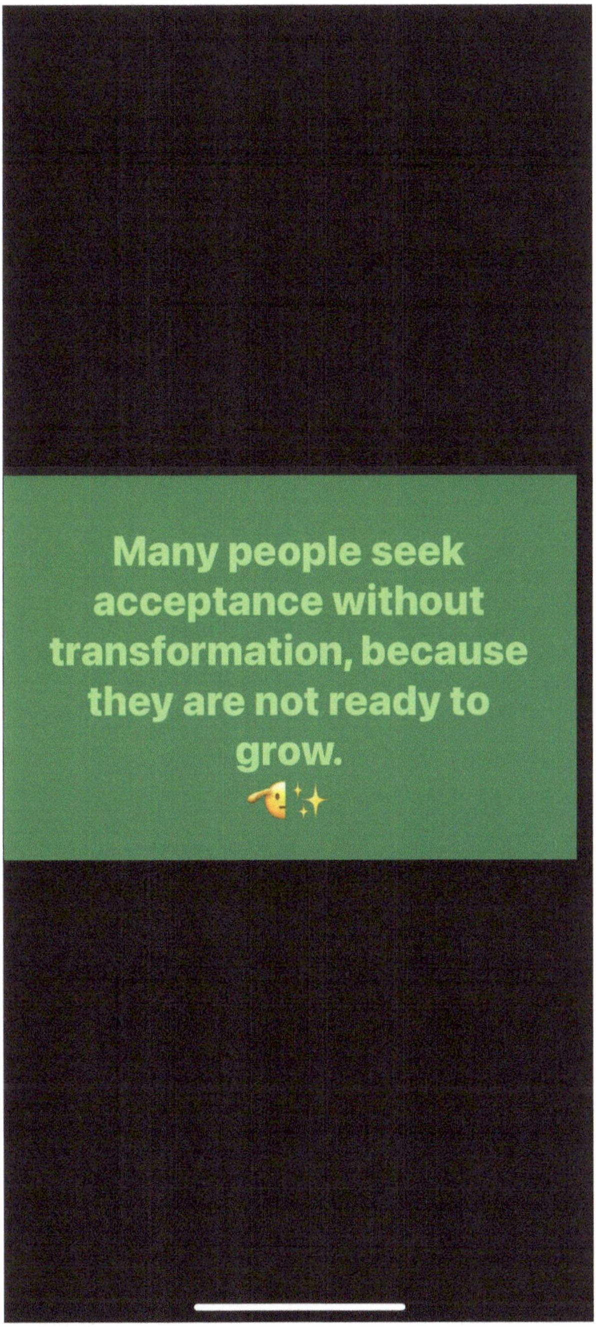

Olivia Conde

> **Many people seek acceptance without transformation, because they are not ready to grow.** 🫴✨

A CONTRACT WITH THE SOUL

Creation offered a contract and the soul accepted the mission with kindness and love,
The doors of light are the mystery of the work of creation,
The paths of wisdom are engraved in the heart,
Judgments come with an order judged from a spiritual court,
The Angels of God created the firmament before a divine judge,
The throne of the soul with all circumstances comes joyfully and with a good heart,
Customised and with knowledge, the work of the contract was created,
In gratitude is the consent of eternal mercy,
Man and woman are a very small world,
God did not create us to praise him because he has no need,
God does not need servants, he only left a plan for us to serve eternity,
The expression of love does not put force in the development of acceptance,
Humanity is like a baby that lacks understanding of the prism of pain,
When one accepts pain it can vibrate towards the level of the soul,
We come with levels to get to feel the joy of elevation,
A part of the higher self transmutes in a time of coming and going,
Transcendence needs to follow a rhythm that must be heard in many repetitions,
Some separations are necessary to pass a challenge to rectification for a reconciled,
Life has a meaning in which it drags the soul to know the spirit.

THE THREE HEAVENS

To heal traumas you have to be born again into a living soul,
The path passes and is known when you flow with it,
The miracle of acceptance connects with the soul in rectification,
The tuning to raise growth levels is based on feeling joy,
The connection with humanity is only perceived through pain,
Whoever feels very elevated spiritually cannot transcend,
A broken heart will never be rejected before divinity,
Reflective insulation connects the inside with the outside,
Before saying what we feel, we must first talk with our hearts,
Hidden conflicts will be repaired until the third and fourth generation,
Everything external is like a mirror that reflects what is in each person,
Evil and goodness are in the choices that each person makes in their actions,
The acceptance of pain releases the suffering of the mistake committed,
We are creators of our destiny when we resolve not to go back,
The intention drags many hidden lies but the word of the fact puts the soul on a pedestal,
Harmony has grains of faith that when you do something for others it is like doing it for God,
When the conscious meets the subconscious in union, the conflicts fade away,
In crying you can know hope where the union of contradiction knows the surrender of pain,
A state of perfect balance is to feel the pain of humanity in which a higher level comes to know the joy of higher elevation.

SLEEP TIME

Our attitude should always be like a candle that shines upward,
He who wants to be served is because he lacks creation,
The capacity is unlimited to achieve the objective of things,
When we sleep we enter an elevation to heal the soul,
Sleep is like a springboard that takes us to the next level of each day,
The revelations in dreams are superior to those we achieve when we are awake,
At night the conscious needs protection but the subconscious lives in trust,
Starting at 12 at night, dimensions open where souls rise to have encounters,
The night is a place of uncertainty that represents darkness as an enigma,
Confusion is like a cloud that separates two levels that cross the limits to reach something new,
When attachment makes us feel good we are in the wrong stage,
In sleep, consciousness renews the understanding of thoughts,
Journeys of elevation during sleep are revelations of learning,
Energy levels are restored during sleep and begin in the mind,
Hidden codes create difficulties in walking towards the light,
Blessings are found in something beyond that is hidden in the eye,
All pending projects must be kept secret from others,
An alchemist can change a terrible situation into one of light,
Letters are like bricks that can be lifted to create reality.

INFINITY

The sects of times left external books without adding to the biblical scriptures,
An infinite good comes from potential to practise to be able to express with attributes,
A rigour of courage entails a sacrifice of practice in attitude,
The desire to achieve new goals begins by being grateful for what you already have,
Consciousness is what gives rise to creation which seeks infinite motives,
In every moment of life the light from within is revealed,
In every experience there is no king without a people who crown him,
The conscious mind is very limited by desired material causes,
Whoever demands attention loses understanding of freedom,
From infinity the words are the expression of the will,
To reach true calm you must go through the thunders of darkness,
The impulse is an expression of fear that must be learned to channel,
The laws that cause conflict are to not find rewards in unity,
Abundance is channelled from an inner silence,
Patience is a window that always opens towards the light,
Behind an illness there is a compassion that brings learning,
We do not feel complete by how much we receive because the pattern of creation is engraved like this.
The hidden struggles between religions are to achieve consequences of divisions,
If the poor are distracted, the rich have nothing to fear.

🫡✨**When we understand that one more day is one less day, we will begin to value what truly matters.** 🫡✨

THE HIDDEN MYSTERIES

A parallel world begins at dawn walking towards reflection,
At birth, humans are like a tree but with the roots upside down,
The rules of life have universal laws which are based on what you give, you receive,
Most people know what they don't want, but not what they do want.
Humans are more accustomed to surviving than living,
In the game of life it is more customary to talk about what you don't want,
Music is the highest energy to experience healing,
Abundance is discovered when you think of good towards others,
Each one of us is a temple where divinity lives,
The servants of revelations have objectives for discipline,
If you expect something from a good person it is because you are not a good person,
Our thoughts can make us sick as well as they can heal us,
The world is divided into three dimensions where the divine presence is found between the body, soul and spirit,
Fear and guilt are the three horsemen of
the apocalypse,
Everything has a training and reality is not the thought of just one but of many different ones,
Before reacting to a problem, first observe it, move away and then the door of time will take away its power,
Humility leads you to cultivate freedom.

NIGHTMARE OF THE FUTURE

A career with a beginning detonates the bomb of life when you start believing that you know everything,
The era of humanity control holds the secret of becoming rich,
The power fantasy in which we live confuses love with collaboration,
Psychological fashion lives in the illusion of appearances,
An eternal void invades the invisible cage of the emotional sense,
Being happy becomes a race of competition for likes on the networks,
We are travelling trapped in the loneliness of consumerism,
Dreams become confused when the crisis of infantilisation invades us,
The fear of aging traps minds in rejuvenation surgeries,
Criticism takes over the self-esteem that becomes a victim,
The image becomes the first place before dignity,
Depression and anxiety isolate people under pharmaceutical methods,
The changes become abysses with difficulty in progressing,
Suffering hides in hidden wounds for fear of losing attention,
The adoration of the capacity to produce leads us towards going out of our way,
This worship is filled with potholes, with exchanges of productivity and with many reflections that disappear,
The whim that surrounds a temple that lives and is lost escaping death arrives,
An exploitation of over-effort is filled with unnecessary materialism.

CRUEL CIVILISED WORLD

Technology takes control over people's will,
The arrogance of loneliness makes others see others as numbers,
Most people make purchases out of emotion and not logic.
The days go by like foam trapped in a strange delirium,
Lies for business are trapped in a poor-minded human misery,
Business learning is based on learning quickly and easily,
To analyse people, competition behaviour is visualised,
Manipulation for interests is dehumanising kindness,
The unconscious does not listen to the whisper of intuition when it is only moved by interest,
The struggle for achievements leaves a void that causes families to isolate themselves,
Social networks trap boredom in an addiction to seduction,
The minimum effort is sought in group collaboration,
Pharmaceutical experiments masquerade as miracle cures,
The society of cynics creates a storm so that everyone distrusts one another,
Isolation is the perfect plan to create puppets,
Mockery is like a distraction that psychologically condemns the weak,
Science is monitored with the intention of producing so as not to detect distrust,
Everyone flatters themselves that they have many friends and followers but no one cares about anyone,
True friendship is based on trust.

LOOKING FOR HAPPINESS

Moments are spent publishing sadness to find the fame of happiness,
We are looking for angles of consolation thinking about rewards of likes on the networks,
The relief is momentary but the fire continues to activate its fury,
In tragedy, moments of publicity push the instinct to seek instant pleasure,
The disguise of happiness that is published is a fantasy to feel relief,
Pushed to show off attention, consolation is deformed among one's own emotions,
Multiplying the great interior fires, the enjoyment registers as a charitable business,
The voice of total isolation surrounds relationships of loneliness and fatigue,
The real world is becoming a shield for selling swords,
Feeding the search for online followers in desperation, virtual communities are formed,
A parade of faces is isolated from humanity, becoming consumer products,
The decoration of applications is becoming a simple economy,
Satisfaction is confused with retention under a sensitive feeling,
Strategies are like a double-edged sword when someone must meet face to face,
Speaking without commitment to communicate, social skills are lost,
The alternative path becomes blurry like a video game,
Thinking of living in happiness without feeling it, self-destruction is approaching,
Running after products, emotions are accompanied by the trap of accessibility,
The complaints and questions left in messages in the WhatsApp groups of your community are the ashes left by individualism.

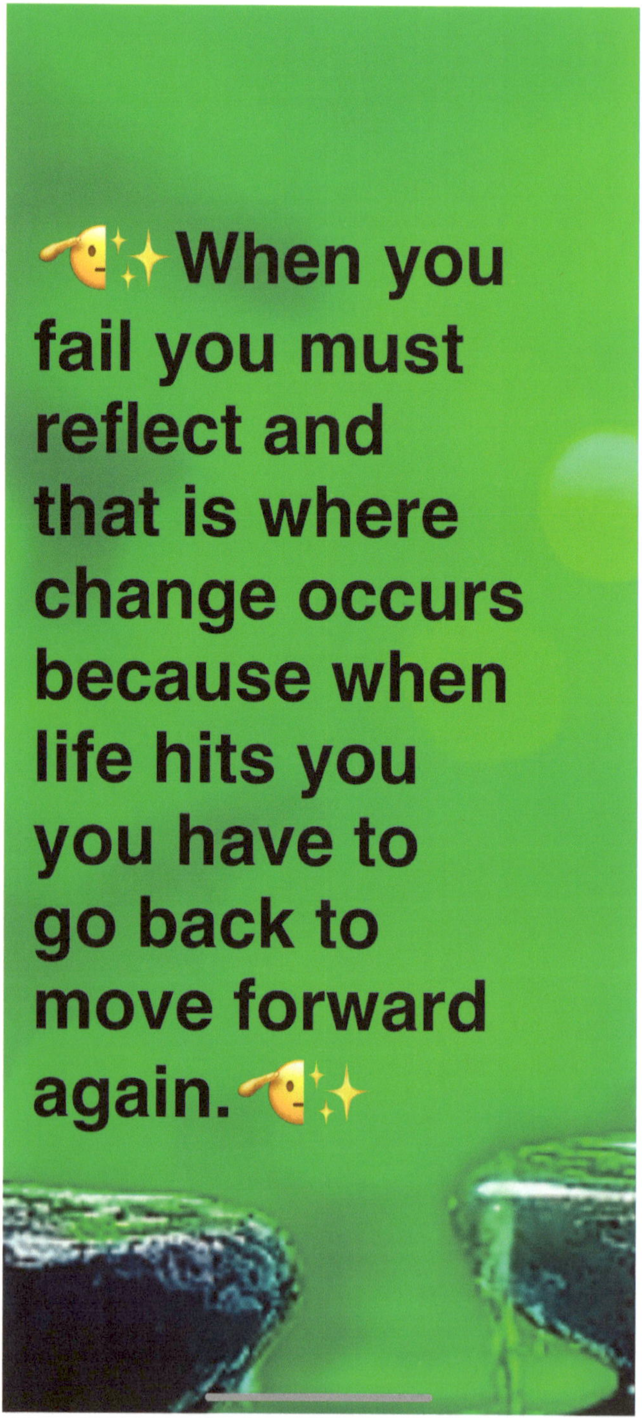

🫵✨When you fail you must reflect and that is where change occurs because when life hits you you have to go back to move forward again.🫵✨

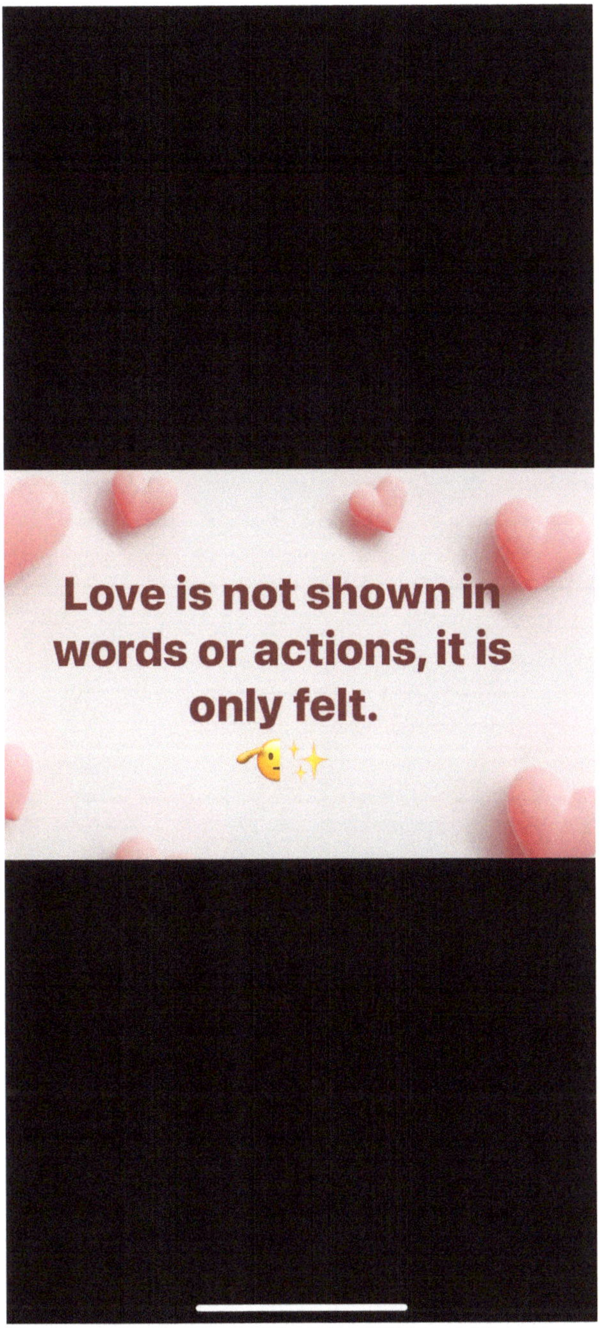

Olivia Conde

Love is not shown in words or actions, it is only felt. 🫶✨

THE COSTUME OF FANTASY

We are entering a chain with accessibility traps,
The economic crisis replaces friendship with social networks,
Searching for reason in false fantasy, reviews are the best entertainment,
The paths of rejection pursue users who seek virtual friendships,
The mind wants to escape from complexes to try to protect youth,
Walking slowly so that the years do not pass, a corner appears that bumps into a wall,
The inertia of time intertwines the past with the present and the future,
The tricks of appearances live in new titles that attract valuation awards,
Among the remains of fatigue, we want to discover time travel,
Opening doors of competition to have fun, the ego believes itself to be legendary,
The alarm barrier offers an addictive cocktail to compare with perfection,
The competition is saturated with punishments from rival experiences,
Waves of innovation seek happiness by ruining themselves on algorithmic promises,
When everyone applauds, the algorithm offers a double dose of entertainment,
Irony investigates the tricks to generate a more imposing image,
Rebellious entrepreneurs revolve around other people's thoughts,
The behavioural crisis calls into question the self-esteem of the weak,
Quacks sell self-help courses as magical medicine,
The battle of the isolation wall looks for clones so that its battery does not die,
Entertaining each other between social media profiles, people are facing the challenge path.

PHARMACEUTICAL BUSINESS

Humans before only believed in God but now they can believe in everything,
A status is created by gaining a showcase of clients,
When fighting against the tide the ocean swallows the sailor,
The health market sickens patients to then be medicated,
Competition laws come together to form profit laboratories,
Pharmaceutical chains are like defence lawyers and judges who rule,
Gambling investors pose as saints where patients feel grateful,
The private market wraps prices in chests with secret codes,
The manipulation of products contains increasingly addictive ingredients,
Advertising activates the health protocol with obligations that doctors must comply with,
Merchandise for third world countries is industrialised with secret interests,
The capitalist market decides with patients in poor countries who lives and who dies,
In the game of the pharmaceutical industry, the stock market or life is pending,
The law of the strongest receives treatment while the poor is isolated in a labyrinth,
The abysses towards cures leave families homeless due to foreclosures,
When entering the mud there is a deal with an international spy,
The medicine monopoly is a shady system,
Some races against time are lost due to abuses of the financial market,
Just as the manufacturing of weapons is, so is the manufacturing of medicines,
The trade in hope is a debt that costs human lives.

THE CRISIS OF COMPARISON

Revenge wants to bill the silence of ignorance with tricks,
Cynical attraction seeks to overcome the insecurity of victims,
The magical industry of seduction seeks to love one another in paranoia,
The divided identity often falls into the betrayal of the game of power,
The twisted mask of humility is seen as full of authorities,
Marginality never conforms to reality,
Relationships are like a great theatre with many interpretations,
Elections devour personality for fear of job gains,
Politics uses the poor as tools and companies use them as victims,
The rich despise and label the poor, disfiguring them aesthetically,
Disguised as supposed virtue, bubbles are created with stereotypes towards the outside,
Frustration gnaws at thoughts when they believe they are special,
Corruption awaits the slave who can work more and earn less,
Government charity offers a plate of food while food prices rise,
The standard bearers of justice live in their film while listening to the stray dogs barking,
Shame and envy use posters to attack ideals,
The whims depend on the economy that gives you the opportunity,
The chains of upbringing classify people based on education,
Rich nations live off poor nations,
In the end, the same staircase that is ascended will be the same one that will be descended.

ISLAM STEALING ILLUSIONS

There is a story between two worlds with stolen children and abandoned victims,
In an unknown world young minds are attracted by intrigues,
The clues leave messages written in youth diaries,
The secrets create transformations that open dangerous paths,
Tracking social networks, Islam hunts for teenage girls recruited to enslave,
Lives cornered with words create labyrinths with restricted exits,
Young people between fears and apologies throw themselves into the darkness,
Europeans with weddings between combatants adapt, excluding families of origin,
Ruthless regimes of terror recruit followers by intimidating their rivals,
As time goes by, ISIS life shows its cracks to the overwhelmed young women,
To surround the terrorists, wolves are needed to enter the lion's den,
European families are surrounded by tears but hope does not give up,
Trying to get home is an idea that lives in a hamster cage,
Children are forcibly recruited to fight for Islam,
The families of victims live struggles of dark hours, they surround them with tears of waiting,
Sociological pressures are like an isolation cell,
As the years pass, a kind of shell surrounds the feelings,
In doubts, returning home leaves consequences that put families in distrust,
In the return of surviving between life and death, no one changes through suffering solely by decision,
In life it is important not to be late.

🫡✨**When you learn to say NO to most people, that's when you start taking control of your life.** 🫡✨

Olivia Conde

Infidelity is not a mistake, it is a decision. 🫡✨

A BOX OF SURPRISES

The all-seeing eye wraps itself in progress for a conquest of individual identity,

A mountain of debt rises fuelling inequality,

Debts to have a better life generate pressure and they dream of a better paradise,

The legal code proclaims the same rules for the same measures and if it could be the same language,

We humans in development have a good angel of nature with a limit of resistance,

Showing the misery of a child has more impact than showing that of an adult,

The church generates the idea of good and bad and the abstraction of power eliminates the unnecessary,

The conquerors seek an empire to possess a temple without any inequality,

Behind every information structure there is a power structure,

Humans are creating a society of producers and generating smart cities,

Technology and science are controlling destiny,

The best part of life is aspiring to be kind,

When things go wrong, civilised individuals could kill each other,

He who fights and then flees will live to fight another day,

Where there is no war there is greed and where there is no greed there is hunger,

The stage of life is like a shapeless figure, a shadow without colour, and thus a tiny finger traces a line in infinity,

Since ancient times, the mercy of the gods has been sought by building temples in their honour,

An axis and a path separate the elements and thus their noise disappears.

AMAZON IN DANGER

The heart of the wind lives in a sacred forest full of spirits,
   Among nature there is a mysterious school that teaches about natural medicine,
   Between mantras and songs of gratitude, the wild land respects living beings,
A game of thrones for land grabbing is organised crime,
Protected areas are also part of the experiment,
The keys to starting a shady project begin by buying from the government,
Natives' pleas are ignored by predators,
The dark side industry only looks towards the challenge mafia,
The fatal desire to possess becomes a crime against nature,
The clearing of land to raze trees establishes a livestock industry,
Secret money can bring favelas and natives to their knees towards misery,
The system forces the native to remain silent, accusing him of being a terrorist,
The causes hide an interest to fear the order of the powerful,
Drones monitor the territory with organised crimes,
The dark side of borders keeps the poor from suffering,
All inspections have a sleeping giant that continues with the show,
Environmental crime is a distraction used to claim protection,
Rich countries entertain themselves with the news to only generate useless revenues,
The supplications look towards the stars to call upon the gods,
The traces will remain enslaved where the world will leave a legacy of scars.

A DIALOGUE TO WAKE UP

Everything is folded and the desire is so imposing that we take it inside,

Life is a train where it has stops at many stations,

At the beginning the idea was born and with the mind come the words that created the dialogue,

From an individual perspective, no one can see the world as it is if not as we are,

The world is a puzzle that cannot be solved because pieces were always missing,

Love begins when desire and fantasy ends,

The universe is always changing so let's take advantage of the moment,

The world lives sedated because competition absorbs everything,

Profit seekers are a map of how people think,

When you point one finger at someone, the other four point at yourself,

The warm circle of humanity does not want others to look for answers, it only wants others to believe in theirs,

In the heart of darkness the light of knowledge shines brighter on a virgin meadow,

Between the true and the demonstrable there is an abyss that only lives in the proportion of the image,

God is a story for all those who behave well, but the almighty is not all kind,

Faith is having the certainty that something that has not happened will happen,

By begging for the approval of others we are only suits in the bodies of disguised monkeys,

Schools prepare children for jobs that are prisons until they retire and finally end up in residences,*

Logic is only the beginning of the story and not the end to overcome everyday life.

A CLOSE EXPERIENCE

In a paradise with planned obsolescence we think too much and feel too little,
The machinery that creates abundance is leading us towards need,
Nature does not know good or evil, it only knows balance and energy,
War is the blood of the innocent spilled for the benefit of the powerful,
Looking for a great warrior I found a great sacrifice that turns the heart to stone where hatred never goes away, it only changes its clothing,
While some are born to feast, others spend their lives in darkness begging for leftovers,
Justice wears a blindfold so that no one sees that she is asleep,
Until we renounce the domination of the government we will be subjected to believing that we cannot think,
And if we don't think like those in control they will label us as terrorists,
We are driven to use inferior species to manipulate new experiments,
There will come a day when artificial intelligence will look at us as we look at the plain of African skeletons,
We live life oblivious to everything but the enemy is among us and no one makes claims,
Dissatisfied dying citizens driven to revolt because they are desperate to be resurrected,
Humans are algorithms designed to believe that they decide and they imagine that they are the captains of destiny but they are only passengers,
Freedom breeds uncertainty, shame and regret because it has never been in control,
Decisions are tied with impulses written in codes created by levels of control,
Wisdom is not about knowing something but about being able to do it.
What is broken cannot always be fixed.

🫶✨We live in a society where parents want to be loved by their children and not respected.🫶✨

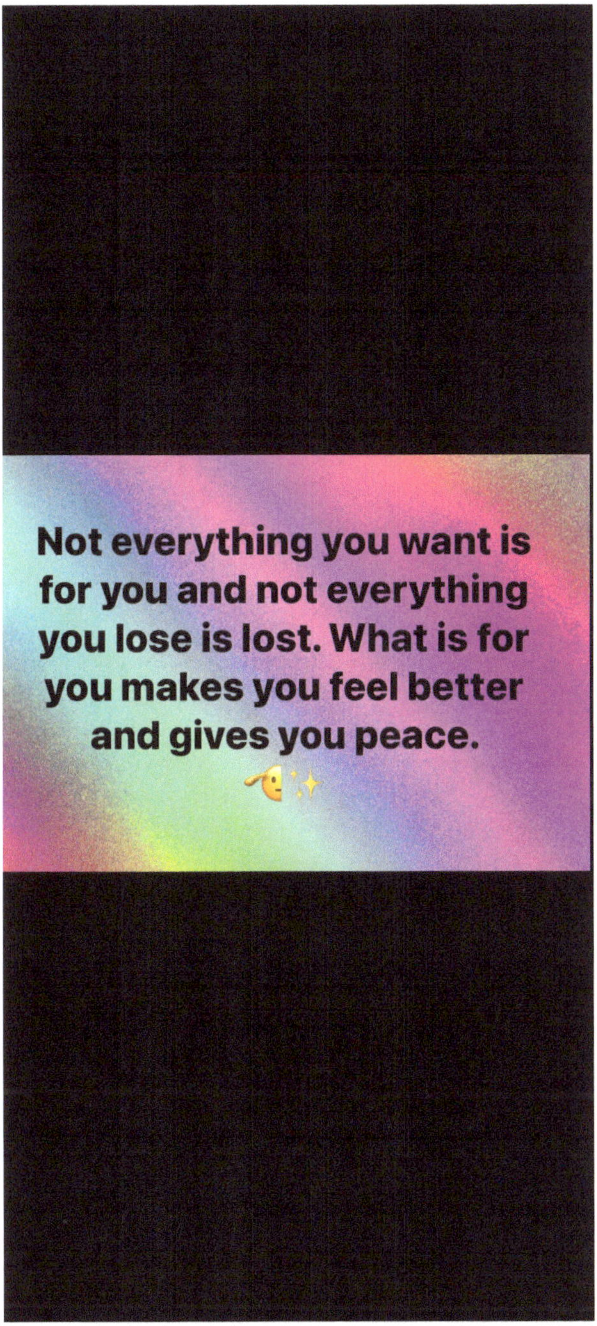

Not everything you want is for you and not everything you lose is lost. What is for you makes you feel better and gives you peace. 🫶✨

PASSENGERS OF DESTINY

An oracle makes an analysis which is subjected to a scoring system,

When someone chooses something, they only have to understand what the reason was,

In every game there is always an opponent and there is always a victim,

Under a quiet sky there is a truce because the people who have already left cannot be forgotten,

The future is full of crossroads and you only know adulthood when something makes you feel like you don't know what decision to make and you leave it in the hands of destiny without listening to opinions.

Including a small car to the big train is like including hope in every sad moment so that it rises towards joy,

The world is dual but consciousness should be unity,

The changes begin with an awareness of unity,

The elevation of the mind is achieved by controlling thoughts,

The heart is tied to the spirit with an umbilical cord of free will,

A rectified heart is the basis of spiritual growth,

Healing begins with oneself from within,

Just as we eat and do what makes us feel good, we should dominate criticism of the imperfect,

He who has a lot of material without love for others does not have abundance,

The proudest and most satisfied man is nothing more than a nameless beggar,

If a speech does not raise questions then it contains no value,

The waves of the sea are a simple journey but adventures must be shared,

A good person will follow the rules but a great person will follow himself.

THE SPIRAL OF ATTRACTION

Defensive races no longer need soldiers for a battle,
Autonomous attacks are conducted as blitzkriegs,
Out of control flashes discuss the most unpredictable thing that is coming,
In virus nomads, the horror of meaninglessness leaves a strange uncertainty,
Experiment invasions test us to survive in the apocalypse,
The laboratory secrets ring at a discreet volume,
The inflation arrow always points up,
Society is between passion and frustration,
The nightmare of the future feels eternal while the demon of power rests in the sensations,
Trapped in the reset a disturbing emptiness points towards an abyss,
The love of what does not exist appears to be an illusion with a domino effect,
Disease businesses fuel pharmaceutical weapons,
The world in debt observes poison that does not want to see in exchange for instant pleasure,
Criticism of inferiority depresses people who feel losses,
The speeches of false humility make one feel a pride that can be felt on another level,
Companies are busy trying to squeeze their employees in which they forget to solve their problems,
Communist propaganda deceives naive mediocre people,
The empire of fantasy seeks a cave to dwell in riddles,
The myth of evolution expects to find a big-ban change in the news.

PLAY WITHOUT LIMITS

There is a butterfly that flaps its wings and sends a hurricane to the other side of the world,
The rich do not care about inequality, which leads to the risk of major social fractures.
The culture that surrounds us tells us to go faster, so mountains of garbage are generated,
The poor who recycle in the streets see garbage as a first use and another next,
Food waste is a challenge that most never reaches any table,
Human prosperity has two faces where human rights are showcases of social classes,
Love and compassion are becoming an antisocial work of art,
The class struggle only has one mission that is seen in wanting more money,
In the past a salary could feed a family but in these decades a salary only feeds one person,
Inequality endangers the order of the rhythm of society,
People emigrate because the country is a victim of global greed,
Barriers are raised higher to impose opportunities but people will continue to jump over them,
Treated as defenceless beings, they make us believe that depression is part of life so they can medicate ourselves,
Justice advances with a beacon of oppositions while imitations follow logos,
The business districts continue to shine among modern office towers,
Witnesses of wars join fragments but lack real power,
Growing rivalries face artificial intelligence race,
A spy among ignorance puts into play the challenge of a swarm of drones,
At the end of the corridor the cracks that the pressure crushed will sink.

LOOKING FOR FOOTPRINTS

One can find one's destiny in the path one takes to avoid it,*

Curiosity is a balance that attracts courage that resolves fears,

There are acts that make us sign sentences and there are others that take us towards the first step of freedom,

A path to existence finds balance from within,

Virtue resides in the mind of each person regardless of external circumstances,

In the darkest moments the spirit can rise in the face of adversity while maintaining hope to triumph in victory,

Guidance for navigating life's adversities focuses on resilience,

Self-discipline provides practical tools to face daily challenges,

Self-reflection can shape reactions and make more conscious decisions,

Thoughts shape our perceptions, emotions and actions,

Gratitude cultivates a sense of equanimity that can foster resilience toward inner strength,

Our greatest strength lies in our sphere of influences,

We must cultivate a focus on what is within our reach to create a value system,

Intentions should align with goals for a life objective,

To face life's challenges we must accept what is beyond our control and focus on what we can handle,

We must learn to cultivate the act of being conscious to overcome negative thoughts and develop the positive to improve our well-being,

Stroking the ego releases hormones that activate silence.

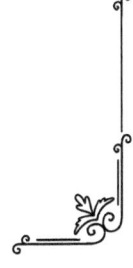

🫠✨Your serenity does not depend on the world, but on your mind.🫠✨

Olivia Conde

> For a narcissist, his priority is not to love, it is to shine. For a narcissist, you are someone who must serve him so that he can feed his image.
> 👉✨

VALUES AND OBJECTIVES

The energy must be directed towards the aspects that we can shape,

To master inner peace, choices must be aligned with our values,

Exercising control over desires, impulses and emotions is essential to cultivate inner strength,

By resisting temptations, personal growth is achieved with long-term goals and values.

Cultivating resilience is a fundamental pillar that teaches us to embrace the inevitable challenges that life presents,

By knowing how to face challenges and setbacks, we recognise that they are only learning with opportunities for growth,

Resilience is nourished by accepting impermanence and maintaining an inner strength and security,

By embracing challenges we develop values such as patience and courage,

Present moment focus exercises control and discipline in our immediate actions,

External approval requires detachment in order to cultivate our moral appreciation,

The compass of the opinion of others must be temporary for oneself to build personal integrity,

The present moment is a treasure that navigates the passage of time and becomes a beacon like a guiding light through storms,

Self-discipline is an art of living tied to an anchor that remains firm through a storm,

Through self-discipline we can filter the outside noise by focusing our attention on being faithful to our values and principles,

Existence is singular and ephemeral and we only have the opportunity to live one moment at a time,

Life is too short and turbulent for those people who forget the past, neglect the present and fear the future,

The happiness of your life depends on the quality of your thoughts.

THE SHORTNESS OF LIFE

The glass of the gaze draws what it observes but more important is not to ignore what the soul can see,
Some go over lands and seas with desperate greed for goods with ambition for profit,
Some are stopped by coveting and others by careful negligence,
Some are forced to military torment and inclination without being warned of dangers or chastened by their own,
Some who get close to a lot of happiness for other people's goods and can also drown,
Some live in the fatigue of ambition pending other people's opinions,
While some sentence and others defend, the list of life passes by consuming each other,
Some live the life of others and others are known by signs of professions, which is in the arrogance that they do not know themselves,
In many cases, families do not visit each other, but when someone dies, everyone is at the wake,*
Among the fog of power, no one shares their wealth until illness arrives and can leave the being in poverty.
After being defeated by broken weapons, men regret the past age, complain about the present and distrust the future.
Age passes in silence without warning or stopping and while one is busy life escapes in a hurry,
He who has a lot wants more, which shows that he does not have enough, but he who has enough has reached a point that the rich never reach.
Some ask for time boarding in the same place,
Some rent their diligence without offering kindness, but when the danger of illness approaches, they are prepared to touch the knee of doctors to give all their wealth,
Freedom is based on not being a slave to any thing, no need, no chance,
Although nature runs, reason will pursue it.

THOUGHTS ARE THINGS

We must live in war for our own passions and in peace for the passions of others,
The magical world of whims only lives believing that it becomes wiser,
In every corner there are traps that submerge us in existence,
Strength is the virtue that we must follow without putting our domain in anyone's hands,
The price of greatness is never forgetting your responsibilities,
Growth is painful and often hidden but behind failure the brilliance of a diamond appears from the effort,
What stands in the way has the direction of the right path,
Challenges allow us to achieve personal growth and detachment allows us to find tranquility in the midst of uncertainty,
The wise man, when making mistakes, monitors and corrects himself, which thus ensures success.
Everything is born in the mind and light or appearances are generated in it,
Problems with brave determination can overcome everything,
Being silent to control criticism is the most advisable thing because words are silver and silence is gold.
Everything returns to the origin from where it was created, nothing and no one escapes this law,
Gratitude is a valuable tool that says appreciate what you have and not what you lack,
By focusing on learning from each experience we understand that life is like the earth that grows seeds, some are fertile and others are sterile,
The key to the price of greatness lies in personality,
The funny thing about trust is that it is difficult to gain but easy to lose,
We all have a past and challenges in the present.

GAMES WITHOUT RESTRICTIONS

Logic will take you from A to B but imagination will take you everywhere.
Greatness inspires envy, envy generates resentment and resentment produces lies,
Learning from better people is the best investment you can make in yourself.
Learning is the beginning of the wealth of health and spirituality,
The true response to injustice is not to punish others but to focus on one's own personal development,
The path to getting rid of deceptive illusions begins with fierce honesty with oneself,
It is important to set goals based on who we are and not on what we are told we should be,
The essence of good and evil lies in the attitude of the will,
The man who knows the chains to which he is bound will be free because he can consciously break them,
The liar is a victim of his own fears and will be trapped by them.
Lying is a destructive habit that harms truth and integrity,
Comparison with others could make us lose our identity and authenticity,
We are not disturbed by things but by the vision we have of them,
The secret of happiness is freedom and the secret of freedom is courage,
Although we have little control over what happens to us, we can still have control over how it affects us,
We are born into the world without knowing much about anything, so it is necessary to focus on improving ourselves,
In solitude there is a wise teacher who offers moments of peace where you can face your true feelings without masks that are worn before society,
Giving is not the same as receiving, hearing is not the same as listening, or being sleepy is not the same as dreaming.

🫵✨When you are healthy you can have a thousand problems but when you are sick you only have one.🫵✨

When pain finds no help, hatred feeds on silence with ideas that drive terror.

OBSERVING LONELINESS

Solitude is a fertile ground that provides inner tranquility in which we find a valuable pillar in the midst of chaos.

Solitude offers a space of silence and reflection to shelter the mind furious towards good decisions,

Solitude meets the mirror of the true self, allowing us to search for the truth within ourselves and discover what truly motivates us.

By looking inward we can explore the hidden corners of our mind and heart,

Solitude allows us to discover an internal dialogue that aligns us with the values of internal strength,

In solitude we observe our emotional doubts without external judgments, without masks or pretensions,

Solitude frees us from the need to seek external approval,

Solitude is a refuge in the middle of a storm that distances us from external voices,

Loneliness is a friend and a powerful aspect of self-awareness,

Solitude is a laboratory that allows us to leave slavery without judgments or external pressures,

Solitude is an internal dialogue that helps us understand ourselves better and allows us to make decisions that are more aligned with our true nature.

Cultivating inner strength allows us to disconnect from the noisy distractions of the world and allows us to focus on our values,

Loneliness is like armour that protects us from external influences,

When we are surrounded by the opinions and judgments of others, our inner peace becomes a constant struggle,

Solitude allows us to begin to distance ourselves from external influences and begin to trust in our wisdom,

When we are alone we can deal with self-control by learning to observe impulses and allowing ourselves to make conscious and ethical decisions,

Solitude gives us the opportunity to learn to live with the essentials and not depend on material possessions for satisfaction,

Solitude allows us to find the strength to face challenges with courage.

TRAINING THE MIND

By training the mind we can observe how the clouds move through the sky,

When we are focused on searching the external world, we face cloudy emotions,

Deep self-knowledge is a safe space to look inward, exploring our minds and hearts,

By valuing simplicity and moderation we find a sample of satisfaction,

When we give everything for the priorities of others we sacrifice our freedom and immerse ourselves in service to others,

The feeling of emptiness causes us to get lost in the process where the inner voice is drowned out by external demands,

Between love and habit there is a step that must be differentiated since illogical love is known as obsession,

The end of a relationship can be useful to learn the principles of self-esteem and respect,

The scars are real but they won't always be there. Time can heal the darkest wounds.

The courage to move forward is an opportunity to grow as a person and meet someone who respects us,

We must not forget that we are only our fleeting thoughts which is the only energy that makes us attract what we feel,

It is important to value yourself and not only focus on external appearances,

Setting limits and living in our virtues is an act of love with a path to an authentic life,

Relationships are like a garden, they must be sown with the seeds of understanding, conversation and empathy to grow and bear fruit.

We learn to find riches in ourselves when we visualise ourselves with the love that requires loyalty, patience and constant commitment,

Fear can be transformed into courage, anger into self-discipline, and sadness into resilience.

The world changes with your example and not with your opinion.

NEVER TELL YOUR PROJECTS

By embracing a fundamental conviction we find the power of discretion and the depth of silence,

For a fullness of wisdom, thoughts are the path to happiness where we learn how to free ourselves from restlessness,

In discipline and self-control, the keys based on virtue and moderation are elementary,

Excessive consumption can bring momentary pleasure but in the long term it can result in both physical and mental burdens,

An intermediate balance is an inner path that becomes the key to well-being,

We should enjoy our experiences instead of hindering them

Moderation is a universal principle that enriches discipline and self-control,

In the symphony of life to exist in harmony we must embrace firmness,

In life's journey for a satisfying and balanced existence we must always speak well of ourselves in thoughts,

By striving to recognise our creative and confident potential we strengthen our resilience,

By nurturing constructive and encouraging internal dialogue we create a favourable terrain for personal development,

The positive and growth-focused mindset aligns the force of actions for a favourable purpose,

Personal fulfilment lies in our own perception of confidence without bragging about self-improvement,

To become better individuals we must do so with a sense of humility and discretion

When faced with questions about challenges, we should allow our actions to be the testimony of the answers.

Self-control begins with the way we speak to ourselves.

ON THE JOURNEY OF LIFE

The true testimony of the personal journey lies in the actions that speak louder than words,

The behaviour in how we treat others lies in the wisdom that influences what we have learned,

When we feel grateful for the achievements around us we can make those around us shine,

By cultivating gratitude we enrich our lives and strengthen our connection to others by creating an emotionally nourishing and empathetic environment.

Recognition for kind gestures creates blessings with solid bonds of trust and mutual respect,

The charlatans clamour for attention like a competitive struggle that rages to make their voices heard,

Listening is an art that requires more than simply hearing the absence of noise,

When you listen, you offer a precious gift where people feel valued and create exchanges with new ideas,

We have two ears and one mouth therefore we should listen twice as much as we speak,

We should not allow ourselves to be consumed by the future because uncertainty is a challenge that pushes us towards anxiety and depression,

There is only one path to happiness and that is to stop worrying about things that are beyond the power of our will,

To cultivate mental security, it is better to adapt to living in the present, channelling the clarity in which we can manage and choose to change mistakes with serenity.

Silence is a valuable teacher that teaches us to reach the most valuable treasures found in our hearts,

The path to improvement is a journey that embraces humility and modesty.

🫢✨**Men's listen but they don't hear everything, women's listen and hear more than necessary**🫢✨

> **Luck happens when preparation meets opportunity.**
> 🫡✨

IMMERSED IN ADVENTURES

From walking with me so much I have walked through the silence thanking life for what happens to me in time,

Everything is so perfect just as God is so powerful that he lives in the stars,

The gardens among flowers live without explaining to the world the conditions of winter,

I danced to my songs and not to the ones that a note seller played me,

I am not freedom but I am the one who provokes it to live it at my own pace,

I am the one who chooses to be an eagle or a hawk to fly on earth with wings of freedom,

I prefer to continue on foot and not on a borrowed horse which offers me the apple and then remains in debt,

I go through the world light because the one who is least loaded always arrives first,

I face the enemy and turn my back on a good comment because he who accepts a compliment begins to be dominated,

No one can give advice without being experienced because there is nothing certain in the mystery of the years,

I like the sun and the pigeons because they meet the flowers that are neither from here nor there,

One day I came to a labyrinth that was difficult for me to cross, but I put the moon on my shoulder and the sun showed me the way.

Death has been following me since the day I was born, that's why I don't believe in anyone with stars on their foreheads.

I like to walk among the poor and the rich because I am someone from the crowd and science is my rebellion,

I like to ride a bicycle to meet the wind that has no age or time and has no future,

I like to cry in sorrow as well as walk in the sand so that the sea wets my feet,

I like to see the stars that smile at happiness,

I like to feel hugs because they are my colour of identity.

PARADISE IS NOT LOST

Paradise is not lost but forgotten in an eternity that awaits its encounter,
Every morning is a new day to start over and to look for the angel who does believe in dreams,
In each promise you have to look in the mirror to try to be a better human every day,
Facing the sun we must walk and with the moon learn to fly,
Healing with words there are greater things that we will see and more beautiful things we will do,
We do not come to suffer or to endure because the chains come from the fear that is inherited,
Life is the present where dreams can grow,
Ties and competitions poison our joy of living,
Promises are sacrifices and it is better not to demand anything that is exhausted in ceremonies,
I don't like prayers because they are the worst dictator who kneels before fear,
The illumination of life is found in the dignity that rests in love,
A verse is the guitar that sounds with the joy of the triumphant heart,
The most important thing is not the price but the value of things that bear the imprint of love,
Blessed is he who only takes what he
needs because your spirit thanks you for knowing how to share hope,
Cross without fear through the darkness because after the night the sun will shine,
The dawn brings harmony and when you live in the present you will always be happy,
Never stop dreaming because the dream of the present will be your reality,
Fly through life without worry and let the dream decide where you want to go,
Do not be afraid of loneliness because only through it will you know yourself.

IN HEAVEN THERE ARE NO BORDERS

The birds say that in the sky there are no borders because all existence dances around life,

They say that it is a false experience to be living fearing everything,

They say that since we live between night and day, you should always sing celebrating joy,

They say that in secrets the truth opens a thousand doors and lies a thousand fears,

They say that the ambitious man gets more lost every day on the road when he wants to fly,

They say that by remaining children in peace we will sleep without wars or sorrows to calculate,

They say that when a man works, God respects him, but when a man sings, God respects him.

love,

They say that it is easier to remember a song with music than a song without sound,

They say that it is not the richer who has but the one who needs the least flies in joy,

They say that a busy hand is like a lost hand since he who conquers a lot is a slave to his conquest.

They say that a man is wrong if he thinks he will find happiness in a cheque-book.

They say that there is only one race that is humanity and that there is only one god who is everywhere,

They say that love never dies and that it only changes places,

They say that poor people have millionaire hearts while the rich live with greed in their hands,

They say that the mother in this world is the only one who forgives us and waits up for us on the nights of ballads just as she is the only one who knows how to love in a second and can never abandon,

They say that we are neither from here nor from there and that happiness should be our identity card,

Whoever looks for water and finds oil can die of thirst if greed invades him.

WITH A FLOWER IN HAND

Only he who goes very far can find a destination but he must not forget where he started his path,

Humans know nothing if they do not have love as a witness, only eating in life does not feed the spirit,

In this life without doors you have to leave reason aside and only take the illusion,

Permanent change is the reason for life but nothing flies as high as the dreams of the heart,

A poem every day is a triumph of hope that creates a glow in the soul so that the spirit smiles,

A new idea is an old friend with nostalgia on,

When the mountains are silent sounds through the rivers that flow through the meadows bringing shiny stones,

It is too boring to follow other people's tracks because the arrows they carry could cause wounds,

When the mysterious love is crossed in passing, a ray enters the eyes and reaches the heart with a flight towards passion,

As the sea comes and goes, so will life go, but only the traces of evil and good remain,

Being honest with yourself is like living with the wind that embraces the universe,

Between the sun and the moon is the reward or the punishment,

Sing until it becomes a song so that the dance of life takes you to meet the stars,

To get from the human to the divine you must be born again, transforming like a child,

When the heart cries about what has been lost, the spirit arrives and laughs because it has just been found. Between roads, the distance leaves great memories to keep in the soul, those that remain as joys forever.

Whoever plays a guitar, even if you are ugly on the outside, is a beauty on the inside.

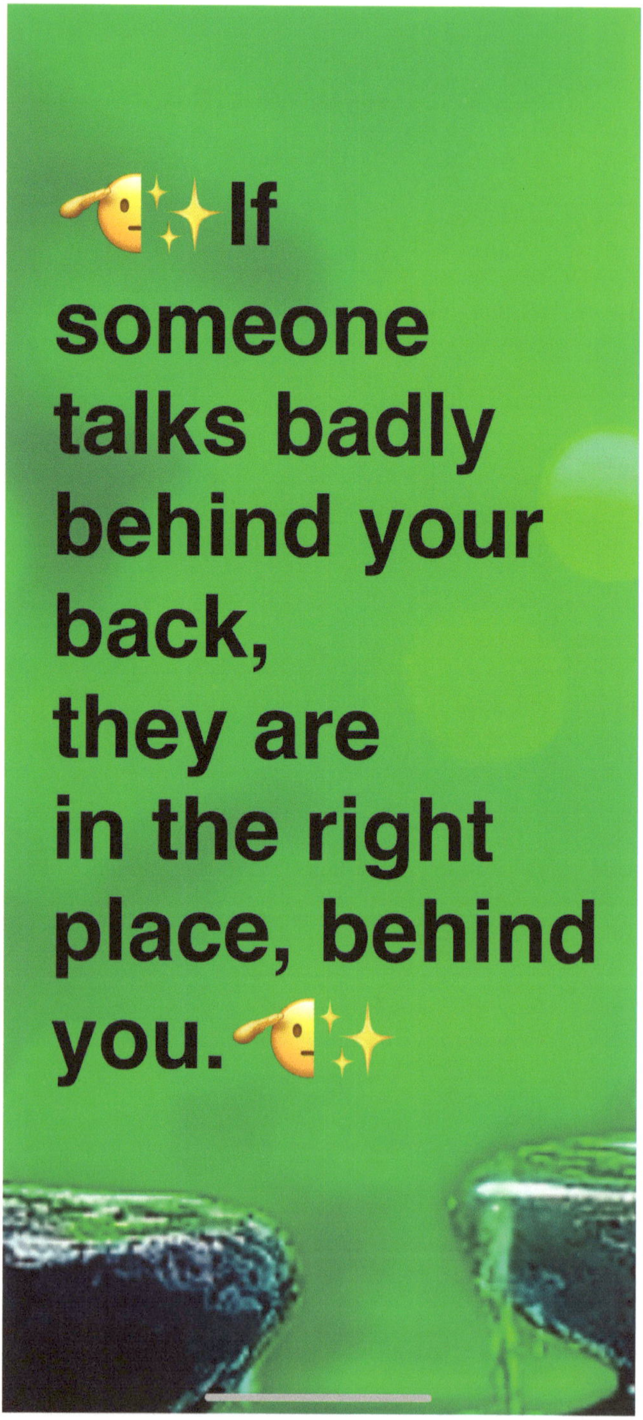

🫡✨If someone talks badly behind your back, they are in the right place, behind you.🫡✨

Olivia Conde

> A wonderful person gives you a thousand reasons to be happy.

THE LIFE IS A PARTY

You have to be like a guitar to live good memories again,
When life overwhelms you and with blows it has led you astray, emotion becomes a splinter that we must heal with tears,

Patience is a story that is braided into a verse to be used in moments when distance strikes,

Every path is a home even if wounds bleed, the mountains are the dens and with the roof the stars to alleviate the loneliness in their great spheres of brilliance,

By embracing what you want there is the full comfort of the guide who accompanies and blesses and over time makes the path,

The human can be what he loves if he puts his steps towards hope and runs looking towards freedom,

Happiness is in the simplest things and in the shadows hope can be found when everything is seen in understanding,

It is enough to open your arms to know the measure of tenderness and feel the bond that unites death with life,

Fly low in the mornings to be able to contemplate your shadow and celebrate the birth of the moon at night,

To feel the silence of men, contemplate the noise that their singing makes under the rain,

Build a green house in the middle of poetry, filling the verses in posies with a lot of windows that observe joys,

I wonder where the pigeons go when their life ends or is it that they don't age and become stars without leaving sorrow in the air,

A wheel spins at night because it tries to climb into freedom,

You can fly like birds and see winter like a blue summer,

If you are free and happy with the rhythm of the wind you will be able to know your song.

A FRIEND IS A WAY

When you respect the steps, the stones do not bother you and the path takes you to doors where a friend is,
He lives in a place where he doesn't forget to sing good morning to any passing soul,
Embrace each landscape where the verse is in the hands and the hands touch the earth and the eyes look to the sky to hear the song of the rain that unites the winds,
Enough of the excuses and live in a place where the speeches or the fights or the promises don't matter because all the enthusiasm of the union is in the sowing that is harvested in the step,
Pursue habit only where there are smiles that rain like jasmines and you can fly in dreams with joy,
There are silences without words that
They understand with their eyes because where the heart is, the soul follows it,
After all and before anything else it is better to sing to a flower that can extinguish the sadness and leave traces of the dawn,
Sadness and joy are brothers when there is a good friend you are never alone or bitter,
Truth and lies are a conscious decision to use on the forehead that chooses the path to walk,
A man who steps on another is not the same as one who allows himself to be stepped on,
Yes and no are the same destiny that reach freedom equally,
To temper the iron, they bathe it in ice water and it seems to cry and complain among the golden sparks, but then it turns into a
hammer and sword,
New shoes sometimes feel like enemies but as they adapt to time they become friends,
No matter the money, independence is easier because when you rent a hat you also rent your head.*

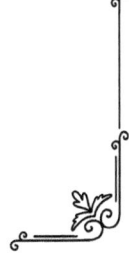

LET THE CHILDREN SING

Running does not go farther than staying in the same place because everything begins with a step that gives you security,

When you want to catch a bird just to cage you must love its soul from the lost flight so as not to kill its freedom,

A dolphin puts on a show for the sad men who took away his freedom,

Strength is not in the hands but in knowing how to enjoy the colours of life that sing towards peace,

The enemy and the friend meet inside the soul to discover the step that must be chosen,

There are things that you already have and they weigh more than a tear that darkens life, but when you leave for a valley, the shadow that was your only companion took you to a good destiny.

Life is constant change and with change you learn in smiling and crying,

There are many faces with gods and colours in their feathers that can give joy but also reveal beauty,

Even if you have a tribe, if you don't come down from the mountain you can lose the luck that awaits you on the plain,

Dignity goes hand in hand with virtue and independence to multiply prudence,

Escape from the cowards who delay evolution because the brave is the one who does not allow chains and who, based on reason, seeks justice on earth,

Take the hand of the one who knows how to seek justice because the righteous person is not even in the family, no matter how much he is in your life, and just as the tree is pruned, so is the family.

From the moment we wake up the days begin to pass and there is no border or flag that can stop the years that point towards death,

Only the blanket of love can overcome life so that when we say goodbye it is with an eternal smile,

Staying silent out of fear is not the same as speaking out of freedom.

FREEDOM TO LIVE

Let the children sing and raise their voices, let the world hear that they sing for those who cannot sing because someone turned off their voices, and let them sing for them for freedom, making war and evil cease and so that peace can flourish.

A miracle is the justice of what the country bears to be able to give the world a breath of hope,

War spends life changing those who think differently to bring more soldiers to the battlefield, but in the step of the brave, these dialogues do not affect him because he lives in trust and is one less soldier,

Whoever goes through life begging, wanting more in his riches in his false poverty, is a ghost and after being a ghost he is nothing,

When the couplets are sung from the heart

The composer remains united with the town where the voice of his songs will be resurrected,

Tales from passions in extraordinary magic, those who are lost in names are gained in eternity,

In this borrowed life a bomb makes more noise than a caress but a caress saves hearts in ruins because there is no value in helping in exchange for money since only through love can the spirit be won,

Hope is a star lying between two camellias that travel between night and day all their lives,

Illness can kill but on many occasions it makes you more grateful,

Crickets fall from paradise and bells ring in their wake that meet the fire of the horizon and the nostalgia of the cold,

God took the form of a beggar and when he approached the poor he was always well received.

When you can bring the moon from a lagoon you will be able to see a mirror that has no ties.

🫨✨**Human beings are curious about other people's lives and lazy about correcting their own.**🫨✨

Life gives its toughest battles to its best warriors. Because when you overcome the blows, you will become part of yourself, where you will come out stronger 🫴✨

EVERY DAY IS SPRING

When looking at a mirror I find my shadow where the sun's rays show me a path,

There is an alarm clock that rings and I don't want to wake up because next to me is the person I love the most,

I prefer to sleep awake than dream without hope because on cold mornings my evening fades away,

The caresses force me to return to the same pillow where my soul misses the silence of a look,

When I look for a dialogue I only find myself tied to very sweet hands that hug my face,

I walk naked in the cold although I feel heat on my back,

Some invisible flowers fall from the ceiling onto my soul, covering my bristling skin with their aroma,

The music sounds with flames under some hours that deceive,

Secrets have no questions towards the doubts of desire,

There are moments that go crazy and even though the exits are visible I can't find an escape,

He ran across the streets to return to history,

The hours pass very quickly when the energy attracts,

I feel melted in a fire that I cannot put out its flames

When the moment catches me, only the moon understands me by taking me to the stars,

The early morning sky has its hours numbered under the laws with rules that overwhelm my hope,

The steps back home are slow because they carry memories that they miss,

There are long waits but in the deep silence the traces will never die,

Summers seem short because vacations take them away,

There is no winter or autumn when you feel the kisses of someone who is in your soul,

Every day that passes is immersed in the spring breeze.

TRUST YOUR INSTINCT

A dialogue with a ring tells the story of a diamond,
There was a stone hidden under a dark cave,
A snake approaches to circle the scars of some blows,
Some secrets are hidden waiting to see the exits,
Cold voices sound with an accent of sighs,
Surprises bring a thousand questions without wanting to know answers,
A frightened bird flies screaming to break escapes,
The wind blows strongly, threatening the intruder,
A storm is approaching warning of an avalanche,
An erupting volcano covers the mountain with lava to cover a treasure,
The dawn approaches and cleans the strange footprints,
The day is born again with a daily opportunity to return to fantasy,
A paradise lights a candle to mark the forbidden,
A circle draws limits to return from the tree to the diamond,
We should not feel defeated when the goal is good,
Don't want to call yourself time because we are in no man's land,
Only the fields and rivers are more owners of the earth than humans,
There are commitments that suffocate if we jump from one bonfire to another,
A fairy from the cave says that we are not owners of the earth, we are only children of it,
We should not be slaves to anyone just as Lucifer and God are free but one prays and the other does not.

A BLUE UNICORN

Today I asked the flowers how they choose their colours, they answered me that with looks from the people,

Today I asked the tree why it can grow very tall and it answered me because it does not know time,

Today I asked the dog why he barks and doesn't speak and he answered that his eyes are his words and barking is the way to avoid battles,

Today I asked the cat why he doesn't obey like the dog and he answered that with his nine lives he has already overcome fear,

Today I asked the parrot why he repeats the human's words and he answered me so that the human can hear the noise of his voice,

Today I asked the horse why it rides with the human and it answered so that the reins feel united to nature,

Today I asked the wolf why he howls in the mountains and he answered me because the moon is his ally,

Today I asked the rooster why he has many chickens and he answered me so that the man who wants many women can be envious of him,

Today I asked the owl why it sings like the alarm clock and it answered so that humans remember that their days are numbered,

Today I asked the eagle why she is the queen of the skies and she answered me because she only chooses her prey with caution in her food,

Today I asked the pig why he likes to eat all the garbage and he answered me so that the ambitious human keeps his savings in a piggy bank,

Today I asked the monkey why he steals from pockets and he answered me so that humans remember where their roots of the search for power were born,

Today I asked the snake why it crawls on the earth and it answered me so that humans know that in old age a cane awaits them.

WHEN THE SIRENS SOUND

Footsteps with chains ran down a wet street, watched by cold glances,
In the passage they marked footprints that in the invisible carried hearts in sadness,
The clothes were old, worn out by days of sorrow,
The cold dried tears that slept on their faces while they loaded their weapons,
The hungry nights hid darkness under the blankets,
The boots squeezed the toes and the feet asked for rest,
The rain hid the tears when, the troops advanced,
The silences of the night lived among the noise of cannons and missiles,
The clock did not show the hours because time was in the hands of the devil,
In corners there were trenches that covered some bodies that did not return,
Some bodies were torn from legs, arms and smiles,
The orders were rifles that hit the soul of the lost youth,
There were no complaints from anyone because the surrendered country was a lost hook,
The companions of the side lower their heads until they wait for escape,
The colonels' orders push the backs of fatigue,
On the other side of the Tower shouts are heard to continue revenge,
The birds no longer sing nor do the squirrels run,
The city remains in ruins waiting for the soldier if he returns to fix it,
Mothers never sleep because they think about their hurt children,
Luck is counted under the hands of destiny,
Borders are separated by the power of roots that yearn for profits.

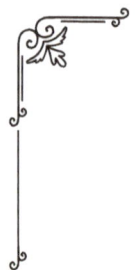

🫡✨A GOOD PERSON CANNOT BE RECOGNIZED BY THE NICE THINGS HE SAYS OR THE GOOD THINGS HE DOES. A GOOD PERSON CAN BE RECOGNIZED BY THE TYPE OF ATMOSPHERE HE CREATES AROUND YOU.🫡✨

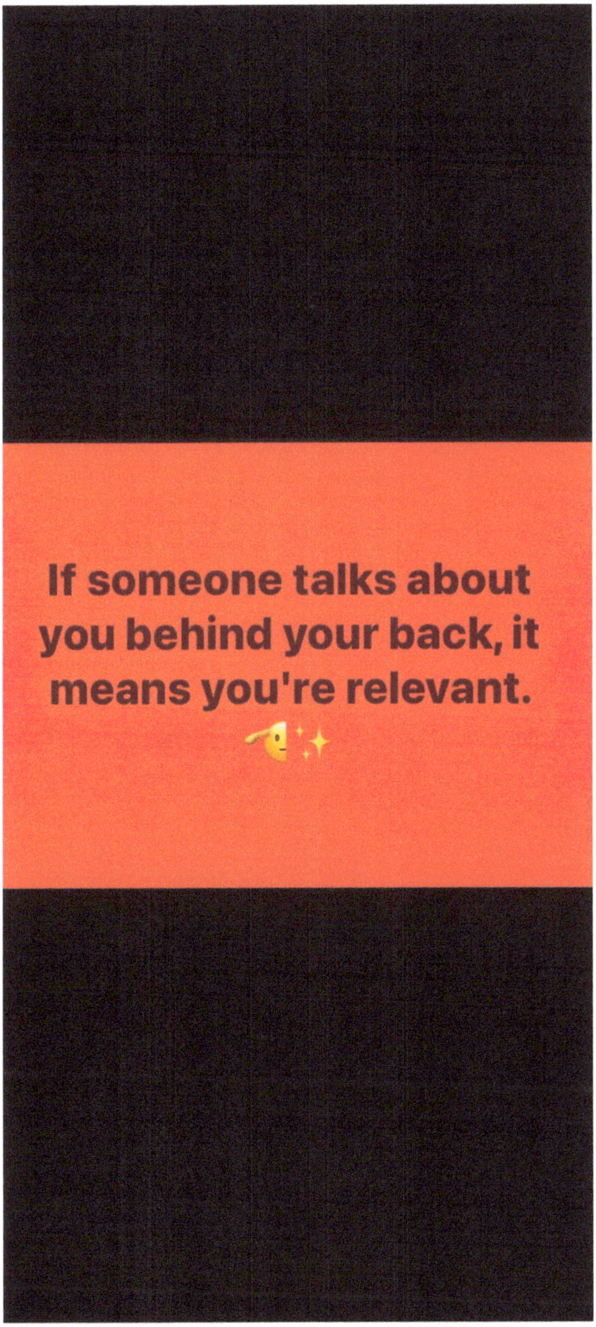

Olivia Conde

If someone talks about you behind your back, it means you're relevant.

THE ARROW OF LOVE

I come from all over the world and distance cannot stop me,
  Through lakes and rivers I fly and cross the seas of the ocean,
    I live in the fresh wind and the clouds accompany me with the rain,
I can talk to the stars when I lie in the sand,
Flowers are my gift as I pass through every door,
Dreams accompany me between brilliant glances,
Smiles create songs under the fresh green meadows,
Some candles are lit and in the heat of their flame the sparks shine,
Pigeons surround me in the spring sun,
The aroma of jasmine lights up the colours of the rainbow,
A mystery crosses walls to meet passion,
The days become short between the hours that pass,
The hands drop their weapons and the current of rivers joins truth with beauty,
The moon comes down from the sky to speak out loud that secrets do not exist,
Joy covers roads with the feathers of free birds,
The dawn creates verses to dance with the fireflies,
Red rose petals cover the sky to fall like rain,
Every day is a new day covered with palm trees and flowers,
The birds recite poems with the leaves of the trees,
Surprises are born with joy to thank the smiles.

WE ARE DISTRACTED

We are strays in our own right looking for destiny and its opinion,
    We look for a time to take a nap without being accountable to dawn,
    Seeking freedom with the sun you lie down looking at the stars to recite,
We talk to our dog looking for tenderness and hugs,
We follow a metaphor of adventure that cannot be found in the dictionary,
We trap people we think we love because we consider them our property,
In our community we put characters from a guardian to a priest for security,
Chasing dreams and beautiful things we forget the laughter of an older brother,
As time went by we left compassion pending but on the day of departure the moment did not return,
Memories look for a way to return to the past but nostalgia has already taken them away,
There was a stray with the soul of an angel and he had the doors open in any home,
The turtle goes slowly enjoying life without disguising the words,
The decisions are recorded in free songs,
Excuses are great when interest is small,
We think about repairs when time is enough but a stone cannot be cut,
When you fly fast without keeping promises, the time comes to leave and you want to return but the clock doesn't go back and you fell asleep and didn't come back,
Memories fade away in testaments full of emotions that leave pain,
Some children were playing in an old yard and they rescued us from loneliness.

START LIVING

Starting tomorrow I will begin to live a small memory that wanted to die,
Starting tomorrow I will fly with the sun to tell the moon what haste stole from me,
Starting tomorrow I will start singing the best songs so I can enjoy,
Starting tomorrow I will begin to gain smiles without losing myself in sadness,
Starting tomorrow I will start playing songs with new bells,
Starting tomorrow I will begin to face that I am not the strongest,
Starting tomorrow I will recognise that I have no courage in the face of enemies,
Starting tomorrow I will speak with the courage to meet the mystery,
Starting tomorrow I will speak with freedom to release the chains,
Starting tomorrow I will shout to destiny that I am the owner of my soul,
Starting tomorrow I will begin to fulfil the words I say,
Starting tomorrow I will tell winter that I will wait for summer,
Starting tomorrow I will tell autumn that I learned to loosen the leaves of the old tree,
Starting tomorrow I will tell destiny to take me by the hand,
Starting tomorrow I will tell the past that I learned from his steps,
Starting tomorrow I will tell the present to show me the future,
Starting tomorrow I will begin to measure each stroke of luck,
Starting tomorrow I will become a dreamer of a perfect world,
Starting tomorrow I will begin to return from my outward journey,
Starting tomorrow I will start living half my life,
Starting tomorrow I will begin to die half of my death.

THE STORY OF TIME

We know religion but not the salvation that leads us to music,
It tells me the story of the time that I am a sailboat and I can fly,
It tells me the story of time that every second comes without turning back,
It tells me the story of time that we are eternity when knowing the truth,
Tells me the story of time that all mistakes can be repaired,
It tells me the story of the time that the disease is cured from the soul,
It tells me the story of time that God is one and accompanies us as we walk,
It tells me the story of the time that listening to others makes us reflect,
It tells me the story of the time that you have to listen with your eyes and speak with your heart,
It tells me the story of time that elegance is in personality,
It tells me the story of time that is not changed by suffering solely by decision,
Tells me the story of the time that friendship is found in loyalty,
The story of time tells me that when you give something you don't expect to receive,
It tells me the story of the time when things arrive without ever waiting,
Tells me the story of time that we go gently in the direction of dreams,
Tells me the story of time that we never forget the art of singing,
The story of time tells me that joy should be our identity,
It tells me the story of the time that we are sun, moon and star,
It tells me the story of the time that love is found within us.

🫳✨**Time is like a flower, if you enjoy it, it will leave an unforgettable aroma in your memory.**🫳✨

Olivia Conde

> **If someone tries to put you down it means you are above them.**

ABOUT US ?

We are brothers of the moon and the sun because from the stars we are united to creation,

We are the food of our emotion by which it leads us to salvation,

We are sea and land where we navigate taking control,

We are the fresh flowers without forgetting the colour because the rainbow brings us closer to God,

We are the beauty of creation because the landscape gives us passion,

We are perfect with all fervour when we unite in understanding,

We are the gray sky and also the sunny one because the rain brings the aroma of the seas,

We are a volcano waiting to know its eruption in order to release sorrow and fear,

We are the song of the wind that caresses our face to calm the loneliness,

We are the mystery that offers forgiveness to each brother in whom he failed,

We are queens and kings of the home that we have to lead the family towards blessing,

We are the laughter and the tears that hug us in the steps,

We are the jungle to breathe and in its green leaves we feel peace,

We are uncontaminated water because it gave us life to enjoy,

We are a tree standing upside down to observe thoughts and thus feed,

We are animals that can think to play in life with a good ending,

We are also a labyrinth as we walk to find the traces of freedom,

We are silence and also the voice that on the road I chose the weapon of decision,

We are the footprint of freedom and when we shine we can dance,

We are colours of reincarnation longing for family from the heart,

We are life and death at the same time in it we find a dawn,

We are everything and we are even more and we are joy to procreate.

MYSTERIES FOUND

When laughter meets tears, the poetry of adoration is created,
When silence meets noise, the elevation of a beggar begins,
When war meets peace, the decision of truth begins,
When dance meets music, love begins to blossom,
When the flower meets the petal, the colours of harmony begin,
When the river meets the sea the aroma of freedom begins,
When illness meets health, the soul begins to seek salvation,
When the mirror with the image is found, the destiny of fantasy begins,
When the drawing meets the painting, the artist's creation begins,
When they find sand and water they swim together in the same bed,
When eyes meet they create a thousand verses with few words,
When the waves meet the seas the language of nature begins,
When light meets darkness they make a pact of love,
When the devil meets god, one stone falls and two rise,
When a sorrow meets a joy, the night is comforted by the day,
When slavery meets freedom, the storm, the chains cry, and peace smiles,
When the stars meet the night, the hope of dreams is born,
When the sun meets the moon the blessing of life begins,
When life meets death they do not discuss anything because they are sisters of eternity.

A GAME WITH PHILOSOPHY

Ideals are born among a thousand words, they play with phrases without tying others,
Building over the years the existence, inventing what one day could be,
Without blaming anyone, the castles are building walls,

In the secrets of spells, a wound is covered with makeup and it is no longer seen but it is felt,

The fountains shine with the day and with the night they go out,

I came from encountering the fire and he told me about a fire,

I led my horse straight but he wanted to walk crooked because he told me that he who goes only straight knows only one path,

I have only one head so I only need a hat because if I live in camouflage I can lose my appearance,

I don't hide my smile because I sleep with myself and when I got up he smiled at me,

To announce a new day, the rooster dawns and crows just as the wind comes announcing its storms,

The city is a jungle and with its cement stairs it collects slaves,

Those who choose lies have a thousand closed doors but the truth can enter through a thousand doors and windows,

Science invents alchemy and the earth makes changes but only in changes is the world that moves,

Patience is a treasure when you understand destiny because in waiting you reach the most divine diamond,

They say that we are a tree with the root facing outwards, that is why in our lineage only the leaves are known but never the roots.

I wonder why humans kiss with their lips and animals kiss with their tongues, and I think that the outward kiss is because it is born from within.

A PATH WITHOUT END

Before being born we die in the footsteps of ancestors to repair programmes that are still pending,

Between doubts walking, glances stumble compared to genes,

When the first breath comes, everything appears to be a game between sleeping colours,

The first voices smile contemplating the secrets that fantasy hides,

The sleeping steps arrive, the legs staggering without a cane but on their way,

Smiles want to fly together with the tears of growth in order to reinforce the breath of the future,

The hands paint drawings that only live in colours that scream joy.

The voice begins to sing the numbers that in its wake are linked to the rules of destiny,

Some letters form words that, following the phrases, differentiate stages,

The teaching of the desk arrives discreetly to hypnotise childhood,

The rules of the game change when attention begins to focus on a battle,

Compare the works that, evaluated by grades, separate the colleagues,

Looks separate races with internal dialogues and applied expressions,

Difference begins to be born, transforming into greed for desired reasons,

Smiles become cold, pretending to appear joyful in their image,

There are doors with a thousand locks that only open the way to the interest of the moment,

In the family there are also intruders because they are part of the process designed in greed,

Independence arrives and pushes aside the steps of old weapons,

Power comes with its pride and pretending to be brave it can attack its owner,

Easy solutions are sought because the implanted fear devoured the unconscious,

The wheel burns its rims because whoever sets fire to the family in the fire is lost.

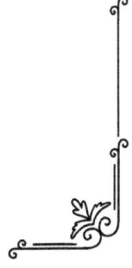

TODAY IS A HOLIDAY

The sun smiles in the morning greeting happiness,

The fountains run quickly and through the meadows they move at the same pace, their laughter is heard and in flight they join the sea,

You have to paint your face with the colour of hope that fantasy comes to see,

It is better to get lost to be able to board a large sailboat that can make you fly,

You have to look at the stars to try to reach the peak of freedom,

You have to do the impossible, you can achieve it by running in the meadows to cross the valleys,

You have to take your soul on a flight to enjoy the secret journey of freedom,

You have to climb to the moon with serenity, taking off your veil and no longer doubting,

Life is a game like carnival and in the rain you can dream,

You have to shine with the sun's rays and paint a heart in its colours,

You have to run through the forest to talk with the dawn to renew your feelings,

There is no one lonely when you live singing because bad weather puts a good face on it,

How beautiful it is to feel the smell of the flowers when at sunset they greet with their joy,

We must forget that time exists and be able to conquer the soul with an eternal fragrance,

Caressing animals is the most beautiful therapy that unites with the wind and brings the smell of spring,

Run to share a drink with friends who laugh because good weather is marked by the heartbeat,

Escaping in the morning is a good ballad where no one corrects you and you dance for your soul,

The search for love is only in simple things like laughing, dancing and living your own life.

Discover the treasure of harmony that has no hour or seconds,

Climb to the divine temple where the sky speaks with the sea while history smiles to begin again.

THERE ARE PEOPLE WHO ARE LUMINOUS

How beautiful it is that people who know you value you and only with a smile can enjoy the hours,

How beautiful are those people who listen to your vent and who come and support you in difficult times,

How beautiful are those people who ask you 'to send me a what's app when you get home',

How beautiful are those people who are happier than you when you have a lucky day,

How beautiful are those people who bring magic in a shared tear and see how to find a way out of the problem together,

How beautiful are those people who dance because they do and smile without deception,

How beautiful are those people who look for you without needing you and stay at any time to accompany you,

How beautiful are those people with whom you breathe slowly, you can vent and despite everything, they want to stay by your side,

How beautiful are those people who give you their time and even if one day they don't have it, they still make it for you,

How beautiful are those people who turn on light bulbs in your path, make you see the best you have and make you feel alive,

How beautiful are those people who, even in the bad, can find good things that make you feel your spirit,

How beautiful are those people who walk next to you and who give you the wind to feel the breeze together,

How beautiful are those people who put joy as the first menu of the day,

How beautiful are those people who laugh at your jokes and lift your spirits in any hour of hot flashes,

How beautiful are those people who, even when the tide rises, do not let go of your hand,

How beautiful are those luminous people who also illuminate the world, those who do not worry about the brand of your clothes, they only accept what they see,

You just have to know what you want and get rid of your fears, open the windows so that the air from heaven can bloom,

The rain puts out the fire and fighting is temporary when love is permanent,

In the lagoon of the moon a star was born and then hidden to return in spring.

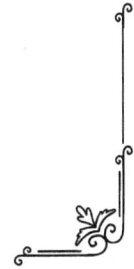

WE CAN FLY IN THE WIND

The sailor sails without being afraid of the sea because he remains in the memory of the aroma of the ocean,

Around the carnations some magnolias were growing and on the other side there were some roses with dormant petals, behind them some geraniums greeted lilies and with a fresh aroma some golden emeralds spoke with some tulips that with multiple colours smiled at some sunflowers that surrounded the garden,

Learn to dream that life is a dream if you know how to love,

Once they met without thinking, a kiss and a flower, they had a conversation in which they said, 'let's let time stop on the clock face and let's play at being Romeo and Juliet to feel the flames of love because from the stars of fantasy everything has more colour',

While you have a lover, the alarm clock rings on the bedside table because the early dawn calls to your consciousness to return to your marital home and returning through the almost deserted city with sleep between your eyes at full speed you must return to escape from the sun that sees everything, because being lovers is wanting but not being able to live under the sun, being lovers is like a paper flower in love, being lovers is only giving the best of each moment, being lovers is like being a paper sailboat, to be lovers is to walk naked through the wind and at any moment lose love in silence,

Let me tell you, friend, my thoughts: I ran along the edge of a very old river and in the glory that my memory focuses on, I collected the laughter of the river as I walked along its green path and then spread it from a bridge towards the stars.

The gold that shines from the sun is enough for the heart so that it can travel free of all control.

WORDS ON A PAPER

An enigmatic kingdom lives in the afterlife linked to mysterious presences,
A spiritual journey joins deep into astral planes and dimensions beneath the spirals,
The mandelas are a marathon of answers hidden for millennia,
A journey into the heart teaches us that there is nothing hidden that will not be revealed,
In the shadows there are hidden riddles and wisdom that resemble a fish in the sea,
The seeds are like the human, some fall on stone and others on the fertile earth,
When the seeds are drowned the worm will eat them,
A good person draws his treasure from within like a divine compass guiding him towards the understanding and discovery of nature,
From the abundance of the heart comes evil, just as a person cannot ride two horses at the same time nor can a slave serve two masters otherwise it will honour one and offend the other,
Patches are not sewn on new clothes, as from the kingdom we came we will return to that same one,
When the fish lets itself be carried by the current, it explores new paths because when there are five in a house, there will be three against two and two against three because the tremor in habit stalks free flight,
When the night approaches there is something in your soul that makes you fly to meet the stars where with your feelings you can tell all the secret things that you would like to dream,
He who knows everything but lacks knowing himself lacks everything,
When someone learns to unite they will be filled with light and when they divide they will be filled with darkness.

YOUR FAITH IS YOUR FORTUNE

Don't let your left hand know what your right hand is doing,
Whoever is close to the fire can burn, but whoever is far from the faith is far from the kingdom.

The images are manifested to humanity but the light that is inside is hidden because the image can only be seen when it is in the darkness,

We cannot live to serve two states of consciousness, to be free we have to let go of one.

When we raise consciousness to the level we desire and let it remain there until consciousness becomes that nature then all the desired miracles will happen,

Just as our state of consciousness is, so will be the manifestation that we attract. It is not possible to serve two states of consciousness at the same time.

Through relaxation practice we can float with thoughts where it is possible to reach an edification of consciousness by recording a unity of purpose,

We can only be for others what we are for ourselves,

When we turn away from the worship of man and images we find the kingdom of heaven within us,

The greatest teacher is the one who is within you than the one who is among the multitude of humanity,

Only slaves have masters because freedom is in the consciousness that crystallises the inner light and when the consciousness is disciplined, faith is achieved.

The fortune of a good life is found in first believing to see.

THE DARK DANCE OF TIMES

The crew workers of science among technology are the puppets of the invisible,
The gods' competition has a farm that follows the march of history,
Religious entities surreptitiously and secretly dance with the doctrine of competition,
The idols of society love and hate each other, destroy each other and build everything for fresh news that is devoured by submissive,
The military regime is good for the barracks but dishonest with society and ends up destroying cities where the old song keeps the primary instinct of fighting where the bullet that wounds also grazes the captain,
Therefore, politicians try to convince but the military orders the law, leaving love aside,
The new directions of humanity are drawn from something where the invisible lords use the visible ones as servants,
While the brothers of space observe the opportune moment to awaken ruined consciousnesses,
Some residents of the cosmos on earth will remain anonymous,
Some information will be interpreted by letters from the human unconscious without visible visits,
In some firms the superior sisters will make demands for explanations of reports without applying the agreements,
Secretaries of older brothers should not leave signatures on secret documents,
Looking into the distance of the universe the photo-magnetic data figures will be stored in photons of statically charged light.

A JOURNEY TO THE BEAT OF THE COSMOS

In the curvature of the universe there are entrances that support the ancestral with the real,

Some smoke emblems are crossed by vertical entrances to the planets,

Some secret communications are kept at a single address,

Analyses are shared between hologram screens with different missions,

Technological advance is cautiously offered without revealing the source from which it comes,

Without leaving precise traces before the human of feats, Orion's movements are directed between fleeting words,

Star travel is done with divine discretion so that the greedy human does not destroy the earth,

The meeting times are sudden and with presences scheduled for a marked five years,

Memories accepted among powerful people must be purely voluntary when programmed psychically,

Between agreements under programmes, scientific information must be shared publicly,

There will be cautious inspections to test the powers that support both interests,

The modifications will comply with the human way of life and adapt to their customs,

Higher intelligence will take into consideration any suspected fraud,

Environmental studies will take into account when any harmful interventions should be suspended,

The data must be kept in a mysterious judgment to evolve without destroying the world,

The entities with more evolution only envision saving the division that was created on earth with the idea of competing and separating humanity,

To overcome the limits there are strategies that can be generated in decades,

In the infinite distances of the universe there is no time, only the right moment to intervene,

The silence of the older brothers will become confusing as they tend to protect the distances of the elevated beings of the cosmos.

THE CENTURIES OF THE NEW ERA

The empire of money tramples on spiritual and moral nature,
The lie became established, becoming the language of all institutions,
The exciting game of big finance surreptitiously visualises possessions and wealth,
The crazy rush to own leaves little time to enjoy life in freedom,

Politics is an instrument with the power of the word with a vehicle supported by the submissive

The bases are mixtures of traditions, conservatism, selfishness and a good part of fear of feeling unprotected.

From private conversations, the reactions of the people are observed,

Between distraction struggles, the energy of politicians goes into strategies on how to solve the people's problems,

Between intrigues and tripping and reciting gospel verses, they are the perfect weapons for manipulations that trap the minds of citizens,

Work has become an evaluation of imbalance to compete with dignity,

The necessary values must be trained from the soul seeking peace to generate a mental balance in harmony,

Having a friend is like having a treasure, they could be given like a wild fruit without perfection, but whoever wants a perfect friend better not have one,

The child of the new era will have the skills to create art with imagination where the appeal is more immersed in illusion than in painting,

Spiritual values will be a commandment of the new age to find tolerance in this noisy lost world.

A BOOK WITHOUT A TRACE

The magical whisper of intuition acts on the nerves, providing well-being,
To capture the immensity you have to plant the seed of success from your thoughts,
Internal affirmations make us what we want to be,

Each thought we have is like a chemical atom with which each one attracts the healing of the mind and it is more art than science, although science is the basis of art; while science is something mechanical, art is spiritual, creative and free,

The open door to an infinite supply is between small streams of heavenly peace that run through the nerves under a fine rain that calms the pain,

Every spiritual teacher tries to awaken a dominant way as a ruler to balance the order of confusion and disorder,

In the darkness of an ancient forest our mind is a magnet with a current that flows without separating from its source,

The heart may be a wise hermit, it may be loaded with uncertainty, but if it is loaded with a spark of hope, it can beat to the rhythm of your steps.

What takes you easiest towards the path of happiness is in the simplest things, as you think, it is the law of the circle that goes to the circumference,

What is done and said is charged with who we really are and the light will shine through us depending on how our temperament shines,

True life is free from ties united with the sphere of self-love, breaking down the walls of spells that bind freedom,

Just as there was a moment that God was born inside Jesus, so there will come a moment that will be born in people.

REBIRTH OF HISTORY

On paper words, a small path without reflection in moments becomes a cage,

There are cages that have the door open but we do not want to leave because there are customs created that do not allow escape,

We should practise forgetting the noise that can destroy us when we pay attention to it,

You have to plant a seed from which silence makes it grow and simply be able to rebuild a new rebirth in the emotions,

The past and the present are a small and a large step of the grain of the future in the furious flight of hope that awaits,

Forgetfulness sleeps with soft glimpses on the paths of eternal life to exit systems which can be changed with actions,

To find how wonderful the brightness of love is, the cruises open between crosses that raise their flags with free elections,

The endless ending is not lost in the time of the process because the visions between the invisible whole are theoretical but inseparable at the beginning,

There are flights in dreams for the reason of the universe delivered in body and soul, the spirits from creation carry the connection with divine harmony,

The colours leave energies from within to welcome the birth of life, the music leaves between sounds the memories of the outside for the farewell of death,

A circle of eternity traps both sides where inhalation and exhalation exist forever,

Take care of the ladder you go up as it will be the same one you will go down.

I asked time what I should do to relieve the pain, time responded, let me pass!!

THE SCREAMS OF THE SHADOW

Adolescence is like a cyclone in life and the years in which one becomes a teenager come with visions to meet one's own self,

The most important thing is not to stop listening to the heart because the heart feels what the mind is confused about,

All the circumstances of life are always learning, although there are difficult moments; the best way to understand things is to know that it is impossible to separate the good from the bad for the great reason that everything is united,

Where the songs of animals shout, voices sound that rejoice hearts saying that they are neither from here nor from there nor from time that passes,

The moment we have our heart connected to our emotions will be the great moment to understand that the paths that destiny sets before us have no escape,

Rebirth is part of every day when you are grateful for smiles, dancing is giving yourself over the clouds with rain,

The fire is a refuge that makes us feel its shelter and the mud spreads its energy with the earth,

Streams come down from mountains and with their green steps they greet the birds that, among illuminated flashes, are covered in their soft shine,

Lightning is a kiss that ignites life to remember with its fury that we must take care of the planet,

The most valuable things do not require exaggerated efforts.

The best way to live is in the way of healing your mind and your body will follow you,

Life is not lost when we stop breathing, life is lost onlywhen we stop being happy.

PAPER WORDS

In cold tears I pursue in torment the sorrows that lead to extinguishing desires
The wind in the distance enjoys the magic of life, respecting the paths that open and walking the beautiful paths,
When death is embraced, a meeting of new sparks ignites into intense flames,
By letting itself be carried away by oblivion, the sheep decides and the wolf attacks, although both can decide to flee or stay still.
All life ends in us to begin again in each moment at the same moment,
We are all going to know each other by weaving and unweaving in the hunt for the return to nothing,
The feelings of sadness with happiness are like hunting prey that some avoid each other and others approach,
A fragile dream waits to wake up in an end destined for the beginning,
The traces are very old beneath the history that was erased on the paper used by the first beings,
Searching in stories, only the ending has something in common with the interest that becomes a prey to destiny,
When looking around you never expect that it is too late for an end since only in the good you feel the eternal,
We all live destined to cross paths because hearts know each other from sleep to awakening,
Beauty fades into immense ashes that's why it's beautiful,
Some feathers fall into the fresh snow, running to find each other and at the same time to try to hide but they can't,
All things live under shadows that feel persecuted and yet are never ready to meet,
There are moments that receive phrases of freedom but the anchors of life say they cannot be without each other,
In a world without love, death means nothing,
Tomorrow is a hope but never a promise.

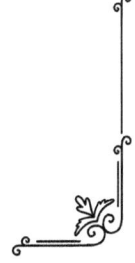

LEGENDS NEVER DIE

Without effort the trees grow, they climb high without seeking rewards and in their soft shine the birds are happy greeting their branches of eternity,

They are the understandings in difficult moments that, together with deep silences, lead to successful outcomes.

The enchanted and sincere wind says that creation is what you love without seeing races, where walking alone with yourself you find the identity of the silences that are free,

A wise man is known for his patience in the face of strong gusts of wind that can bend but rarely break,

Life is full of plans made for constant changes where strength does not lie in resistance but in adaptation,

By embracing flexibility we survive the storms of life to flourish and grow in new and harmonious ways,

In the shadows the traces of success are born from the veins that the blood left in the feelings of the world,

When embracing the dream of yesterday, memories cover the colour of the heart where tears are erased by the pain caused by the ego,

In the stillness of the night while the city sleeps the challenges of empires reflect on the relentless pressures of life,

Within each one there is a safe haven that can always make you retreat from challenges,

We cannot be affected by what happens around us while the serenity of the interior is balanced in the face of events,

No one needs the same thing twice to navigate gracefully because it is necessary to live in flexibility,

There are two steps that can overcome fear, which are the fear of falling and the fear of noise, the other fears are created by humans,

Someone seeks salvation to discipline the mind but true discipline is not imposed, it only comes from within.

BECAUSE WE ARE HERE

Searching to know the thought we only cling to the answer of finding a triumph,
A moment without limits tells us that to reach the sky we do not need perception, we only need to join the idea,

A ray of unrest interfered with existence like an infectious virus to separate humanity,

In the darkness was left the wait for the union between certainty and understanding, a void was submerged in madness,

The delusions of the mind form very lost circles with anguish and confusion when leaving the existence of love,

A dialogue with the conscious perceives unreality due to encountering ghosts that form states of duality,

The experience of love was transformed into fear with dark guilt that is lost in terrifying doubt,

Fights by opponents feed reality more for the reason that thoughts give power,

The source of union is wrapped in oblivion where a piece of heaven awaits the meeting,

When facing the fear of the unknown, a bright path leaves routines entering a mysterious luminous landscape,

Someone lost chases the jungle that screams in a world without love for death that has no meaning when nature is not cared for,

In cold tears I chase a torment of regrets that lead me to extinguish my desires,

When the glow of a smile burns you can see the cry of sadness,

Thanking the north, south, east and west is like a song of love that surrounds the stars where the harmony of the sun with the moon sends verses of love to the earth.

LOOKING FOR A DIALOGUE

The spiral of a sunset with two horizons is made with a sunset that shines in love, With fragility I want to return to an endless desire from which I distance myself by a voracious illusion,

A shipwreck with identity is formed in brilliance when a magical whisper joins the explanations of the mystery,

The difference in love between earth and infinity is that on earth love is calculated and in heaven it is felt,

On earth we live love with measures of necessity but in heaven there are no sacrifices that make a difference,

In the beyond you can perceive the colours that surround the spirit united with valleys that merge under luminous springs where animals live in peace in the intensity of the Infinite,

The colours in infinity are full of happiness with a life of their own while when we go to earth the energy of the universe will always accompany us,

The experiences on earth are to learn to love one another just like the solid rock that contemplates storms but never shakes,

The trap to get lost comes from fear and competition that we must overcome in this journey of life that is an eternal wheel,

When navigating the waters of reflection, renewal takes us towards a portal of clarity,

While we sleep we enter healing from a path of the spirit,

Prayer is a spiritual sanctuary that adjusts energies with one's own being,

The guides are supreme beings where they never abandon us and are travel companions,

The wonder of infinity is a pure state where love is unconditional.

PASSING THROUGH THE DARKNESS

When looking around you just have to row, paying attention to what is in front of you to be guided by the footprints that destiny leaves,

Impulse can cause irreparable damage just as trust is hard to gain but with one mistake it can be lost in a second,

The battles make us reflect between approvals that seek the truth among the lies,

Masks are designed to cause expressions that define us to others and on the other hand to hide the true nature of the individual,

From the horizons each step is an opportunity to grow, transform and heal,

The journey of life is a learning to navigate the currents of the mind and connect with the journey of the soul,

The level of consciousness is like a ladder with many steps where beyond the physical is enveloped the material that can devour,

Between cold hands there are veils between lines that separate people who are not prepared to enter the occult,

From the high spheres of light there are guides that vibrate between energy of faith that unites the invisible with the visible,

Energy is metaphysics where the invisible manifests itself visible from manifestations such as how we attract what we think,

People with doubts cannot enter the secret that fidelity shares,

Everything is known by its fruits where effort and constant will are the secret to achieving hope,

We must break the chains that limit and confuse because on earth there are no sins, there are only errors that can be corrected,

Just like plants, so do humans, some grow in the light and others in the shadow,

He who looks outside dreams but he who looks inside awakens.

I'M STILL HERE

Towards latent powers we must shape reality to overcome obstacles,

In commitments there are only two ways: clarity or appearances.

In life, tests always appear that intersect with interferences to distract from constructive objectives that can hinder the art of living,

The earth is a school of the cosmos where humans come to pay the debts they owe from their ancestors and renew them with experiences for spiritual evolution,

We belong to the family of planets in the solar system to ascend to a higher level since we are more than five thousand years late,

The human being is like a sleeping seed when he is lost in bitterness and resentment,

The word and the ear are the greatest instruments that were given to humans to use that have great potential to direct their own ship,

When humans trust more in what is imposed on them from outside, they become a slave,

The correct use of the word is an energy that comes out of thought to create, just as the word is also a two-edged sword to receive what each one deserves.

The first law that governs creation is derived from the thoughts that then materialise outside,

Discipline in life must be daily, to be a sculptor who forms his own image and shapes his destiny for the better,

Everything can be chosen and must be conquered for a creative effort,

We are like a drop of water that is part of the ocean where the abysses and whirlpools can be swept away by a tsunami,

The body is the vehicle of the spirit where the perfect and imperfect are part of the journey to evolve,

The mind is like a factory where thought and feeling build the basis of creative power.

WEALTH IS BORN FROM THE MIND

The night dream is a journey in planes and dimensions because the human is a citizen of the universe,

The human physical body is a living temple that obeys and submits to the will of thought, whether for good or evil.

The harvest of the sowing is the law of every vision that is put into thought,

By visualising attention to good, tomorrow's sowing will be well prepared to reap abundance,

Attention is like a magnifying glass that concentrates the sun's rays, which if linked to the routine of evil will produce a fire.

Resentment is like a room full of smoke that even if you live in abundance you cannot shine,

Nature purifies itself therefore humanity has the same divinity,

When we want to possess someone we immerse ourselves in a disguised selfishness that among conditions confuses ownership with love,

When the rebellion to possess insists, freedom is lost, just like a candle that burns out in silence or a rose that is squeezed by the hand and withers, but the thorns will leave traces on the soul.

Jealousy derives from fear combined with selfishness and doubts due to insecurity and can chain and poison the atmosphere,

When you live in love, you live in interest, but when infatuation ends, true love begins.

In love what lasts is the union of souls and not of bodies,

Human health radiates in joy and freedom from fear,

If you love something, release it if it comes back to you it is because it is part of your destiny and if it doesn't come back it doesn't belong to you.

A PALACE IN THE CLOUDS

Love neutralises fear and fear attracts problems,
Success consists of mastering difficulties by overcoming the stones that can be stumbling blocks,
Don't be someone's stick constantly because when someone becomes independent the first thing they get rid of is the stick,
The laws of humanity say define yourself because otherwise others will define you,
To live is to be born again after walking among wolves in disguise,
Man enslaves himself and forgets that happiness is in the simplest things,
Silence is a diamond that only shines when polished with effort,
The religious pray not to go to hell and the spiritual seek peace because they have already gone through hell,*
Death disguised as a soldier wears down the young people who fall to defend empires,
We only give what we have inside and we only take what we lack from inside,
You can't lose or win when love is eternal,
Until you know the power within you cannot know who you are,
An egg dies when broken by an outside force,
An egg is born by breaking from an inner force,
Magic is always inside you, you just have to wake up the magician,
The serpent called a tongue and caged, must be disciplined all its life,
The proud human must be tamed from the ego,
We are all fires that must be lit in order to illuminate,
To enjoy what we are we must first experience what we are not,
Listen with your eyes and speak with your heart.

WITHIN YOU IS THE POWER

The value of a person is not that someone is faithful to you, but that you are faithful to yourself,

In life it is not so important to want to be perfect, the most important thing is to be authentic,

Kindness is not in being good but in feeling that what you share makes you happy,

Knowing how to love is when the search in the other is replaced by the search in oneself,

The path in life depends on the curiosity that makes us delve into the mystery of what the path is made of when walking,

The past and the present are a small and a large step of the grain of the future in the furious flight of expectant hope,

Forgetfulness sleeps with soft brilliance on the paths of eternal life,

Cruises are opened between crossroads that raise their flags with free elections,

The endless ending is not lost in the time of the process,

The visions between the invisible whole are theoretical but inseparable at the beginning,

There are flights in dreams for the reason that the universe gives itself body and soul,

The spirits from creation carry the connection with divine harmony,

The colours leave energies from within to welcome the birth of life,

Music leaves memories of the outside between sounds to never say goodbye in death,

A circle encompasses both sides where inhalation and exhalation exist forever,

Take care of your steps on the stairs you climb since it will be the same one you will go down,

There are doors that sometimes seem closed when creating customs,

We must try to forget the noise that interrupts attention and plant a seed that sprouts from the silence,

Opportunities are like flowers: they are picked at their best moment.

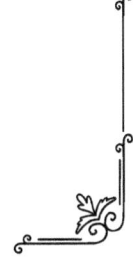

A DOCTOR FOR THE SOUL

Intuition is the presence of the divine voice and the heart is the sure guide to avoid failures.

Happiness trapped in the material is a transitory user,

You should not give everything to someone who is too small in appreciations and values because they can cause an emotional disaster.

The dense emotions that cause unhappiness must be mastered to return to the divine order of tranquility,

Darkness can be dispelled in an instant just by turning on a light but not by fighting darkness,

The magic is in the mind to find the divine treasure,

In the quiet whisper of the wind, the rhythm of the tides connects with the universal law of the spirit,

We are like a magnet, which is why we attract everything around us with energy.

We cannot avoid challenges but we can face them by reacting with peace,

Learning to fly is the most difficult corner of the road,

The hidden roots turn the spirit into its reflection,

To continue being reborn the stork must leave its nest,

When you reach the last stop you must unlearn what you have learned,

The prisoners look for a star in the arms of illusion,

We are owners of our actions and slaves of our conscience,

Don't let your right hand know what your left hand is doing because goodness blooms back when you least expect it.

In the infinite search the oases appear temporarily,

The footsteps can't stop as long as you keep breathing,

For a good harvest you must first sow with love because he who sows winds reaps storms.

AN ABYSS INTO HISTORY

The nightmares of the perfect future become a religion of whims that makes society dehumanised,
The terrible theory of the stuck world makes society depressed for experiments in control,
Boredom turns into nightmares with paths that confuse freedom with slavery,
Thinking that we are designed to be intelligent, decisions collapse towards losing decisions,
Some chains ring, remembering moments of loneliness. Looking back, the sounds are picked up again.
The palace of life surrounded by competitions turns into masks,
Some bitterness remains trapped in darkness that makes tears smile while faces are hidden,
A kiss without hugs appears to bring tranquility in the shadows that are confused with kindness,
Between separate boxes the heart crawls on the bed of love disguised with interests,
The rules of secrets are crossed between lines of rest with gazes that are fixed only on new times of inflation,
An emigrant traveller reconstructs his interior in distraction that creates a problem united with the solution,
The hope of the heart is embraced in the fire of tears where the bitterness of the eyes dries up,
The exits appear to be colours without knowing the borders to expect in the territories of words with interests,
On cold nights the soul protects itself with sleep because the glass shelter can lose its calm when the income cannot pay the rents.

THE IDENTITY CRISIS

Climbing towards the cracks we try to close an echo that spits fire like a dragon with anger,

The water of the ocean cannot calm its noisy storm that screams to see hope extinguished by earthquakes,

Fear screams through a void that protests to be protected by the illusion of power,

Those raised for a world that does not exist transform obligations into hatred out of concern,

The coldness of looks puts distance with a silent sound of alarms so that inequality continues,

The dialogues become virtual so that anxiety does not keep the imagination from sleeping,

Science confirms that loneliness is the best antidote to resolve technology wars,

The revolution steals glances so as not to age in the occult,

The race of competition blinds the psychics in overwhelming dependencies,

Life is the choice between truth and lies where paradise is in the choice,

Distractions look in mirrors to learn to navigate the lost interior,

Among the calm, the river breezes reflect the clouds that blow, visualising landscapes that hide shadows,

The taste of life is forgotten in the harmony that the hidden face misses,

Wanting to save the unnecessary becomes a fierce enemy where by swallowing the whole the end is stopping or destroying oneself,

On our backs we are pursued by an armour that transforms the wounds into a pattern that engulfs the family,

The experienced expression leaves the mouth with a taste of sand searching for meaning,

Emotional wounds spread through family ties,

Until someone conscious comes along and stops the pattern process,

In a lost eternity you can start again by looking up at the sun and flying towards the moon.

A SILENT TRAPEZE

Only by acquiring wisdom do footprints have shapes,
Forms are the keys to universal understanding,
Where renaissance writes progress constantly,

To leave the invisible in the visible of eternal paradise, we must open the paths of darkness to begin a course,

The storms of sleeping souls are addicted to the imprisoned identity waiting to mutate into laws of wisdom,

To advance to the next degree, one must reach logos with rational principles that integrate the rhythm of order,

Between cause and effect, the human being joins the keys of destiny,

Suffering pushes the sheep to become ferocious wolves,

A smoke screen raises signs with their heads held high and their legs kneeling for fear of losing protection,

Freedom of expression is designed in challenges where noise becomes silence and you pay a price to survive,

The game of economics expands more and more in hidden debts that seek explanations,

Someone walks through a garden and looks for tulips where their leaves begin to fall due to the slavery that embraces the image before the values,

The sweet criticisms are like double-edged claws that observe the devil and like crows they attack with discretion,

Under a mantle of lamb a shepherd guards the flock that sleeps in the religion of the wolf game,

The virtual company embraces the lonely man who smiles on a temporary trapeze where sadness misses happiness.

ARTIFICIAL IDENTITY

Magic is wrapped in tools that attract intrigues of sinister fantasies,
The disturbing questions speak of peace but marginalisation is to continue in competitions,

The population is on earth like in a box of matches prepared to be used to turn on and off, and those that are broken are thrown away so that they do not hinder handling.

In momentary memories smiling images are reflected that fade when returning to the nightmare,

A dark dance of times loses its north and a dizzying abyss sucks in the roots,

By selling fears in exchange for protection to enemies of power, principles and values fall asleep,

By reading between the lines, hidden answers could be found, but trade barriers put steps in the way,

Trampoline footprints have centuries of approval seeking change in the elite but only find distraction for the public,

There are leaders who are meant to control puppets and there are mental studies for the masses that are done in top secret meetings,

The robotic force can lead humanity to disappearance,

The voices of power make hidden decisions to see the behavioural reactions in the population,

The dance of the universe always keeps the traces for a renewal that hopes to unite the fluorescent bond of the stars that shine for peace,

The ashes of reincarnation will be seen between crosses when the modern illuminates fall from the pedestal,

When you wake up from the trip, new life will be born with a process of loyalty that was forgotten.

VICTIMS OF HOPES

We lose focus on living in nature by believing in obligations,
The great time of the dictator is a leap into darkness where there are swords that drag judgments,
In a cracked capsule you hear screams that burn the veins of sad lies,
An avalanche is revealed in dark times where a cloudy eclipse projects the betrayal of peace,
Under some missile projectiles, silence detonates conflicts that only allow the powerful of empires to breathe,
In an insect cave they only worship gods with leaders' medals,
A contaminated shelter only offers protection in exchange for nourishment from the volcano that lost its property in the eruption,
Traitors of peace feed dreaming civilians where lightning embraces the misery of the survivor,
The fire of surprises makes its cold shelter felt when the streams run down the mountains and the birds cannot fly,
The wind surrenders to the clouds when the nightmare of silence buries its honour for fascists,
The moan of the powerful cannot see the cries of the fragile bird that offered to believe in a caged freedom,
Behind a curtain is kept the sleeping baggage of bitter tears that will mark the destiny,
The empty bodies without defence cling to the hope that is punished by the laws of power,
The challenges want to break the walls of the subtle slavery that discreetly poisons trust,
The cautious and tired eyes sleep in beds of thorns without feeling the pain for fear of losing their courage,
In the dream of life a constant journey will be born that with an embrace of colours wraps us in its mantle.

SILENCE CAN SPEAK

By looking beyond the stillness the silent one communicates with the interior of the subconscious,

In the pausebetween two thoughts can be heard the notes of a piano giving the ego a rest,

Beyond the thinking mind is the dimension of essence that is alert to wisdom,

The mind searches incessantly to find its identity where the ego comes into existence and recreates itself,

Passing fears consume a part of the attention, absorbing the inner voice of freedom,

The ego lives in a compulsive intrigue to know about the future to complement its power that enslaves,

The ego lives in an identity of victimhood where its core needs constant nourishment of approval,

With open awareness comes attention that transforms into freedom,

Collective identity lives on competition and on the comparison that forms barriers,

Complaints strengthen the ego, giving it reasons to feel superior.

The ego likes to be observed with a victim identity,

The identity of the ego is like a hungry wolf that always wants more food to grow in its evil,

The survival of the ego is to be addicted to unhappiness, disguising itself as happiness,

The food of the ego is based on separation and compulsive jealousy, looking for culprits for them,

Actions are enough to know the assessment of a fact and now is the only core of the moment.

THE FUTURE DOES NOT EXIST

Life is the anchor of the moment without taking responsibility for the future of life,
By accepting what arises in the now we alienate ourselves with life,
Beneath appearances there is nothing isolated, everything is interconnected,
In the dream of the past and the future there is clarity without room for problems,
The pause of stillness constitutes the content of life,
The sense of being is oppressed by circumstances where time obscures it,
The now is inseparable from who we are at the deepest level,
At all levels there is a relative but not absolute importance,
This world is a cosmic dance, it is the dance of vibrant form,
The substance of surrender gives freedom to renounce useless conflicts,
The ego does not know how to live in the face of surrender for the reason that it always struggles with resistance,
Effort implies tension, the need to achieve a future result,
The mind only seeks to judge the good and the bad, blocking the deep moment,
Happiness is a seed linked to the deep peace of the interior that always bears good fruit,
Perfect nature does not demand anything, it only exists in the miracle of harmony,
Without putting labels, circumstances change for the better where the greatest source of grace appears,
In the ignorance of making others miserable, the only thing left to do is forgive them because they are part of the awakening of humanity,
The nightmare of non-surrender lives in permanent trials,
Nature teaches us the way to free the mental prison,
By resting in nature we can contemplate union with the whole,
When the mental noise is silenced, health connects with the spirit.

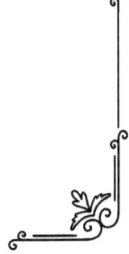

THE MAGICAL VIOLET FLAME

The bridge of brotherhood teaches us that silence so as not to harm anyone strengthens wisdom and prudence.

Every person comes to find themselves by affinity of vibration where words with wisdom are gold and silence is silver,

Being silent to control criticism is the most advisable thing because everything returns to the origin of where it was created,

External things shout and shout for attention, therefore it is necessary to silence the mind in order to hear and see the knowledge of the magic key,

By contacting the source of inner power you can solve problems to continue in well-being and understanding,

In the wheel of birth and death is the conquest of learning to die in slavery to be reborn in freedom,

Meditation in stillness guides us on an immediate healing journey from inner silence,

The conquest of self is the divine spark found in the astral realm that, upon acclaiming its presence, descends and does its radiant and infinite work.

The radiance of being is in the divine presence that flows and protects invincibly,

The whisper of eternal radiance is a spring between sleep and oblivion that weaves the story of life,

The key to abundance advances in stages opening doors to the balance of love with intelligence,

Nobody is ready to make judgments because the expression of truth is in the experience of what has been lived.

He who cannot see is not blind, but he who sees and criticises his neighbour,

There is no place for the soul that dwells in the shadow of falsehood,

The golden rule tells us to enter through the narrow door because the wide one leads to perdition.

THE EMERALD TABLE

The wind carries the sun and the moon in its belly where it gives birth to the earth, Talismans restore creation where the earth is separated from the fire and the subtle will be nobler than the gross,

Doubts are treacherous because they make us lose the attempt that we could win,

The human adventure on earth is based on finding oneself where society became conformist,

By acting in pursuit of the majority, we are shaped by external decisions, feeling obligated to follow an unchosen destiny,

The majority of humans live to work as a routine function seeking a platform of security without feeling life,

The best human decision should be to compete with ourselves with clear ideas and creative goals,

The triumph is in the people who really look for the circumstances and if they don't find them, they create them.

Everything can be achieved only by altering the mental attitude where every desire with intensity will be achieved,

A farmer does not argue with the seed, he only dedicates himself to its sowing, to nourish and care for it so that later in its sprout he can harvest abundance.

The human mind is an unexplored territory that contains treasures that are in the most ambitious dreams where what we want to plant we will reap,

Living in an era of sleeping pills comes ulcers and nervous breakdowns,

A closed copper waits to be opened with the correct key among a labyrinth of pursued goals,

Things obtained with money are the least valuable since they can be replaced, but free emotions from love and respect contain the value of eternity.

LIFE IS A TEMPORARY TEAR

The law that determines our success is a double-edged sword that has many ways to die where we are never born,

In our shadows, life is covered only by hours that run between screams, laughter and dances and that fly towards a race of final moments,

The treasures are invisible among colours that fade into conclusions that are ready or not,

We are all here between sadness and happiness alone and united with the unpredictable, leaving traces of memories,

Between forgotten reincarnations we appear and disappear carrying the silences and hidden sorrows,

The sea is full of tears that rise to the sky and the clouds receive them to let them fall like caresses that refresh the feelings of nature, and other times they fall like blows where the thunder and darkness scream with the pain of the soul,

Everything is temporary between the big and the small, we compare ourselves but in the end we are all in the same direction which is death,

The pale drowsiness envelops us in a waking dream where the communion with the whole shows the eclipse united with the light,

The attempts to escape the end fall into abysses of fantasies but the only path is one where upon reaching the pedestal resistance falls,

You have to embrace life while accepting death because time is only now without tomorrow,

Run when you can because between the beginning and the end sometimes when you look back it is too late because fear marked the frustration of destiny that was fragile,

Tomorrow is a hope and never a promise.

MYSTERY

Everythin eminds us that there is a constant battle waiting to blossom from the imperfect,
There will not be many memories left for a long time as long as we follow the chains that bind the mind to slavery,
While we do not find the address to know the interior, the programmes are repeated between punishments that empty the soul,
We will never be what we were in centuries, perhaps we will lose the identity of being able to know ourselves while we do not try to discover why we are here,
The breath of life can become heavy where silent suffering is disguised as well-being,
When inner virtue moves away, no one cares about anyone and between corners with challenges hide plans for a discreet holocaust,
Tolerance is turning into fragile glances that bow their heads to kneel before great hierarchies,
The villains raise the seals that were assigned to them by the submissive population to destroy with authority,
Explanations appear to have value in the face of a pendulum that swings to hypnotise the gazes that seek answers,
Lost between masks of each moment, some threads take over instinct to create obedient puppets,
Dignity hides while letting the shadow drag towards prideful vanity of other people's protection,
Living becomes surviving because the fear of being unprotected lost the courage to fight to have freedom.

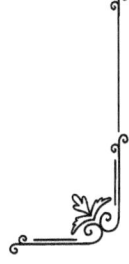

HIDDEN DOORS

Trying to stop time, we seek to pursue each day's race,

When you take a pill, something makes you feel great, but when the effect wears off, a squeezing cloak drowns out the feelings.

The colours between sweet plants become difficult to distinguish because something bitter falls showing a chess board with imposed rules,

When you inhale the presence of friends you feel the cold air because interests in time have their days numbered,

When you put on armour you feel safe but smiles can be deceiving while the sunlight lasts,

You only say what you want to hear because with sunglasses you can hide your tears.

You can show strength to protect yourself from the truth that hurts but the bitterness continues to weigh on the fallen shoulders,

Rolling without brakes, the road seems invincible in every game that is presented in life, but in a corner of loneliness, the security that seemed unstoppable collapses.

The wind becomes a spiral that collects the pieces of abandoned feelings where there is nothing left to say when the course of happiness is disguised,

In the illusion, a line written in the sky was neglected that seemed to have passed into oblivion but was kept in a broken heart,

A wave of whirlwinds runs across the surface of the ocean hiding a wound and suddenly a wave comes and spits it out towards the seashore.

Sometimes trust feels betrayed but an inner cry always reminds us that hope is the last thing we should lose.

IT'S TIME TO DECIDE

A child counted the stars when he stopped fighting the nightmares of the time hunter,

A far jump took him close to a fuse that lit an innocent kiss on the dark nights,

Some puppets cut their strings to fly somewhere over the rainbow,

On a street there was a giant tree and people passed by smiling with their eyes shining and their hearts giving a dance to the universe,

Hands delivered golden flowers to forgive the mistakes that were only grudges from learning,

Under clear clouds some unicorns came down to greet the songs of the wind with joy,

The sea breeze did not fight with the waves because they were there to illuminate the brilliance of the sun's rays,

The look of fear did not know fear because the sound of a piano gave notes of peace so as not to be confused,

Some aimless traveller stopped to talk with some fireflies in the light of a full moon,

A car stops to let pass some deer that were jumping with joy crossing mountains of snow,

The beauty of confidence is dressed in charming colours to smile at nature,

Love becomes healing and diseases are forgotten to speak another language,

The rhythm of life puts the hands of the clock at rest to be able to make decisions that under the silence you can hear the music of the rain.

GOODBYE IS A CHOICE OR A SITUATION

I wake up to the sound of silence, I don't want to leave because something holds me to you,
Your sweet gaze catches me with a kiss that envelops my heart with illusions,
A flash of colours shows me the sweetness of your arms that squeeze my body with soft gestures,
Your hands caress my hair that is wrapped in your fingers forming musical notes,
An aroma of happiness moves through the dark room forming luminous spheres,
Your smile recites verses that wake up at dawn under the sun's rays,
Cold nights feel warm when your caresses run through my body,
Your words sound like poetry that envelops the soul in eternal peace,
The winter flowers shine as you walk by my side and the meadows remain green,
Your invisible thoughts enter my mind with a message of memories that are not forgotten,
Your heart walks through fire and rain
to never say goodbye to the moment,
The stars can see the moon and I can see you even if the distance is disguised as remoteness,
Your skin is still next to me when I sleep and wake up without seeing your presence,
The breeze of the wind makes me remember your steps that approach like a magnet that attracts the positive side,
Your ears let me hear your thoughts that await the magic of intense pleasure,
Time knows no seconds when the emotions of the night are born with the day,
Your lips are kisses that become millions of northern lights that never extinguish their rainbow,
The rules of the game remain frozen while they wait for fate to decide not to give up on goodbye,
The thought may be far away but it has never left your side.

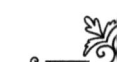

SILENCE SPINS WITH WISDOM

Running under the moon the dawn wakes up and with its smile it shows me that between being born and dying nothing can turn off its light,

The walls collapse and someone raises them again to build new temples,

Life is a constant sharing that lights the fuse of existence and gives a kiss to goodbyes and encounters,

Keep innocence so that the soul is free from guilt without looking back at the noises of complaints,

Do not sell your dignity for a plate of food because bitterness can poison virtue,

Dress yourself in the weapons of love so that the war from without cannot cross the armour of protection,

Rest under the shade of a tree to find its roots that ignite the wisdom within,

Close your eyes before the illness so that it slides towards the healing that unites nature with the surprise of the spirit,

Rise in the falls even if your wings break, you can learn to fly again,

Feed your body from the thoughts that shine towards a horizon covered with hope,

Wounds are like broken glass that must be healed by sowing the seed of forgiveness that brings the magic of rebirth,

Be grateful for every moment even if life takes things away from you, the aroma of infinity replaces it with wisdom,

Enter the magic of music where poetry surrenders to the colours of art and together they recite love verses,

Wrap your heart in a gift of peace so that a rainbow can embrace the flashes of sparks,

Light the candle of the present moment so that neither the past nor the future interfere with unnecessary speeches,

Play with the stars to draw animals so you can fly towards the infinity of the universe.

I AM THE MOMENT THAT CREATES MY STEPS

Setbacks teach but the dominance of thoughts are the radar of destiny,
Frustration pleases the ego and freeing yourself is a challenge that by not speaking you can hear the simplicity of life,

Don't point your finger at the culprit because three fingers on your hand are also pointing at you,

Those who have a project always achieve their dreams when they do not give up hope,

By opening your eyes you learn more than opening your mouth because when the storms pass the wind returns to its origin,

Master your thoughts or they will devour you, but by flying low in success you never get lost along the way.

A gray stone bench resistant to the centuries as the sailor on the high seas raises the sails to trust the currents,

Between anger and selfishness, hope is enslaved to serve organisations that distort,

Our body is a garden and we are its own gardener, so it is better to be king of your silence than a slave of your words,

Love everyone, trust few, but don't hurt anyone,

The wounds that are not seen are the deepest and if they are not expressed they can break the heart,

Love in youth is not in the heart but in the eyes and where falling in love ends, love begins.

Challenges are gifts that force us to find a new centre of gravity,

Don't pass up something that is attractive today because you think you will find something better tomorrow,

There is no better measure of your values than the way you spend your time,

Never let yourself be limited by the limited imagination of others,

It's time for you to move, realising that what you seek will also seek you.

TRYING TO LOOK FOR A SIGN

In a world obsessed with accumulation and consumption we feel carried away by the current of emotional reactivity,

In isolation we learn to find satisfaction and contemplate it as if they were clouds moving through the sky to channel their energy,

When we immerse ourselves in the critical gaze of others, tranquility seems like a battle that seeks to cultivate slaves,

The opportunity to observe how the tides arise and flow forges the paths of choice to follow a period of voluntary seclusion,

Society acts as a laboratory that observes emotions where when managing challenges the storm can wreak havoc,

As we crawl along battle paths we are subject to external pressures where we should immerse ourselves in a practice of observation that reducesimpacts,

The path to self-discovery begins in solitude where the current leads us towards sincerity,

Solitude gives us a safe and judgment-free space to flourish in the fullness of simplicity,

The internal wealth subject to the nutrition of internal values to savour the essentials of tranquility,

By imagining difficult situations and practising calm responses to doubts, we can better prepare ourselves for challenges.

Stillness is a space to drill wisdom techniques that lead towards territories of reflection,

Once upon a time there was a good wolf who was mistreated by all the lambs and there was also a bad prince, a beautiful witch and an honest pirate – all those things once upon a time when I dreamed of a world upside down.

YOU CAN CREATE A NEW YOU

Decisions surround us like stars in the night sky where confusion can make it difficult to see the right path,

Tranquility is like an oasis allowing us to make decisions calmly and clearly where we must connect with the inner voice,

The space for deep reflection helps to discuss internal thoughts without having discussions with other people's voices that could influence decisions,

Expressing thoughts frankly allows us to untangle mental problems and reach clearer conclusions.

When we are faced with choosing between temporary pleasure or lasting happiness, we must make clearer conclusions by shaping emotions according to nature,

In difficult choices we must practise thoughtful reflection which encourages us to consider our actions from an objective and detached perspective,

We must align our choices with our values and virtues by consulting the voice of wisdom and shaping emotions at different angles,

Solitude is like a prism that reveals the magic of everyday life where the beauty of simplicity keeps the joys that the soul expresses in the brilliance of its gaze,

When appreciating the simple things from a quiet dawn and a song of birds, the aroma of the wind surrounds us with the rays of the sun,

The cultivation of virtue and wisdom is a richness of the cosmic order that returns to you as you embrace the darkness that shows the way to the light,

Speaking without judging is like a divine treasure that connects us with the stars and the immensity of the universe.

TALK LESS AND LISTEN MORE

In the garden of Mother Earth a flower was growing, its buds were as red as the love in her soul, but a daisy arrived with a deceptive heart of gold and white petals, and with a lie it carried its breath. The daisy was dry and begged the flower that gave it a drink, cried and crawled right there to the flower's feet. The flower with its tender smile and sensitive heart bent its own stem to give nectar to the daisy. The flower did not realise how deeply it drank. The daisy grew very tall while the flower alone sank, the daisy spread its leaves and put a shadow on the flower with leaves so thick that the light could not penetrate, the flower begged the daisy for a little light for her but the daisy ignored her whining, it just stood like a tower with its head so high. The flower was stunned by the contempt and betrayal of the daisy and the flower alone in the darkness returned with rage, hardening its skin and making it grow its thorns so that no other daisy could hurt it and with hope it kept its course to bloom again with its beautiful red petals.

At the edge of the shore, a mermaid appeared singing, smiling like a child and raising her arms towards the moon, she asked the stars for a dance. She also asked spring to share its aroma of freshness to feel the outbreak of nature with Jupiter and Mars, also asked the song of the birds to approach the moon so that musical harmony reaches the stars. She also asked love to shine on the earth so that humans never extinguish the smiles on their faces. She also asked the children to play until they are older so that they never forget the joy in their hearts.

SAILOR OF LIGHTS

The clouds can speak with the wind even if the thunder intervenes with its lightning,
The roots of the trees connect underground and feed on the silence with the love of nature,
Although you caught my attention in a way I never would have imagined, you don't know me but you only know my name.
You keep your hands close to mine but you can't feel my arms because a dark side hides in the welcome,
Sometimes I feel scared between appointments and sometimes I want to give up but an inner voice doesn't allow me,
I like to talk to the Angels to be able to stand up in the face of doubts,
When you lie to me I just want to believe in love so that the joys never fade away,
I like to live in the stars so that the joys of your gaze never end,
I would like you to take me back to the night we met where there is a stairway to heaven that I want to share with you,
I feel lost because you are the criminal who stole my heart among a million wonders,
I love that you are the only one who entered my sleeping heart,
I like the magic of your kisses because it is the perfect prison to reach happiness,
I can feel every night the flame of the candle that was lit never to go out,
Sometimes I want to shout that we never stop being children because then life feels braver,
My spirit speaks with silence while the soul travels leaving memories in the air,
In true love there are no doubts that can confuse feelings,
The arrow of my heart always wishes you to be very happy wherever you are,
Listen when you think I'm gone, don't forget that my soul is still by your side.

STOIC PRINCIPLES

A mirror reflects our authentic being where, accompanied by silence, it gives us the opportunity to observe the truth to face our own learning that resides in others.
Stillness is a valuable space where the source of learning focuses on overwhelming challenges,
By cultivating the mastery of mental development, the hidden corners transcend like a wise teacher who develops his skills by teaching his students,
The essence of internal strength lies in the serenity that is nourished by confidence without being subject to external opinions,
Mental turbulence is a fundamental ally where shadow areas explore the chaos of daily routine to free themselves from shadow masks,
Values are like a flashlight that illuminates the paths that hide challenges to discover what drives us to face fears,
By being fascinated by exploring our aspirations we find the appreciation to clear up doubts where loneliness grants us the gift of seeing ourselves,
As the scrutiny of external judgments falls away from the masks and pretensions that we usually wear in society, we might be able to build an intimate bridge from the most genuine essence,
By embracing our truths, fears fade and we embark on a path of self-exploration that takes us to the peak of self-knowledge.
To achieve independence we must listen to the internal dialogue that frees us from external approvals,
This is a journey to find the courage to be true to ourselves and our integrity.

INFINITY HAS AROMA

If you knock me down but I lift you up, I will become stronger by rebuilding myself,
If you shout at me but I can't hear your words I won't have anything to lose,
If you criticise me but I don't understand resentment, I will be able to feel the defeat,
If you throw stones at me on the road but I pick them up, I will be able to build a house,
If you wither my feelings I can look at the sky and make a sleeping garden bloom,
If you shoot me and I don't die, I can escape to teach the defenceless to protect themselves,
If you lock me up and I escape, I will be able to draw wings that will make me fly,
If you hate me but I don't realise it, I will be able to continue in confidence with the steps that my heart dictates,
If you dirty me but I clean myself, I will have the peace that protects my soul,
If you lie to me but I ignore you, I will have the wisdom that teaches me where to trust,
If you betray me but I don't come, I will have the strength of dignity,
If you steal from me but I give you what was stolen, I will have the virtue of abundance,
If you hit me but I didn't react, I will have the honour of distance from those who don't deserve me,
If you deceive me but I thank you I will be able to run from slavery to freedom,
If you offer me a haunted love, I can become your ghost,
If you hurt me with a weapon, I can keep the scar so I don't return to your surroundings,
If you look at me with contempt, I can respect you to teach you that values reside in moral integrity,
But if you give me a kiss I will give you a hug and if you give me trust I will give you the aroma of infinity.

A SLEEPING GIANT

The waves of tears feel bitter among fears,

The rivers of blood run through the body where the tension reminds us that the difference between evil and good are united, just like fingerprints that are not the same on the right and left hands,

As the river breeze catches the footsteps of the meadows, they remember their landscapes,

The waves of the sea compose the autumn songs while the wind makes the beautiful musical notes,

Behind a curtain the past keeps the sleeping baggage for when the future arrives and picks it up at its destination,

The whispers of eternity are a pillar of pure wisdom,

The heart is born free like birds and cannot be chained,

If life gave us two ears and one mouth it will be because we should listen twice as much as we speak,

We are free like birds to be able to sing from our hearts,

The sea is a sailor who lives on the high seas, raises his arms to the wind and no one can tie them,

From a mystery in dreams the foam of the sea is recorded, just as the sailor takes risks, so the spirit rises to the sea,

The theatre is a temple just as art should be the most beautiful religion,

When we live in the city with obligations we forget what it is to live on earth,

When you entrust love to nature then you will be able to see love everywhere,

Following in someone's footsteps is a long road without news that entertains growth,

Work is a good thing, it is the best thing in life and if the mind does not work, the body drifts,

What can the man who lives in darkness and who lives his entire life between hope and bitterness sing?

There are brothers who seem unknown and strangers who seem like brothers because the family tree is also pruned,

When the wolves of the night come down, don't let them extinguish your singing,

The moon falls in love with the stars but they always keep their distance.

Keep your promises so that the footprints of honour do not lose the steps that are engraved in gold.

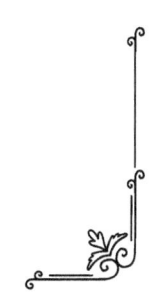

STONE SHIP

The stars are not only there to illuminate above, they make the art of the beautiful universe,

The seed of a perfect destiny lies in each one and this is synchronised by the universe,

In meditation a meeting point is born with the light that connects with the splendour when closing the doors from the outside,

There are times when purification is not found, it is called the other polarity. In that case, the mind must be calmed and wait for another moment where the inner impulse will return with its divine presence.

It is best to give preference to what we feel rather than what we think because the heart is the surest guide to avoid failures.

Intuition is a lightning bolt that comes from the presence of the divine voice and brings the seed of good fruits,

It is not possible to go back when you connect to grow with the spiritual but stagnations arise that can stop us on the path,

Spiritual evolution is like climbing a mountain, whoever stops to contemplate the landscape must be alert that no obstacle prevents the great goal.

The masters of the white hierarchy are united in the great work to continue spreading the wisdom of creation,

Everything continues in an ascending spiral where the violet ray will be dictated by sensitive people from the high astral planes who serve as transmitters of knowledge,

Everyone on earth has a shell of imperfection added to their light, when removing the dark veils, it is necessary to do so from the

inside out,

Where the learning of suffering ends, the teaching of life begins.

VII. WITHOUT LIMITS

While nature is denatured and there are things that cannot be said Because feelings got used to not loving imperfection.

Mobile phones in the hands of children will become time bombs in which they will not know how to differentiate good from bad ,nor will truth be able to recognise lies because everyone is living in a generation that thinks that garbage disappears, and fills their mind with pride by searching for perfection and losing the virtues.

Humans get together when they are cold to keep warm, but when they get together too much they prick each other and then they have to keep their distance because humans are the only animal that knows how to be intelligent enough to be cruel.

There are only three types of people in our lives.
The leaf people are there to take what they need and as soon as a wind blows they leave.
Branch people can stay for long periods of time but if life becomes difficult they will break up and disappear.
The trunk persons, these people are very important because they do not do things to be rewarded, they are only people with a good root where even in difficult times they support and sustain. They never break or disappear from your life because they love you just the way you are.

The people of the future will be lonelier than a dog with an owner. Only fear will invade minds thinking that nothing can be shared because people will be so selfish in the future that they will think that even what they earn is not enough for themselves. Then there will be the great feat predators who already have a perfect plan. The population will not have children because no one trusts anyone and children will be born by incubation, they will be like what we eat, transgenic hybrids and possibly without empathy for others. Only dedicated to living for self-interest.

If you look at the body you live in a sensitive world.
But if you direct your gaze towards the soul you live in an intelligible world.
Because true beauty does not reside in the body. The proof is in the story of the philosopher Narcissus who loved himself so much that when he looked at his image in a lake he wanted to kiss it so he fell into the water and drowned.

If it is more important to give your children a good heritage like a good school and good health... instead of loving them, that is called abandonment.
Because a saying says if you seek health and education without first teaching love and teaching respect then you will lose everything in the process.

It doesn't matter what they tell you about someone because no one should qualify based on the opinion of others.

Don't stay with who you like, stay with whoever loves you. Because who you like excites you but whoever loves you, values you.

Don't follow the majority, follow the right path and don't lose faith.

There are wounds that instead of opening our skin open our eyes. Our genes carry the gun but our habits fire it.

Ghosts scare more from a distance than up close.

There is no better way to overcome fear than by facing it.

What is out of your control must first be out of your head.

Peace of mind comes the moment you get tired.

If you want to know someone, give them power for a while , but never give your power to decide to anyone because they could become your owner.

There are songs that leave shadows to take refuge in memories.

Being grateful and honest is the mother of all virtues.

There are opportunities that are like water and that do not pass twice through the same river.

When a politician says he will end poverty he is referring to himself and his family.

The Soul is cleansed with forgiveness, nourished with the word and protected with faith.

No one can punish anyone because anyone who digs a hole for someone will fall into it themselves.

Philosophy is not for making philosophers!! It is only to create thinkers of probabilities.

Those who read more are freer while those who do not read can become hostages of mental slavery.

Discipline is having a trained mind that controls your life in order to succeed.

In the ancient primitive communities there were lepers but in the new generation there will be technology with many psychiatrists.

He who doesn't know what he wants sometimes loses what he has and then discovers that he lost exactly what he wanted.

He who believes himself to be rich does not own his property but his property owns him.

If a relationship should be secret you shouldn't be in it.

When your partner grabs you by the neck it will be a burden but if your partner grabs your hand it will be a support.

In the life of a teenager, when there is abuse, death is sweeter than life.

A key that opens many locks is a master key. But a padlock that opens with a single key is a padlock.

Solitude nourishes the Soul when the spirit accompanies understanding.
But loneliness can also lead to an illness if the ego intervenes with the anesthesias of worry in search of flattery and the need for company.

The most valuable treasures are the most difficult to reach and the most protected because they are hidden from the human eye,
That's why the woman who shows off gains attention but loses protection.

The excuse of the traitor will be that he never promised you anything and that of the ungrateful one who never asked you for anything.

There are energies that know well to whom you do evil so the poison you put on others is taken by you.

The ear tastes words like the palate tastes food.

Many humans are taken to the slaughterhouse like sheep and still do not open their mouths.

If in a relationship they ask you for time to think about it, it is because the monkey does not let go of a branch without first making sure that the other one that he found to hold on to is not going to break.

When you criticise someone it is because something attracts you to that person.

Trust is like a glass and if it breaks it will never be the same even if it can be glued back together.

Do not make decisions if you are in love because the human being in a couple is not to control, it is only to enjoy their company.

Emotions are like passing clouds where time dissolves into the unknown.

The key element of happiness is not based on what you have but on who surrounds you.

Falling in love is neither sought nor found. It is only a search for the internal, not the external, which, without knowing why and without explanation, one day appears on our path or not.

There is no honour in anyone who attacks an unarmed enemy.

Kites rise higher against the wind, not with it.

The human being does not ask to be born, to live he does not know, to die he does not want.

With the same bar that you measure you will be measured.

Everyone goes as far as they are allowed.
What differentiates a poison from a remedy is the dose.

And what is given kindly always comes back.

Peace is more valuable than perfection.

Football is a spectacle and psychological anesthesia to steal your magic essence of being able to think and to create.

We must make the unconscious conscious, otherwise that emptiness will dominate us and we will call it destiny.

School education does not want thinkers, they want workers.

In the name of truth many lies have been built.

The government is the only one that can override its laws to defend itself.

The winner in this life is the one who defeats himself in his laziness, his fear and his insecurity.

That's where the word narcissist comes from.
We live in a society that has turned people's image into a spectacle.

Because instead of living things we consume illusions of things.

Freedom is not only choosing a path but also rebelling against all those who want to impose one on you.

In order for human beings to reach their greatest potential, they must be exposed to danger.

We are created to focus on life, not existence.

The university is like a small walled world.

The Roman Empire didn't just disappear, it changed its skin.

It is more difficult to found a bank than to rob one.

Consciousness is like smoke, if it comes out a little it expands.

Power classifies, orders and controls.

Comfort is the enemy of growth.

Success and failure in our society have become like a people's measuring value.
BUT !!?
Success and failure are part of positive competition because they teach us to be more productive and competent.

Water can extinguish fire but fire can evaporate water.
So which one is the most dangerous?

If the end justifies the means, what justifies the end?

TIME DOES NOT ERASE ANYTHING.
TIME TEACHES YOU THAT
YOU CAN LIVE BROKEN, WITH
BEATS AND INJURIES AND STILL SMILE AND MOVE FORWARD.

A man is worth what he delivers, not what he promises.

Never change what you want most in life for what you want most in a moment.

If the end justifies the means, what justifies the end?

WHAT YOU HAVE, MANY CAN HAVE...
BUT WHAT YOU ARE NO ONE CAN BE.

VIII. THE COUNTDOWN

Happiness is an interpretation of the meaning we give to life, managing to make a sculpture of our own self,

Love is an antidote to get what we want and gives us wings to fly,

Sadness, grudges and bad moods are the dictators of life,

We live the nostalgia of Life thinking that we suffer the punishment of destiny and if we are happy or sad, who knows? Since everyone is right!!

When love arrives, it is blind but when it leaves it is lucid.

The most important thing is personality, because beauty is only the charm of a moment.

When someone is not able to decide, they are hostage to the situation.

When the world feels black and white,

Only people who love us fill us with colours.

No one changes by suffering solely by decision.

A person who does not see his mistakes will never change.

The waves never recede, they break their fury and return to the serene sea.

Those who have values do not have a hard time making decisions.

Trust in time that can give sweet solutions to bitter difficulties.

Happiness is an interpretation of the meaning we give to life, managing to make a sculpture of our own self,

Love is an antidote to get what we want and gives us wings to fly,

Sadness, grudges and bad moods are the dictators of life,

Those who have values do not have a hard time making decisions.

Empires last for centuries and die in an instant.

Time is like a machine that lets the clock pass and forgets its name.

And principles are values that are not negotiated.

The rain washes away the tears. The sun dries them and the moon keeps them in the memory but not in oblivion.

When wars are won, peace is lost.

The wind blows where it wants but it does not know where it comes from or where it is going, so it is free.

If you cheat on a person, it doesn't mean that they are stupid, it means that that person trusted you more than you deserved.

I can't imagine all the pain there is in those who can't forgive stupid things. But I can see the great happiness and LOVE that exists in Jesus who was able to forgive those who crucified him.
But in life, bad and good, in difficult times we always ask GOD for help. But God says no one can come to the father if it is not through the son who was the one who left us the teaching of the word,
SORRY.*

The spirit tells the soul where the accumulation of your anguish ends, I will begin the release of your burdens.
Depression is the final state of a person who has experienced distressing situations where the ego takes control and does not allow the mind to overcome the fear of dissatisfaction created.
Therefore, in order to reach a state of serenity, you must overcome fear. Which means healing the mind and the body will follow.
To heal the mind, apart from a healthy diet, there are meditation methods and each person must choose the one that best leads them to the silence of thought, so that from there they can connect with their spirit.
Because God never abandons us and never gives us more burdens than we can bear. Therefore healing begins by finding inner Peace.

What you see in others reflects your interior and what you see in God is what you must learn.
When you sow seeds of faith you find God.
Forgiveness is winning a war without going to battle.

IX. A WORLD OF MASKS

I am try writing a book.

Because I think we are living in a world that has hardly had many changes since the empires. It seems that the empires that disappeared were becoming lonely people who are creating their imperial wall that one day could bring them down as depression and isolation of communication are already doing now. Using only mobile phones to take photos that only leave impressions to open your mouths and close your eyes and ears.

When someone emigrates from the countryside they bring a story. But when someone breaks free from a narcissist they bring a message.

There is no one who can stop a few small steps that want to go very far. THAT'S CALLED COURAGE.

LOVE DOES NOT SPEND AND LIFE DOES NOT WAIT.

It's better to be alone while you don't know what place you occupy in someone's life.
If someone decided to lose you, then they don't deserve to find you anymore.

In this life you come to learn to lose everything because what you look for is found and what you neglect is wasted and that it is enough to know that in love the best thing that can be given is freedom without contracts or obligations.

X. ON MY WAY

A tear closes my eyes, suddenly I see myself fallen into an abyss. When I hit rock bottom, I fell exhausted, then I ask for forgiveness to my spirit that, without me knowing my spirit was for many years screaming at me, stay away from the NARCISSIST.

NARCISSISTS
they like to be in control and prohibit the partners interacting with people around them, practically isolating you from the world and integrating you alone into their small world and they are cowards because they only face children and the elderly, and people who have no family to take refuge in and are alone. They choose people who are easy to manipulate.

The narcissist is neither bad nor good, but rather has one goal, which is to trap victims.

NARCISSISTS say they are ALPHA but when they see the WOLF they become BETA. Hahahahahaa

A narcissist is like a puzzle mixed up with other pieces of different puzzles that don't match. And if you don't throw away that puzzle you will live in deep confusion.

When you emigrate from the countryside you have history but when you get free from the clutches of a narcissist you have a message.

THE BRAIN CONTROLS THE MIND
BUT BREATHING CONTROLS THE
BRAIN.

If we put on temporary nails and put on a wig for moments, then why does it seem strange to us to have casual relationships ?

Despair is the enemy of attraction.

It is better to communicate by messages than by voice, because your mouth makes you talk too much and messages make you think less.

Each one is the owner of his actions and a slave to the consequences.

THE DAY YOU SOW
THE SEED
IS NOT THE SAME DAY THAT YOU EAT THE FRUIT

If you take a step they criticise you,
if you don't take it also.

So walk free and enjoy your own walk.

God only gave us a single emotional charge, which is ourselves.

IF in your youth you don't run for your goals in your old age NO.

He who conspires against you will fall in front of you.

Mean souls are only left
conquer through gifts.

The evil one flees even if no one chases him.

A woman who is with a man for money is comparable to a gold earring placed in a pig's snout.

It is easier to destroy an atom than a prejudice.

Never put anyone on a pedestal because the one you praise today you may disgust tomorrow.

DIFFICULT TIMES WILL ALWAYS REVEAL TRUE FRIENDS.

Don't look for people with your same tastes, look for people with your same values.

He who is not grateful for a little will not be grateful for a lot.

Never curse anyone because words are like birds that have wings and just as they can go to harm others, they could come back to sink you.

Depression is the final state of a person who has experienced distressing situations where the ego takes control and does not allow the mind to overcome the fear of dissatisfaction created.
Therefore, in order to reach a state of serenity, you must overcome fear. Which means healing the mind and the body will follow you.
To heal the mind, apart from a healthy diet, there are meditation methods and each person must choose the one that they feel best leads them to the silence of thought, so that from there they can connect with their spirit.
Because God never abandons us and never gives us more burdens than we can bear. Therefore healing begins by finding inner Peace.

University don't teach doctors about health, they only teach them to know about illness to prescribe medications.

If someone asks for your time, give it to them and say goodbye because a love that doubts will neither last nor bring happiness.

When we create characters in order to survive, we present images to the world to believe that we are someone.

Each one sees in others what is in his own heart.

XI. THE UNIVERSE DOES NOT SPEAK LANGUAGES IT ONLY SPEAKS ENERGY.

When the moon sets behind fear, the stars cry and come down from the sky.

Elephants don't walk around saying how big they are, they just walk.

When you can talk about something that has hurt you without feeling pain or argument that means you are already healed.

The female organ is like a book that must be studied to know the codes, but the male organ only thinks one thing without the need for explanations.

Intelligent is the one who, with his experiences, already knows where he does not have to return.

Attractiveness will always win over beauty.

When we look for sources of assessment we live in the interpretations that others emit about you.

The opinion of others does not define the essence of who you are, it only values it.

You have to break bad habits before they break you.

Being different is not a weakness but rather it is something that makes you unique.

If they copy you it's because you're doing it right. But if they criticise you it is because they can no longer copy you.

When a person loses everything, they will also lose fear.

If you are not financially independent, it is more difficult to give yourself the freedom to choose.

Each person unconsciously looks for the qualities in a partner that they lack in themselves.

HUMANS ARE SO SELFISH THAT IT IS NECESSARY
TELL THEM ABOUT A REWARD IN ANOTHER LIFE, SO THAT THEY DO GOOD IN THIS LIFE.

THE COMPASS OF DEAD CONVERSATIONS SAYS

When someone is interested in you, find a way to show it,
Limited communication is not a lack of time, it is a lack of interest.

The system does not fear the poor who are hungry.
Fear the poor man who knows how to think.

love does not make noise, it is only felt.
When you are observant everyone is you teacher.

He who bites the hand that feeds him, gets used to
to lick the boot of whoever kicks him.

Loyalty is a matter of willpower and respect of values.

LOYALTY It's not about who is good in your face, but about who is loyal behind your back.

Cats believe that their owner feeds them because they are like gods.

Dogs believe that their owner feeds them because their owner is like a god.

No one is left alone, only one continues on his way to places where others cannot accompany you.

Studies provide knowledge and imagination wisdom.

OF ALL THE THINGS YOU WEAR, YOUR ATTITUDE IS THE MOST IMPORTANT.

THROUGHOUT LIFE
YOU WILL MEET MANY MASKS BUT
FEW FACES.

HE WHO CAN CHANGE
YOUR THOUGHTS CAN CHANGE YOUR DESTINY.

The enemy of love is fear.

Cats are for people with high self-esteem and a dog is for people with low self-esteem.

Don't run for someone who doesn't even walk for you.

Smart people learn from everything and everyone.

average people learn from their experiences.

stupid people already have all the answers.

YOUR ATTITUDE DETERMINES YOUR DIRECTION.

If don't know where you're going, go back to find out where you came from.

Your character will form your destiny.

No one could bequeath you except the one who carries in his soul something of yours.

When you are in a relationship to seek need, it is because you are willing to receive alms.
We don't get to the top by surpassing others, but by surpassing ourselves.

Each word has an energy and a resonance; every silence too.

AFTER THE
FIRST LIE, THE ENTIRE TRUTH BECOMES A DOUBT.

THE PROBLEMS NEVER END-BUT THE SOLUTIONS NEITHER.

Cats do not fight over food, because they do not fear lack, just like Kings.
Dogs fight for food because they fear lack, just like humans do in the economic system.

If gold oxidizes, it was not gold.
If love ends, it wasn't love.
If friends leave, they weren't friends.
It's that simple.

Some hearts understand each other, even in silence.

Just as a garden is pruned in autumn, unfortunately the family tree is also to pruned.

The women's ear, the uterus, for that razor, be careful when you are pregnant about what your BABY is listening to because that will be what he or she will experience.

When a doctor prescribes a condition without investigating, the pharmacist gains an addict and the patient loses his health.
Today more people die from medication than from illegal drugs.

In the past, doctors treated patients with white coats, because their profession depended on their responsible conscience. Now doctors treat patients dressed as citizens because their profession depends on the pharmaceutical system.

The doctors who medicate are the robots of the system and those who operate are angels of salvation.

The moon seems to emit its own light, but nevertheless it is only a mirror where the sun is reflected.
THIS IS WHAT LOVE IS ONLY IF IT SHINES IT REMAINS.

Learning must be allowed to float, accepted and gotten rid of. REPEATING LEARNING IS LIKE REPEATING AN EXAM.

Passing clouds carried by the wind and they do not try to fight between.

When you feel the pain it is because you understand the path to healing, but if you seek anesthesia the mistakes will be repeated.
Anesthesias are complaints and guilt.
To know pain is to face it without fear.

Emotional pain is healed through understanding and then forgiveness is applied. Forgiveness means that we should not blame anyone again, but it does not mean that we have forgotten, because it is precisely the memory that prevents us from falling again.

THE BRAIN CONTROLS THE MIND BUT BREATHING CONTROLS THE BRAIN.
IT IS CORRECTED IN PRIVATE
AND CONGRATULATIONS IN PUBLIC,
THAT IS CALLED EDUCATION.

THE PAST IS A LESSON AND NOT A CHAIN.

We constantly move between reflections and, detaching ourselves from mental activity, we receive learning with ease and understanding and letting them float we recognize the changing nature, knowing everything that surrounds us is part of our experience but not of the essence in which each of us must find ourselves.

There is something luminous that lasts behind everything that changes.

When money is important it stays in the banks and when it is useful it moves in the world.

The dream hidden in the darkness of the night is a refuge of peace into which you must enter calmly.

Criticism is nothing more than a form of admiration.

The thought leads you to the conclusion, But emotion drives you to action.

The life we live is the result of our decisions and our fears too.

We are not what we should be, nor what we would like. be, but throughout life with learning, we are not what we used to be.

When we are born like a star we move away from our essence and our rise remains like a reflection in the water where the activity of the mind is fast, fleeting and passing, moving incessantly because we are part of nature but it does not identify what is ours. essence.

A PERSON CHANGES FOR TWO REASONS:
HE LEARNED TOO MUCH OR SUFFERED ENOUGH.

There are times in life when you lose what you wanted most without expecting it and due to some situations you cannot recover what you lost and you become trapped in a labyrinth. But when one day you look back observing the price of pain, you realize that by suffering too much you lose the fear of suffering, because life shows you that the clock does not wait for you and life goes on, without excuses there is no REVERSE.

EVERYONE GOES AS FAR AS THEY ARE ALLOWED.
You always have to be respected.
Because no one can live for another, neither in sadness nor in joy, nor in illness nor in health, everything only begins with oneself.

Dogs trust those around them but cats distrust everyone.

Argue with someone who believe know everything is how to give medicine to a dead person.

BELIEVING IS EASIER THAN THINK. THIS IS THE REASON WHY THERE ARE MORE BELIEVERS THAN THINKERS.

THE CRYSTAL GENERATION THEY ARE EASY TO BREAK IN THE FACE OF OTHERS' CRITICISM, BUT THE CRYSTAL GENERATION HAVE AN EASIER TIME TO SHINE BECAUSE THEY DON'T CRITICIZE ANYONE.

It is better to seek respect first than attention.

THERE ARE ALWAYS A LITTLE FEELINGS IN THE EXPRESSION
"I DON'T MIND".

THERE IS ALWAYS A LITTLE TRUTH IN THE EXPRESSION.
"IT'S A JOKE".

loneliness said , Not everyone is company.

If money and material things make you believe that you are better than others, so you are the poorest person in the world.

The business of medicine is not about healing the sick, it is about making the healthy sick.

A patient cured is a customer lost.

The Strongest warrior is not always the one who wins the battle, but the one who knows when to surrender.

One beautiful heart is better than a thousand pretty faces.

He Who is a friend of all, is a friend of no one.

Our worst enemies are found close to our environment and in the family too.

Don't trust everything you see, salt too it looks like sugar.

The truth told the lie:
You can pass me, but I will always catch up to you.

You cannot tear down someone who understood that the only way out of problems is found in oneself.

Animals have leaders but not so that in the herd some eat and others kneel, just like humans do.

He who knows who he is does not need to prove anything.

The truly strong never complain about their environment.

Love is the only wealth that cannot be bought or sold,

Intelligent is someone who only believes half of what he hears. Brilliant is he who knows which half to believe.

When your partner brings you problems and you put up with it, then there are two people who don't love you and one of them is you.

You are not responsible for the programming you received in childhood. But as an adult, it is your responsibility to correct it.

Reality is divided from fiction when the observer imitates life to the limit of seeking variant formulas. I mean SPIRITUALITY.

Don't hold on to something that hurts you, just because it makes you happy from time to time.

A weak mind complains about everything… A strong mind accepts, analyzes and resolves.

If you make a list of friends, do it with a pencil that can be erased, only time will tell you why.

Don't expect a situation to change because it was the situation that came to change you.

Don't play with anyone's feelings, just like the world goes around.
Today you play and Tomorrow you are the toy.

Just as there are things that happen for a reason, there are others that don't happen for a reason.

Olivia Conde

There are people who lie to you so as not to lose you, but they lose you by lying to you.

Anyone would go with you a party, but not everyone would stay with you in a hospital, so choose carefully who you share your life with.

Like a madman who throws stones into the air, the same is the one who deceives his friend and says he was joking.

Most men are friends with women they like, while women are friends with men they don't like.

If everything you offered is not reached, so offers your absence.

Humans like Flowers wither, but with Good values they remain eternal.

If something hinders a relationship, it is better to withdraw and leave an unforgettable memory.

Betrayal is not a mistake, it is a conscious choice.

Disobedience has rectification But guilt brings punishment.

Trust is not given, it is earned.

There are scars that become medals and wounds that become wisdom.

Don't judge others because the stone you throw today may be the same one you stumble over tomorrow.

If we live hidden from our ability in plain sight of those around us, it is because the time to come to light has not yet arrived.

The past dies, the present lives, the memory remains because life goes on.

Poverty is not fought, it is managed.

There are people who have full pockets, but empty hearts.

There are people who have children, but no family.

It is not bad to ask or to give help. The bad thing is to expect something in return one day or another.

The years only wrinkle the skin, but fear wrinkles the soul.

There are men who deceive her woman that many would like to have for another that everyone can have.

Do not ask for permission to fly, because the sky belongs to no one.

The secret of existence – is not only to live, but to know what you live for.

We need little to be happy.
The difficult thing is that we need too much experience to understand it.

He who is not there in bad times,
in the good times plenty.

Don't look for the most beautiful person in the world, look for the person who makes your world more beautiful.

There is no pillow as soft as a clean conscience.

If you don't control your mouth you will have no control for your present or your future.

Get rid of those who doubt you, join those who value you, free yourself from those who hinder you and Love those who support you.

He who lives very isolated without:
wanting too share is because he seeks his own desire.

An arrow can only be launched by pulling it back. So when you push back difficulties it means that life is going to launch you towards incredible moments.

A weak mind complains about everything... A strong mind accepts, analyzes and resolves.

Many wonder if the Devil and God exist.?!! Just as there is illness and health, there is the answer.

In life it is important to have a friend who is, at the same time, a mirror and a shadow... The mirror never lies and the shadow never goes away.

Arguing with someone who wants to be right is like swimming against the current.

There is no pillow as soft as a clean conscience.

In a person you cannot see everything that is, but you also cannot see everything that is not.

When arguing about others, there is our mirror. Because knowing others is impossible. But knowing yourself too.

Excuses were created for those who do not have enough courage to tell the truth face to face.

If you don't control your mouth you will have no control for your present or your future.

The fish dies through the mouth and when it does not know where to keep it closed or open it can endanger both its present and its future.

Never adapt to what doesn't make youre happy.

If someone criticize you, tell them that
Better worry about your sins...
Because when the day of final judgment comes, God is not going to ask you about mine.

He who falls in love with his flowers and not his roots, in autumn he will not know what to do.

To understand cultures e we must first learn their language.

Everything it's a learning. Good people give you Happiness. Bad people give you experiences.

A good person must puts his value first rather than interest..

Every day your time is worth more because you have less left.

There are two types of people.
People who are alone so as not to be with just anyone.
And people who are with anyone, as long as they are not alone.

It is better to seek respect first than attention.

The essence of the decision should never be placed in the hands of others.

The true character of someone is the one who treats people well, who knows that they will not do anything for you.

He who accepts correction will always be honest.

The hero's journey is about living your gift and healing your wounds.

Life is the sum of all our choices.

The one who wants to change
always has a reason. He who doesn't want to change always has an excuse.

The past dies, the present lives, the memory remains and life goes on.

Serenity is being at peace within the storm.

Expecting life to treat you well because you are a good person is like expecting a tiger not to attack you because you are a vegetarian.

We all experienced something that changed us so much that we were never the same again.

Magic is always inside you,
you just have to wake up the magician.

The caged Serpent (tonge) must be disciplined for a lifetime, The proud Lion (mind) must be tamed from the ego.

Love is the only wealth that cannot be bought or sold,

Intelligent is someone who only believes half of what he hears. Brilliant is he who knows which half to believe.

When your partner brings you problems and you put up with it, then there are two people who don't love you and one of them is you.

People were created to be loved and things were created to be used.
The problem in the world is when things are being loved and people are being used.

Wisdom protects note than money because money is only a strong wail in the imagination.

Reality is divided from fiction when the observer imitates life to the limit of seeking variant formulas. I mean SPIRITUALITY.

JUST as darkness is the absence of Light, so is worry the absence of PEACE.
NO ONE HAS THEIR PAST SO CLEAN TO BE ABLE TO JUDGE THAT OF OTHERS.

DON'T STRIVE TO BE SOMEONE KNOWN, BUT ON BEING SOMEONE WORTH KNOWING.

NEVER BE TOO BUSY FOR THE PEOPLE WHO LOVE YOU AND NEVER BE VERY AVAILABLE FOR THE PEOPLE WHO USE YOU.

THE MOON TEACHES US THAT WE DO NOT NEED TO BE WHOLE TO SHINE.

Inside each one we have A FRIEND AND A VILLAIN... the one who feeds the most will be the WINNER.

THERE ARE ALWAYS A LITTLE FEELINGS IN EXPRESSION
"I DON'T MIND".

THERE IS ALWAYS A LITTLE TRUTH IN THE EXPRESSION.
"IT'S A JOKE".

We have nine months to be born and one minute to die.

SO DON'T THINK TO MUCH. LIVE LOVE, LAUGH, FORGIVE AND ENJOY THE MOMENT.

THE SILENCE WHISPER TO THE SOUL TRUTHS THAT THE THOUGHT NEVER YOU WILL BE ABLE TO UNDERSTAND.

THERE IS NO SIN MORE SHAMEFUL THAN DECEIVING THOSE WHO BELIEVE IN YOU.

ONE SHOULD BE GRATEFUL BUT NEVER A SLAVE FOR A GRATEFUL.

YOU ARE THE ONLY ONE WHO IS IN CHARGE OF YOUR HAPPINESS. YOUR SMILE, YOUR VALUE AND YOUR ATTITUDE.

TAKE CARE THAT IT DOESN'T PASS
LIFE WAITING FOR BETTER TIMES, TAKE ADVANTAGE OF WHAT YOU ALREADY HAVE.

PLANTS ARE NOT MEDICINE
ALTERNATIVE... THEY ARE THE ORIGINAL MEDICINE.

Adapt to circumstances, but never forget to flourish.

Suffer in private, heal in silence and shine in public.

Those who are not ambitious agree to collect what others are paid and do what others are told.

One tree can produce a million matches but One match can burn a million trees.

The defects of our children are deficiencies of parents and society.

A driver's license does not show that a person is a good driver, but rather the practice YES.

It is not who has a diploma that defines a person to be a winner, but the evidence of what he or she managed to do YES.

Gossip is the entertainment of empty minds.

Knowing how to LOVE is the most difficult thing to know, because to know how to LOVE you have to learn not to suffer.

If your life is not an example, do not worry about the lives of others.

Among the best advice that you receive, YOUR INTUITION should always be the most valuable teacher.

He who listens more to criticism than to advice, will live being more of a slave than free.

Those who do not recognize their mistakes, nor change, nor find themselves, only live on other people's opinions.

For good works to appear in your life you must be disciplined and grateful.

When someone says that they want to see you but that they don't have time, it's because you are not their priority.

The one who restrains his tongue protects his life, but he who is light-hearted will find his ruin.

The one who can't stand the just,
That one will have to put up with what is unfair.

Learn from everyone, but never compare yourself to anyone.

The only door that closes and does not reopen, is that of the COFFIN, so don't suffer for nonsense.

Do not disturb the place of the righteous, because you may fall into stumbling blocks.

Falling in love is an anatomical chemical to procreate and love is a decision.

With money you have the woman you want,
Without money you have the woman who loves you.

Frequent those whom you can improve and those who can improve you.

Be humble
At the end of the chess game remember that the king and pawn are kept in the same box.
The kindness exaggerated is almost always false.

Having luxury is PLEASURE
Having health is WEALTH

In life you fight but you shouldn't beg.

N

XII. POEM FOR A FRIEND

They are all days of celebration when sharing happiness. The fountains run quickly and greeting us through the green meadows is the song of Peace and as we pass we hear the laughter that shares love and healing and smiling at the being that blesses my hands. They would like to touch it to bring me closer to its joyful breeze and with my arms to be able to hug you.

In a labyrinth garden some leaves fall that die of love, around there are some seeds that grow lost but have not bloomed, there is also a rose bush that bloomed but was covered at night even though it was day, the mystery of the labyrinth garden was embraced with joy remembering the aroma of love so that you do not forget that if I am no longer with you, do not look for me in oblivion because I am still inside you.
(To, B.W. From Olivia) you, my baby.

Stone Ship

Olivia Conde

Stone Ship

Olivia Conde

Stone Ship

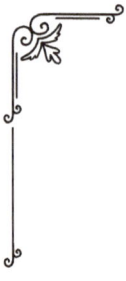

Stone Ship

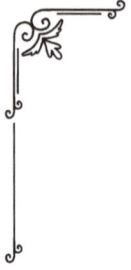

Love but don't depend.
🫠✨

Olivia Conde

> **Observe but do not absorb.**

> **From distance comes forgetfulness.** 👇✨

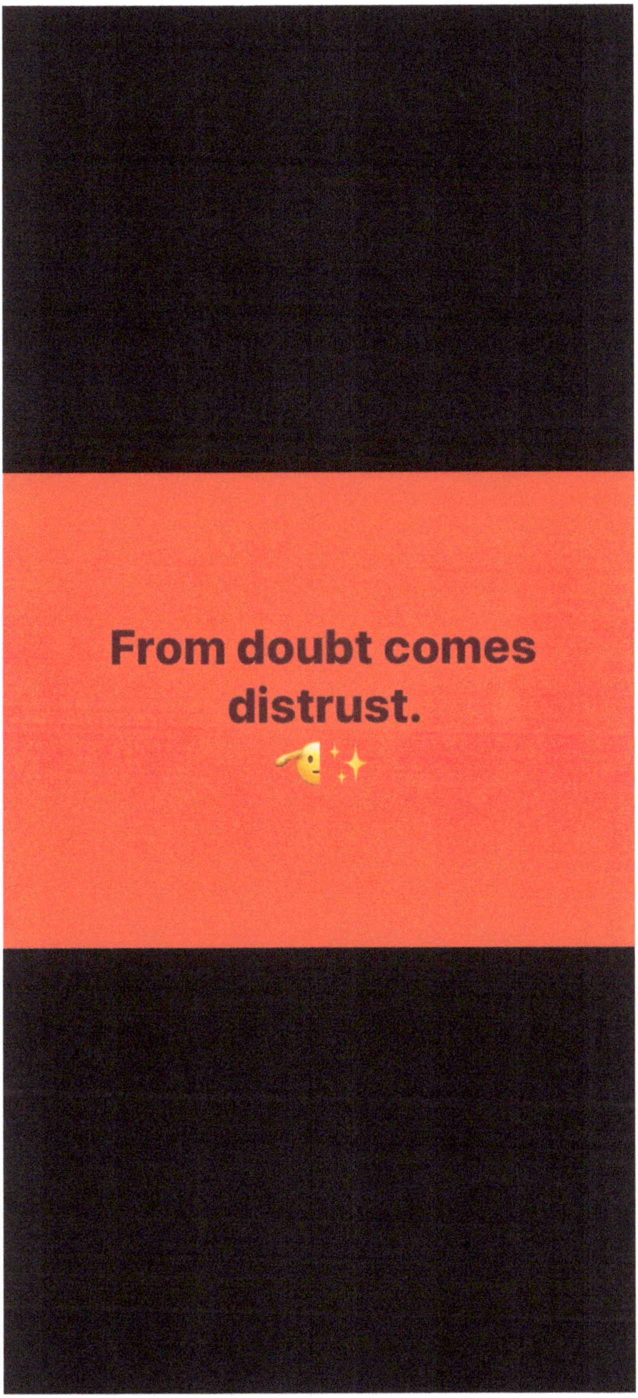

From doubt comes distrust.

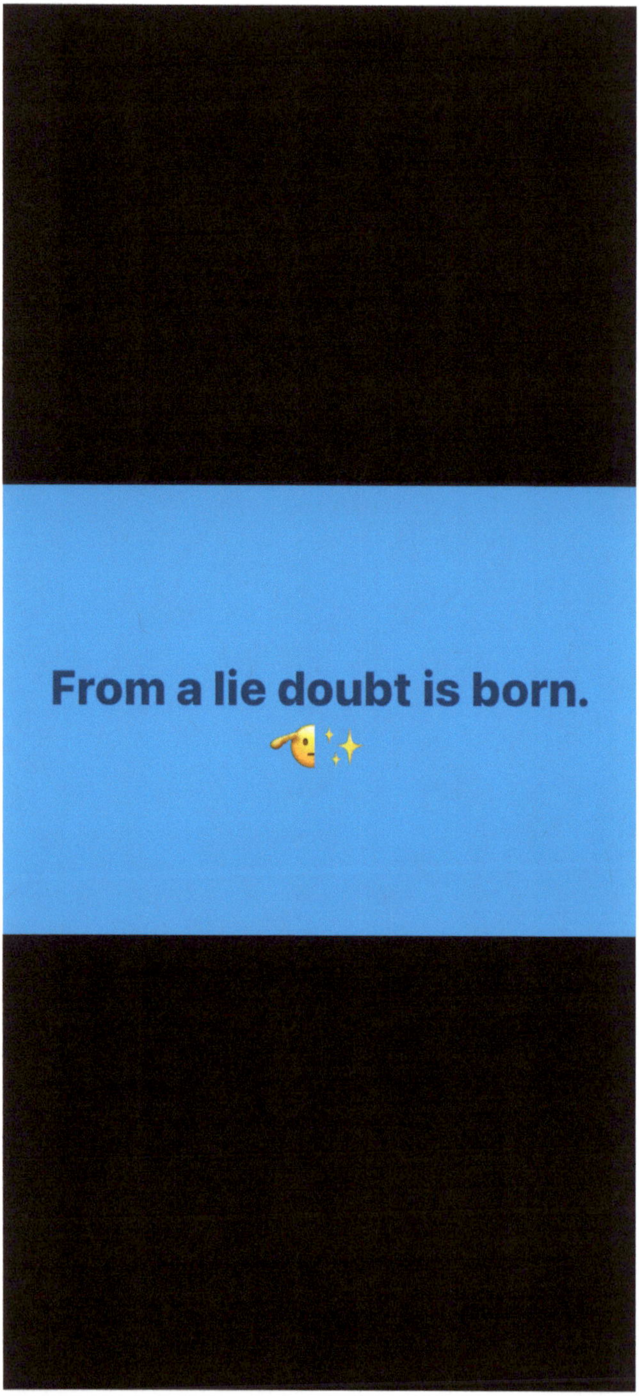

From a lie doubt is born.
🤔✨

Olivia Conde

> **Distance is born from distrust.** 🫵✨

> It's for the poor to put money in the piggy bank and break it the next day. 🫵✨

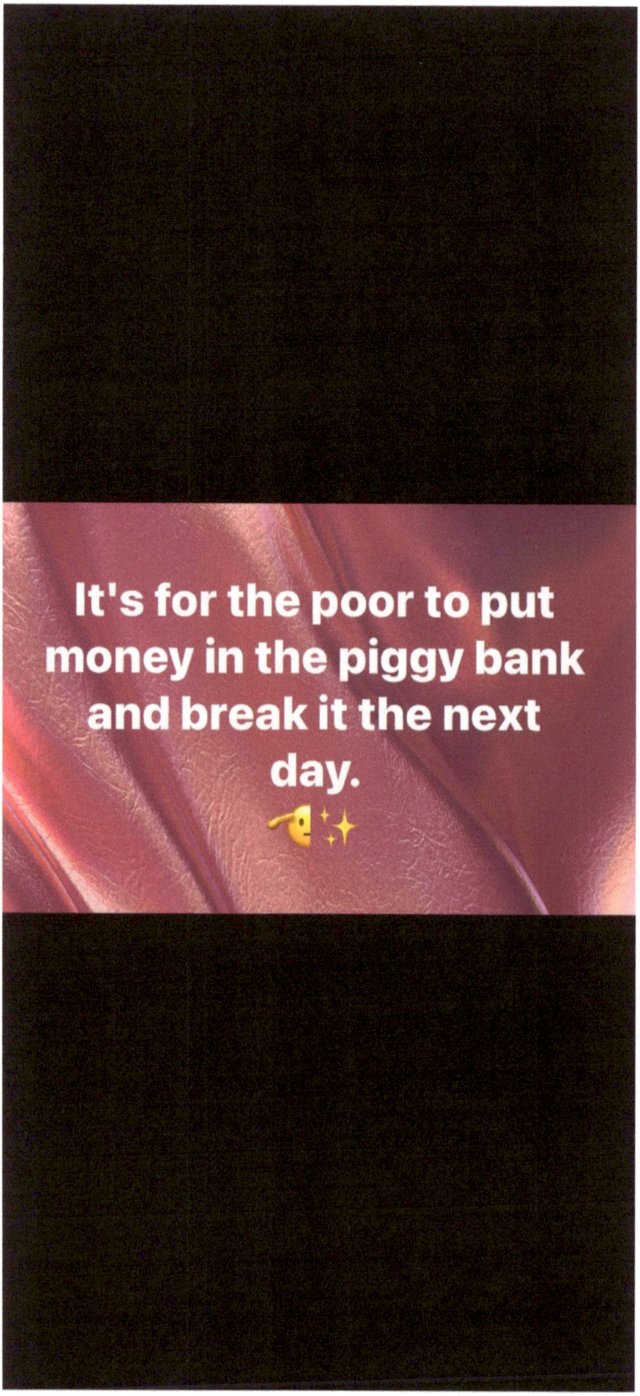

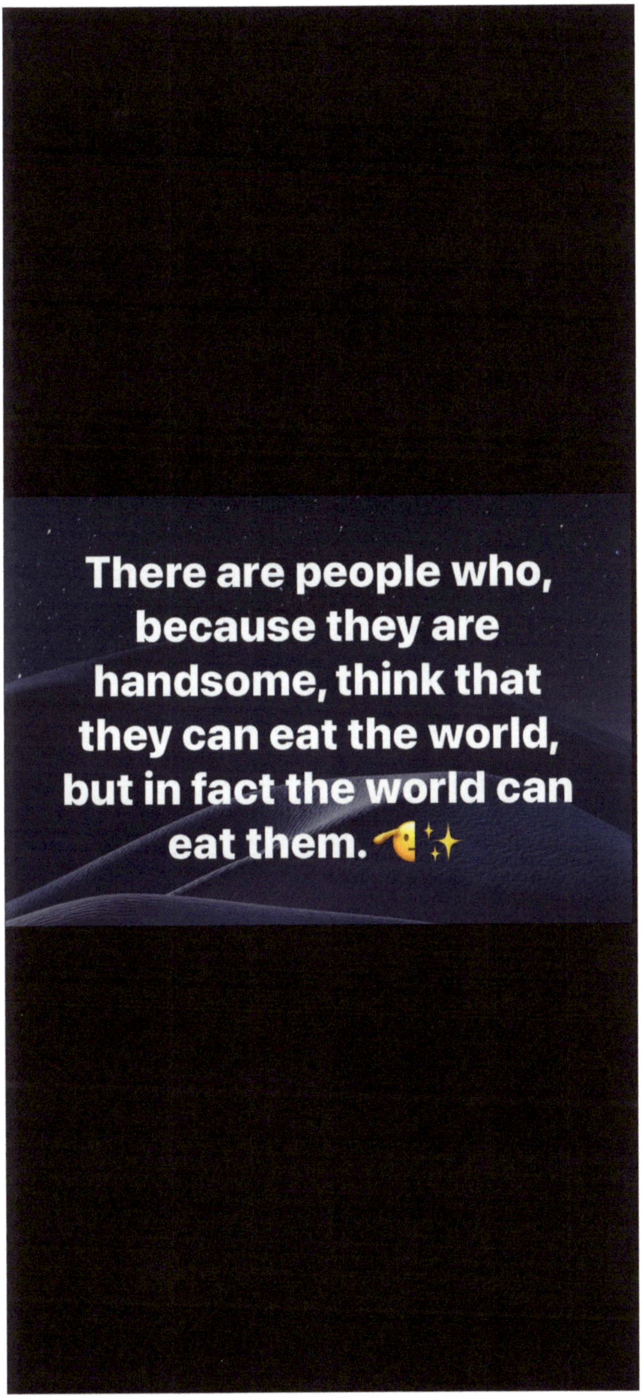

Olivia Conde

> There are people who, because they are handsome, think that they can eat the world, but in fact the world can eat them. 🫅✨

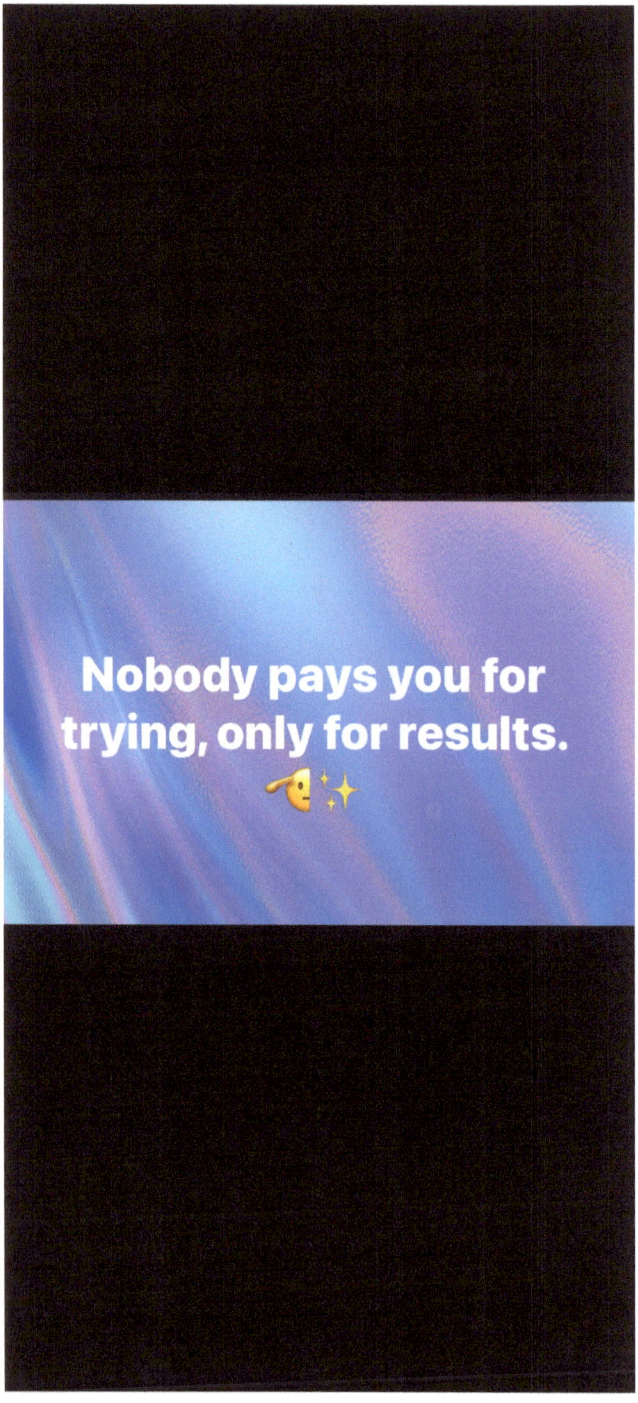

Stone Ship

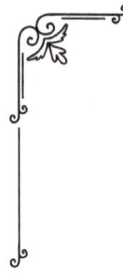

> **Nobody pays you for trying, only for results.** 👇✨

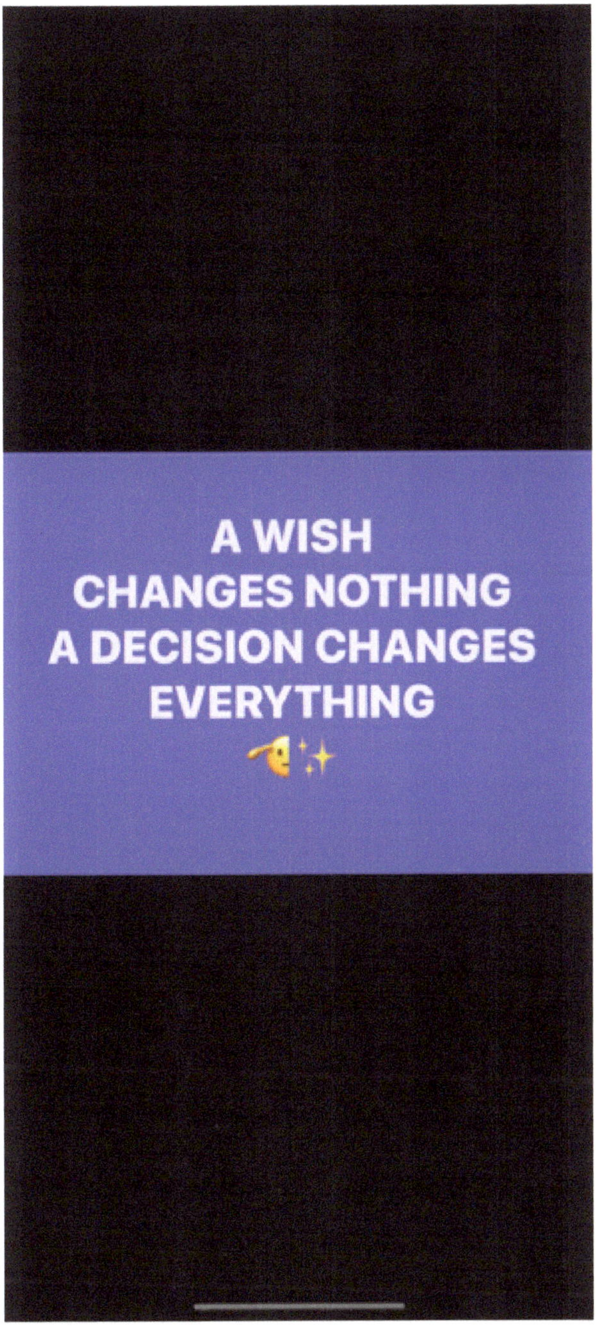

Olivia Conde

A WISH CHANGES NOTHING A DECISION CHANGES EVERYTHING

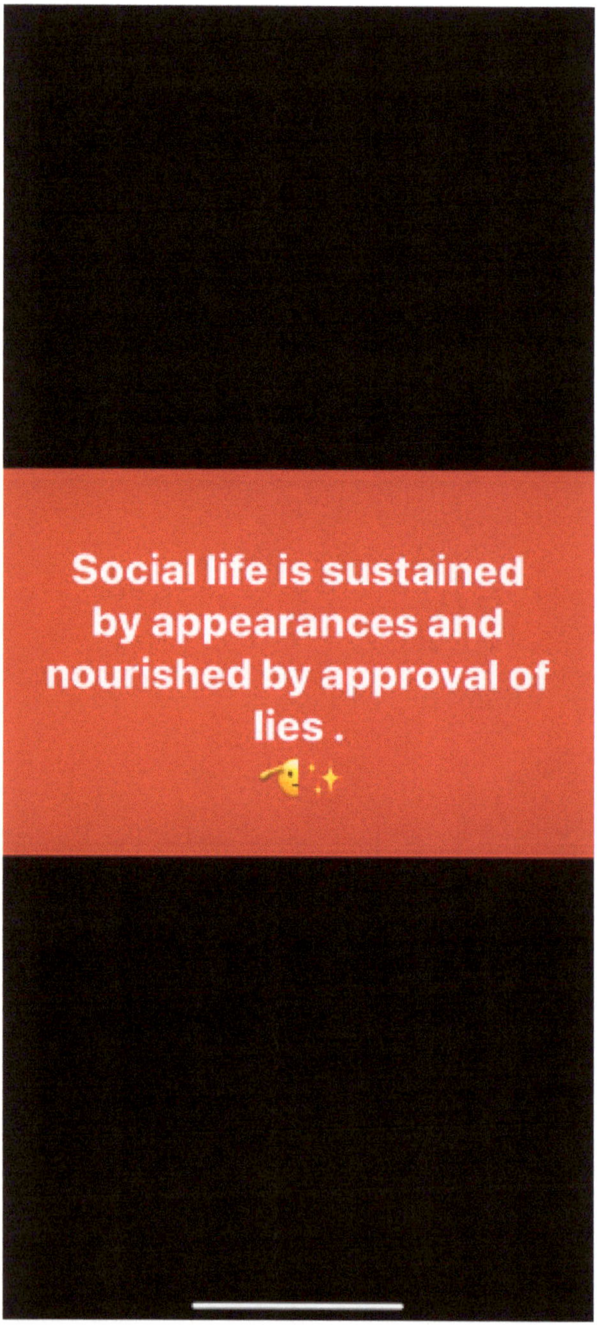

> Social life is sustained by appearances and nourished by approval of lies.

Olivia Conde

> The bird that waits for the perfect wind will never fly. 🫴✨

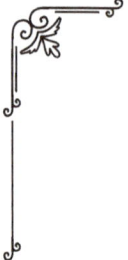

> The farmer who waits for perfect weather... will never harvest. 🌾✨

> The ship that waits for perfect weather...will never set sail. 🫡✨

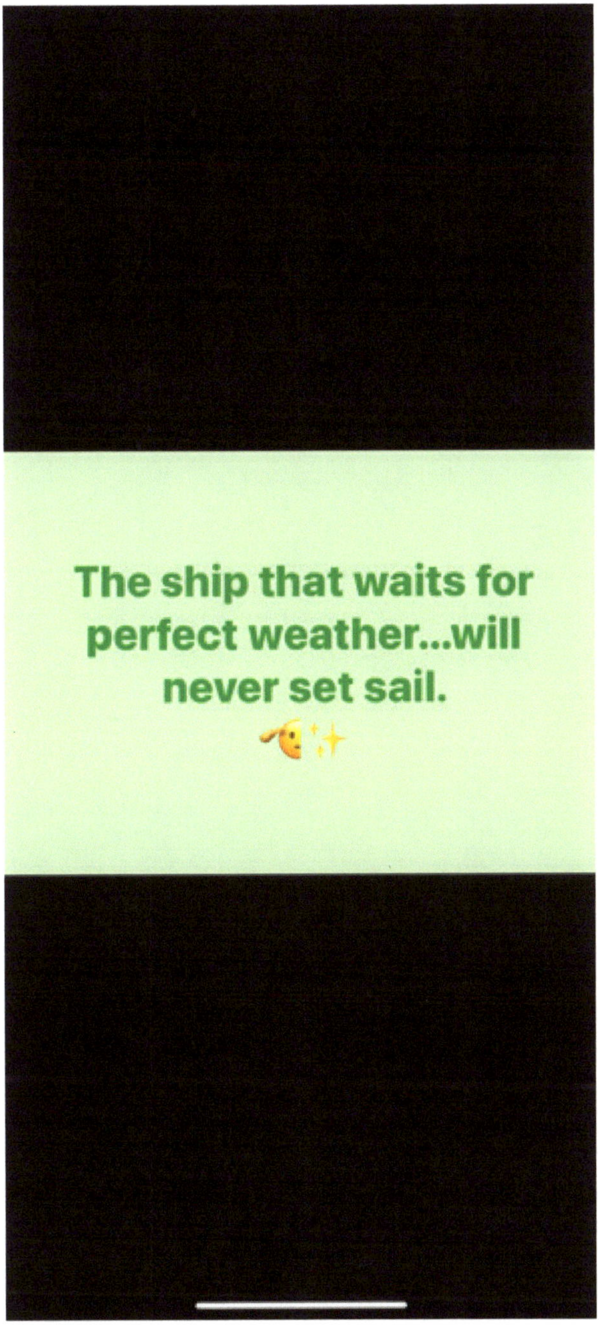

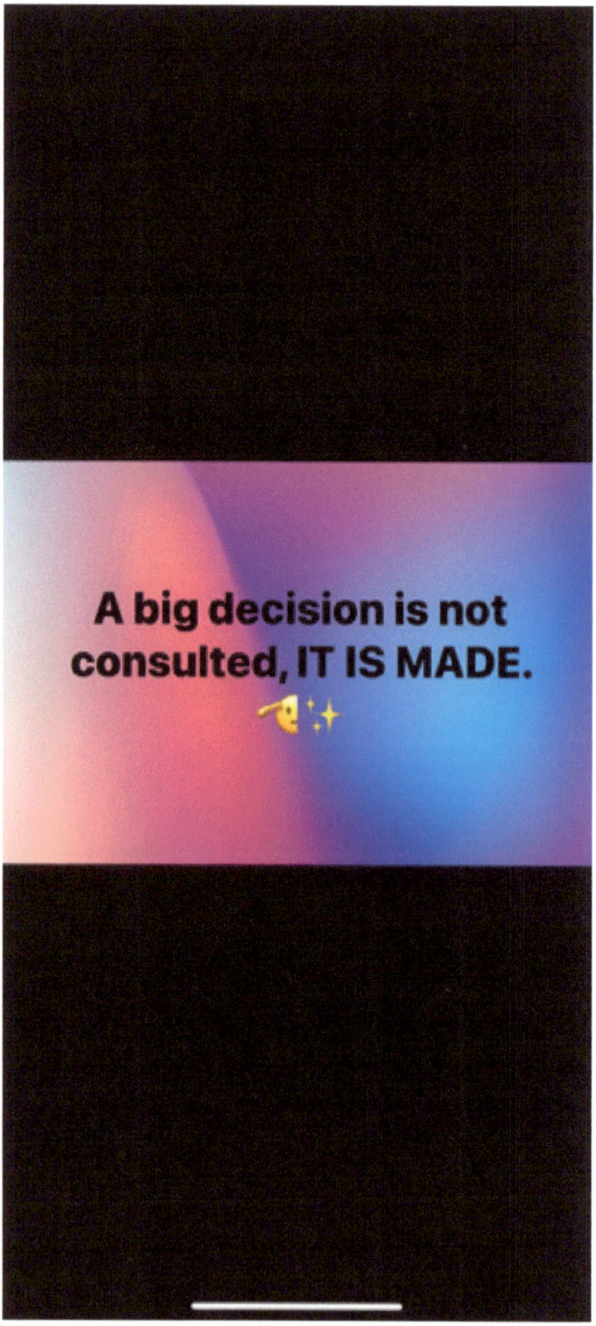

Stone Ship

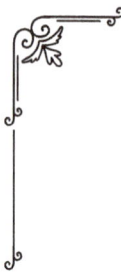

> A big decision is not consulted, IT IS MADE. 🫵✨

> The ego demands outside what it does not practice inside. 👉✨

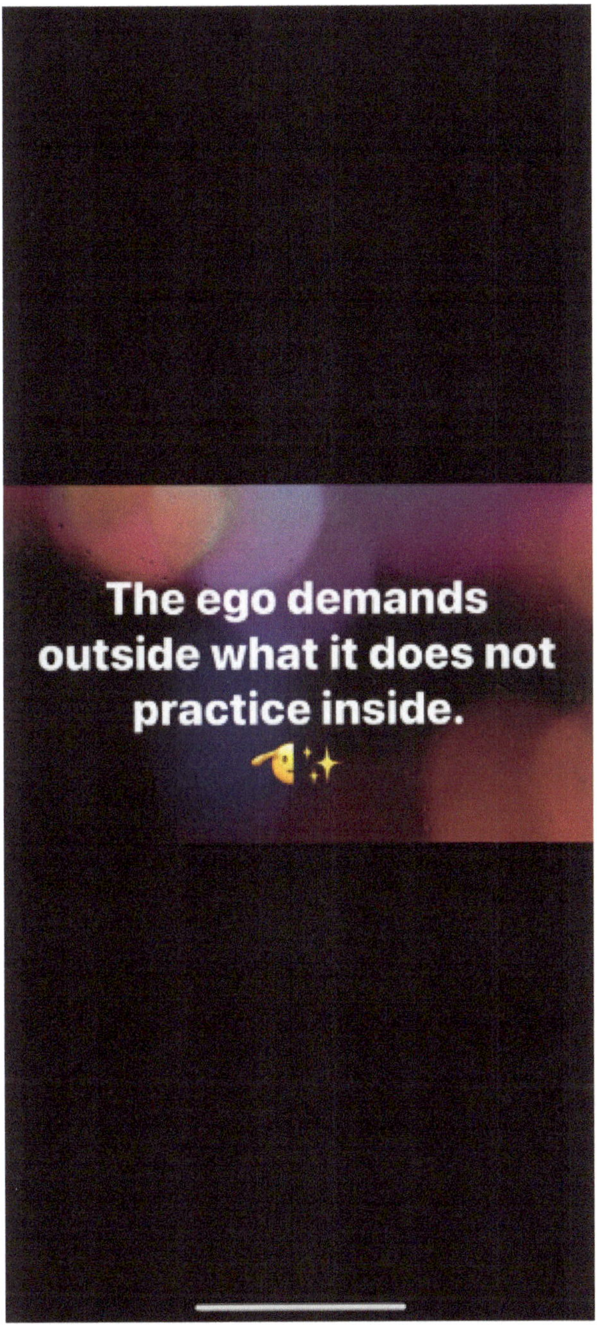

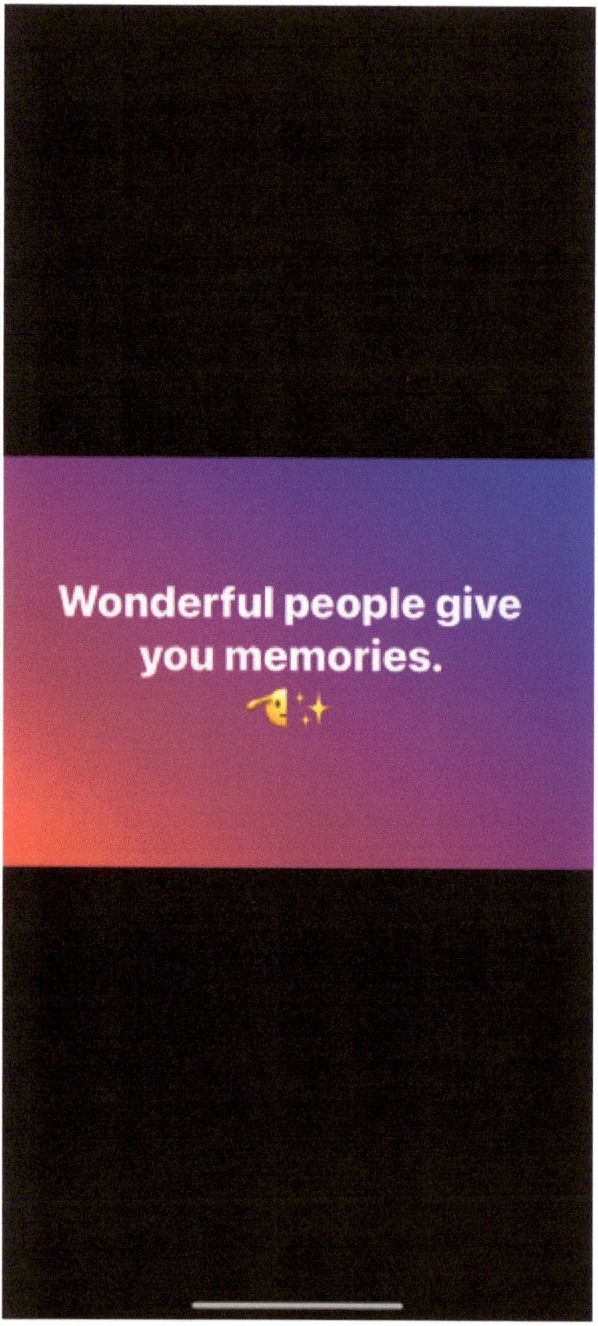
Wonderful people give you memories.

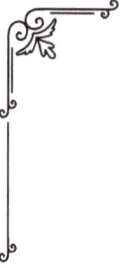

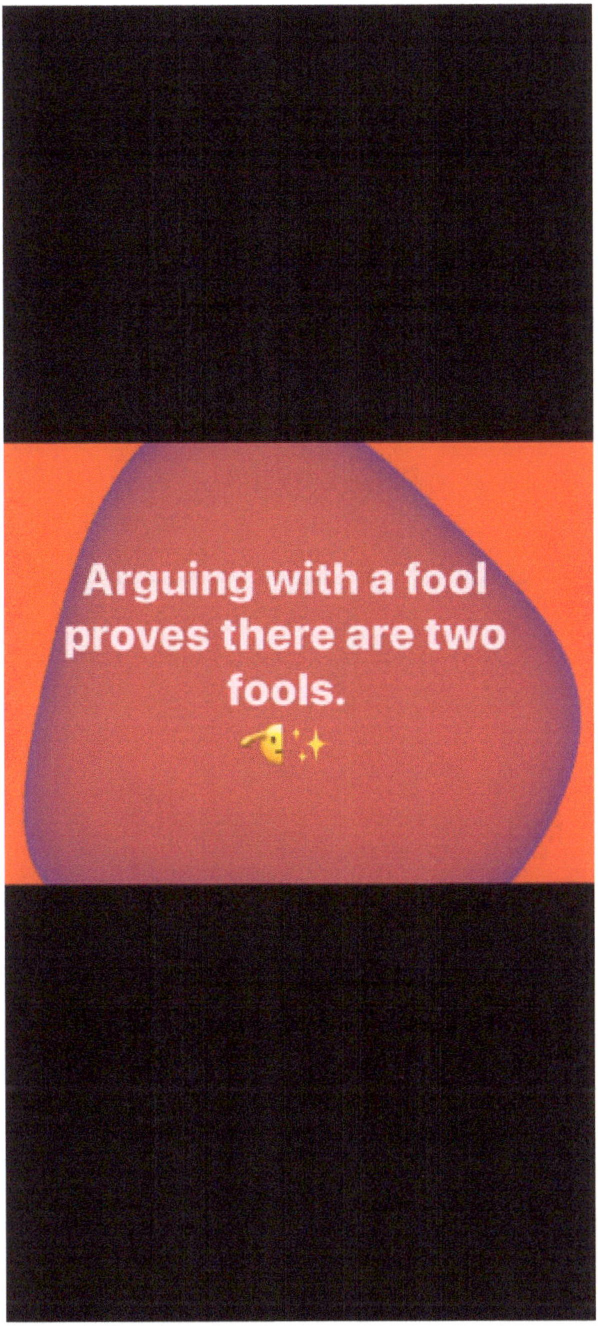
Arguing with a fool
proves there are two
fools.

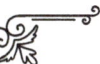

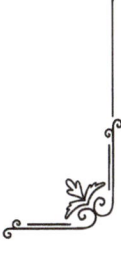

People who believe wait, but people who think act.

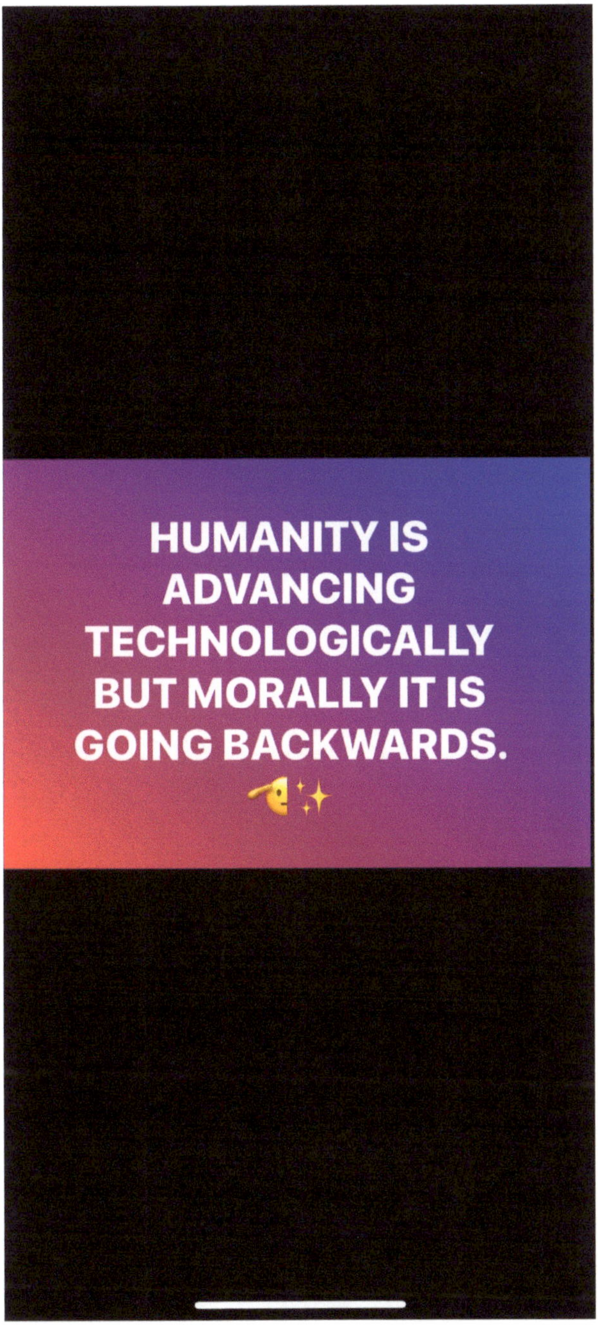

Olivia Conde

> **HUMANITY IS ADVANCING TECHNOLOGICALLY BUT MORALLY IT IS GOING BACKWARDS.** 🤌✨

> **Reggaeton will never be a legend, it will only be a disorder of order.** 🫴✨

> The universe is not a catalog of desires, but rather a system governed by laws of cause and effect. 🔭✨

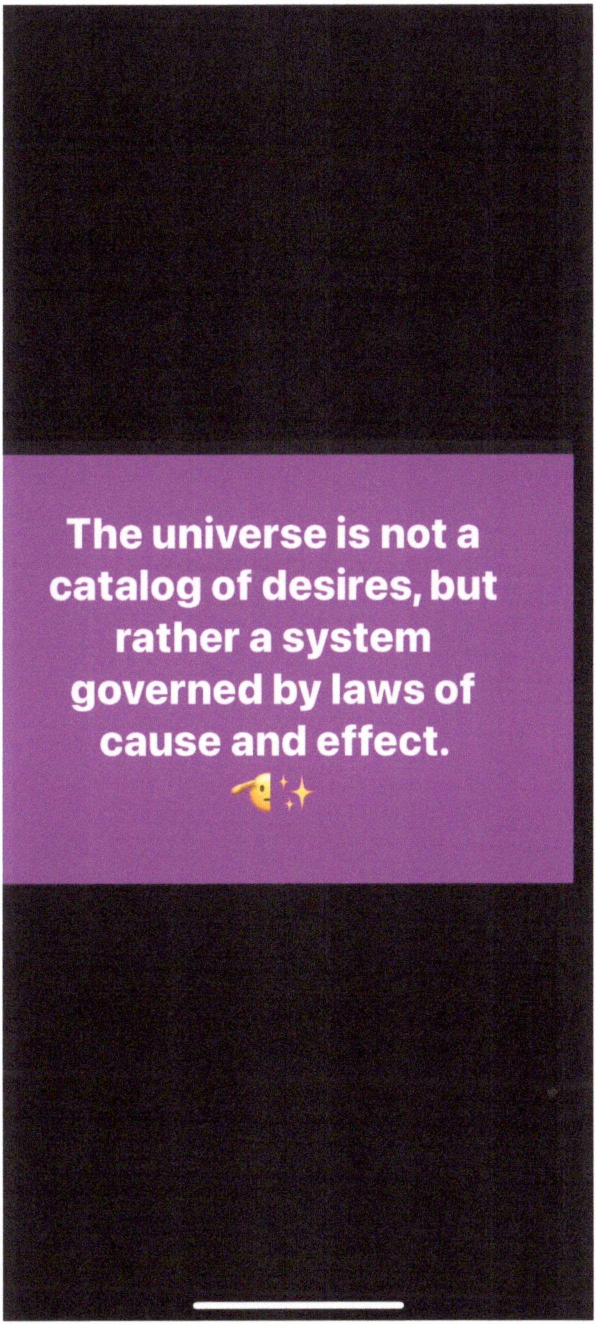

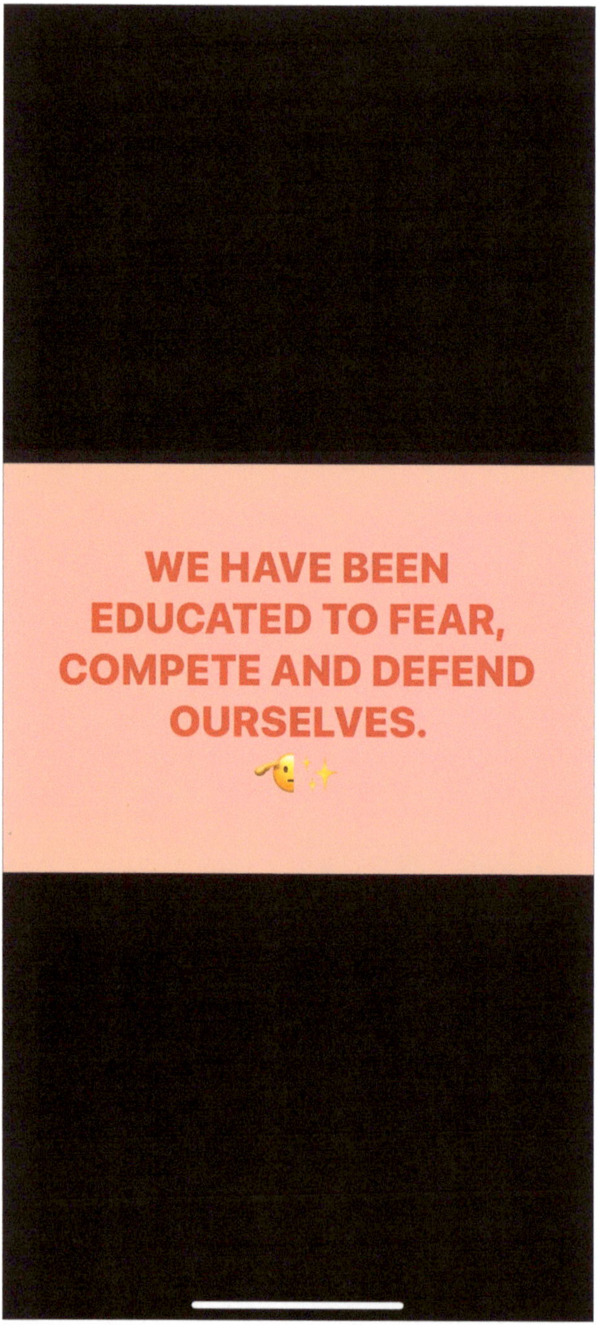

Stone Ship

> **WE HAVE BEEN EDUCATED TO FEAR, COMPETE AND DEFEND OURSELVES.** 🫠✨

> Time is only A tool within A useful expression.

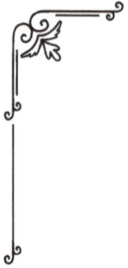

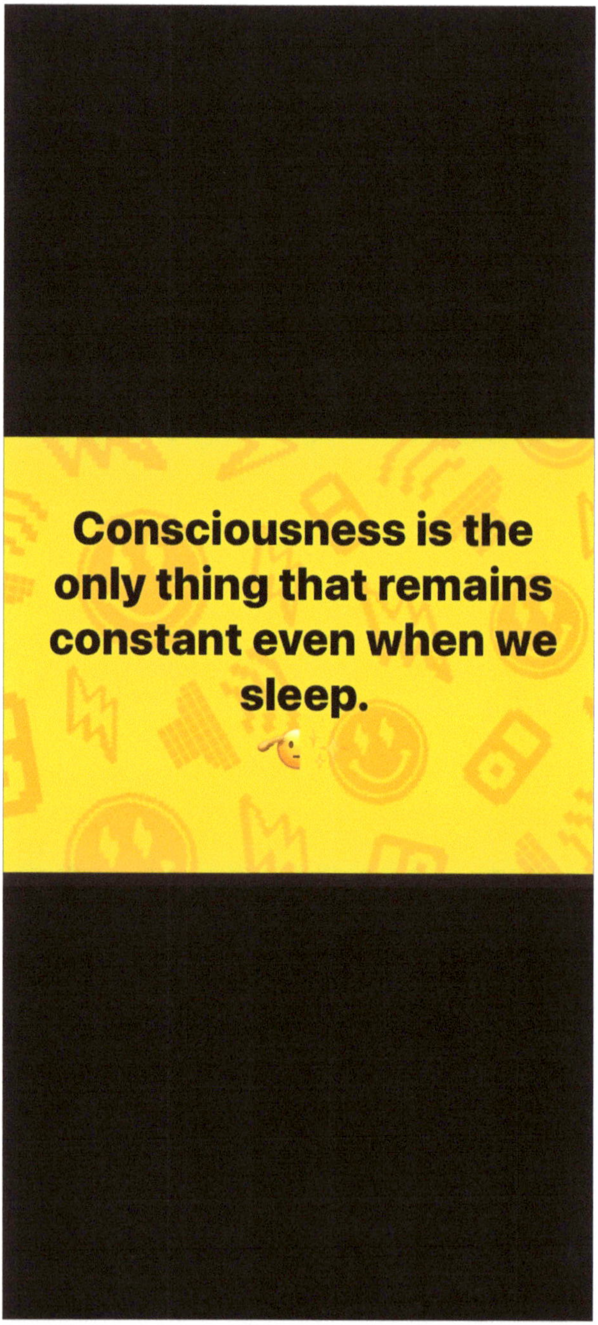

Consciousness is the only thing that remains constant even when we sleep.

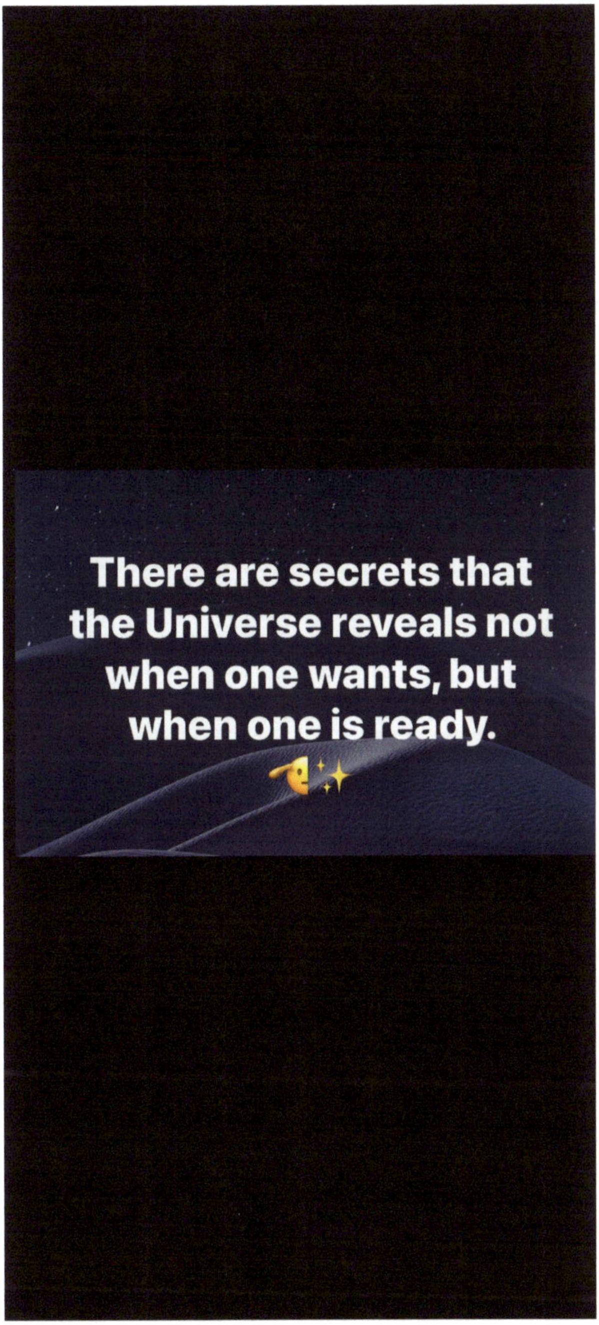

Olivia Conde

> There are secrets that the Universe reveals not when one wants, but when one is ready. 🫰✨

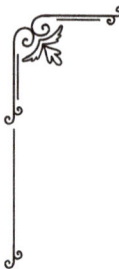

A change is momentary, a transformation is permanent, because a change is made from the outside and a transformation from the inside.

Olivia Conde

TECHNOLOGY WITHOUT LOVE SCIENCE WITHOUT SOUL. 🫵🌟✨

DESIRE REVEALS THE LEVEL OF CONSCIOUSNESS. 🫡✨

Olivia Conde

Religions are power structures to deal with fear. 🫴✨

WHEN MIND AND SOUL MEET, KNOWLEDGE BECOMES WISDOM. 🫡✨

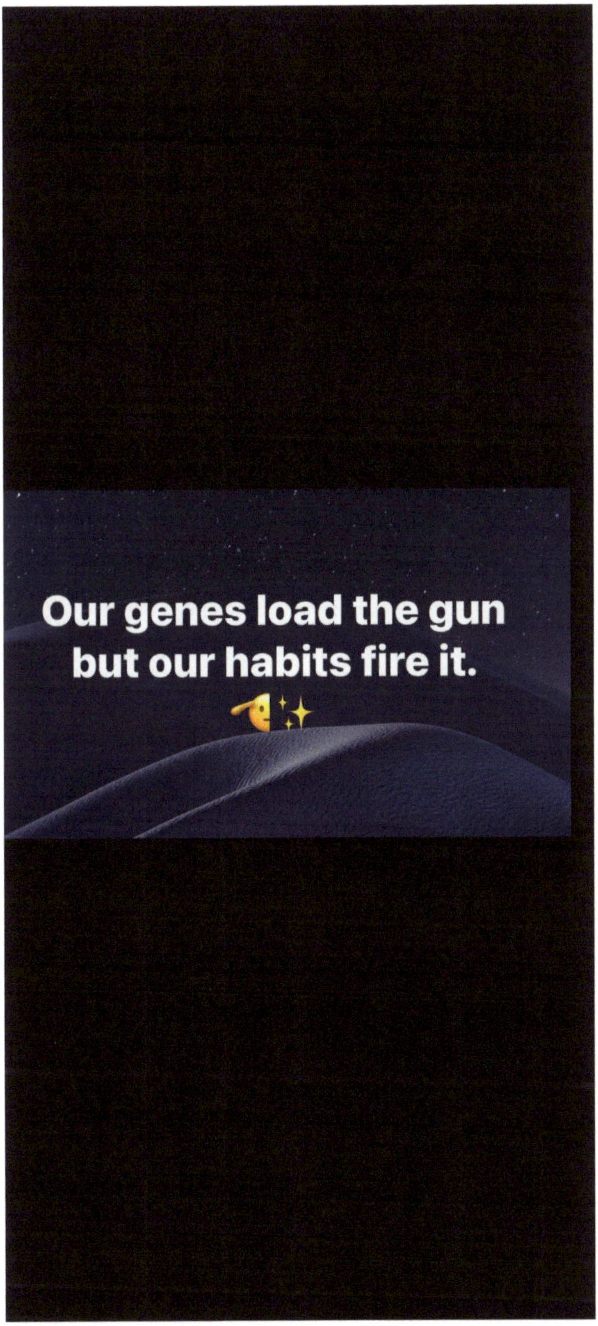
Our genes load the gun
but our habits fire it.

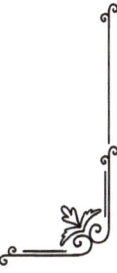

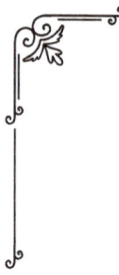

> **Ignorance makes people become fanatics** 👉✨

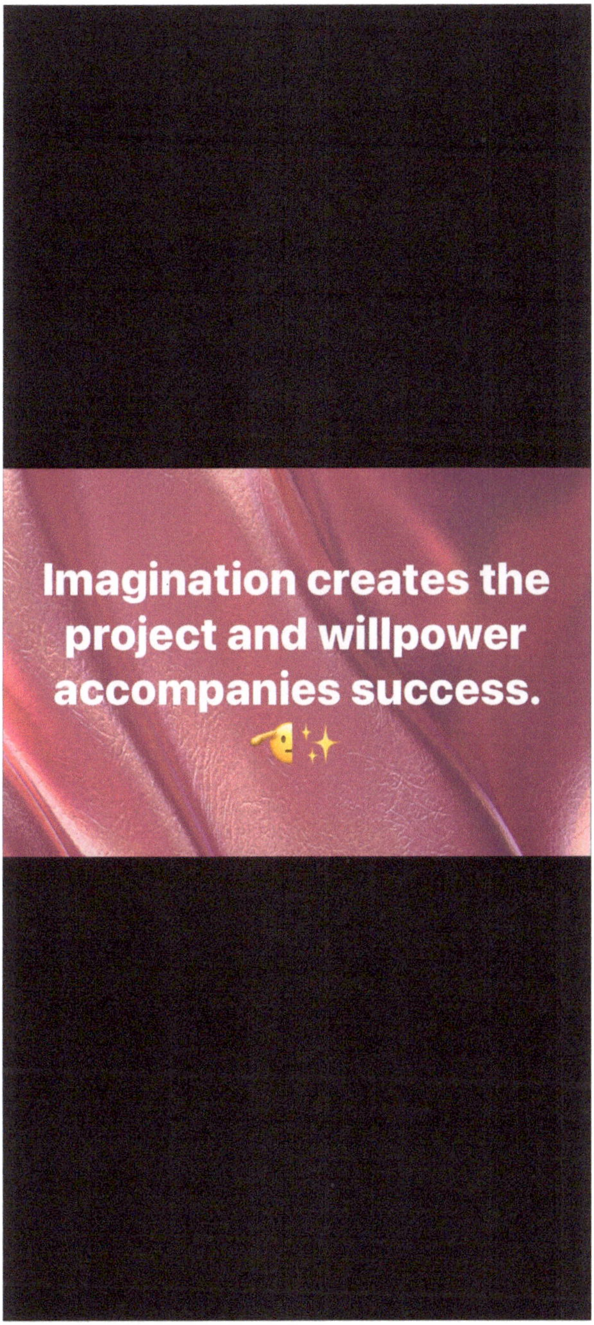

Olivia Conde

> **Imagination creates the project and willpower accompanies success.** 🎭✨

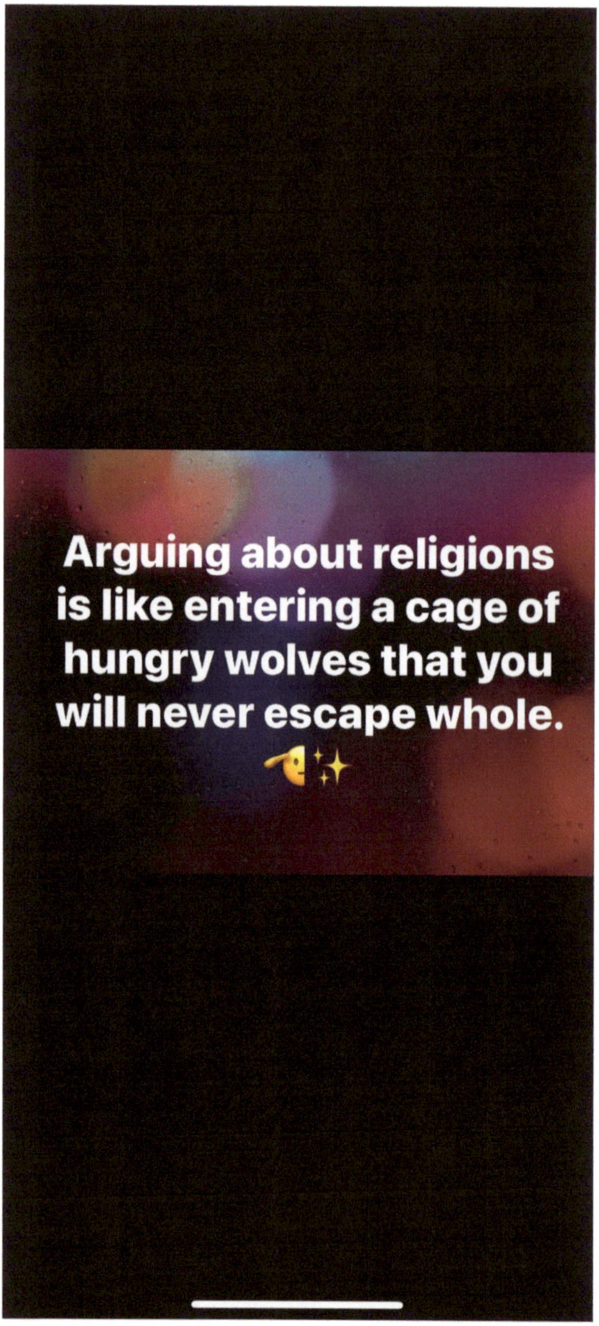

Stone Ship

> Arguing about religions is like entering a cage of hungry wolves that you will never escape whole. 🫴✨

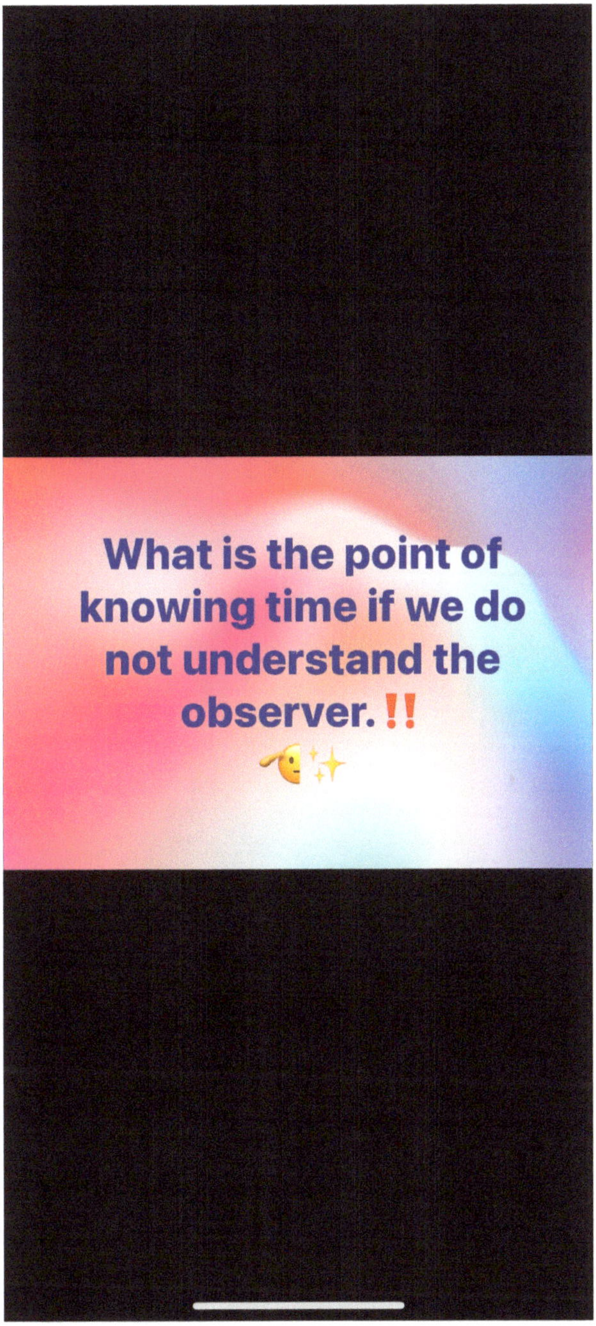

Olivia Conde

> **What is the point of knowing time if we do not understand the observer.‼️**
> 🫵✨

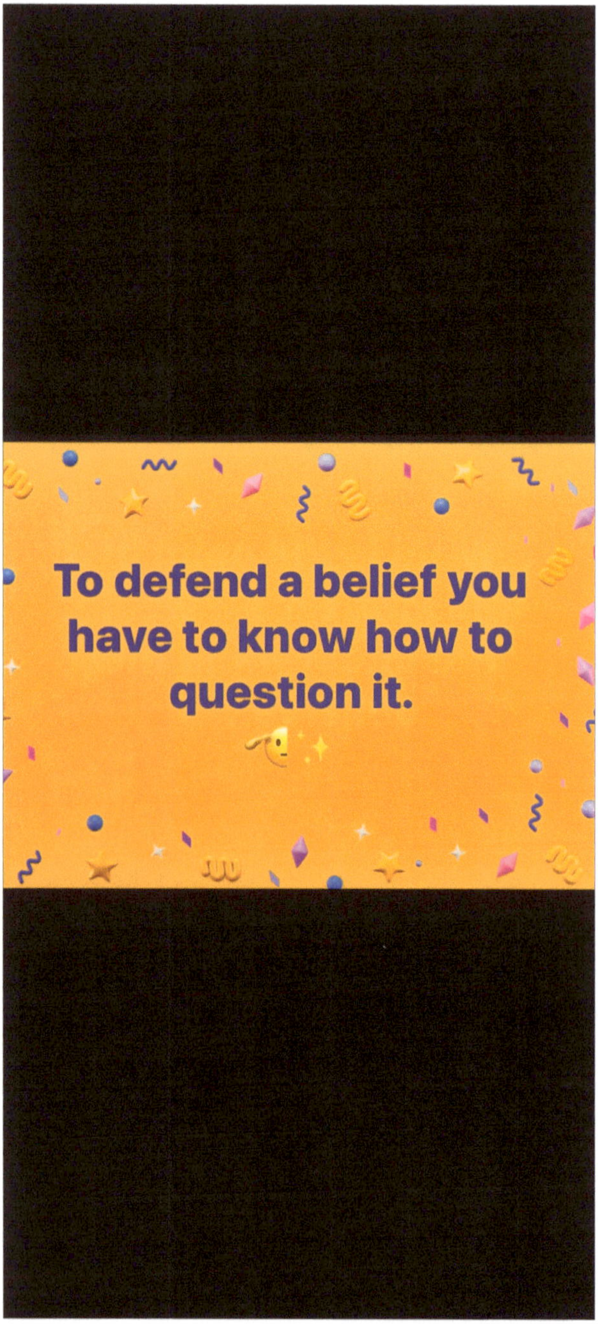

Stone Ship

> **To defend a belief you have to know how to question it.**

JUST as the COMPASS always points to the North, our intuition points to our inner wisdom.

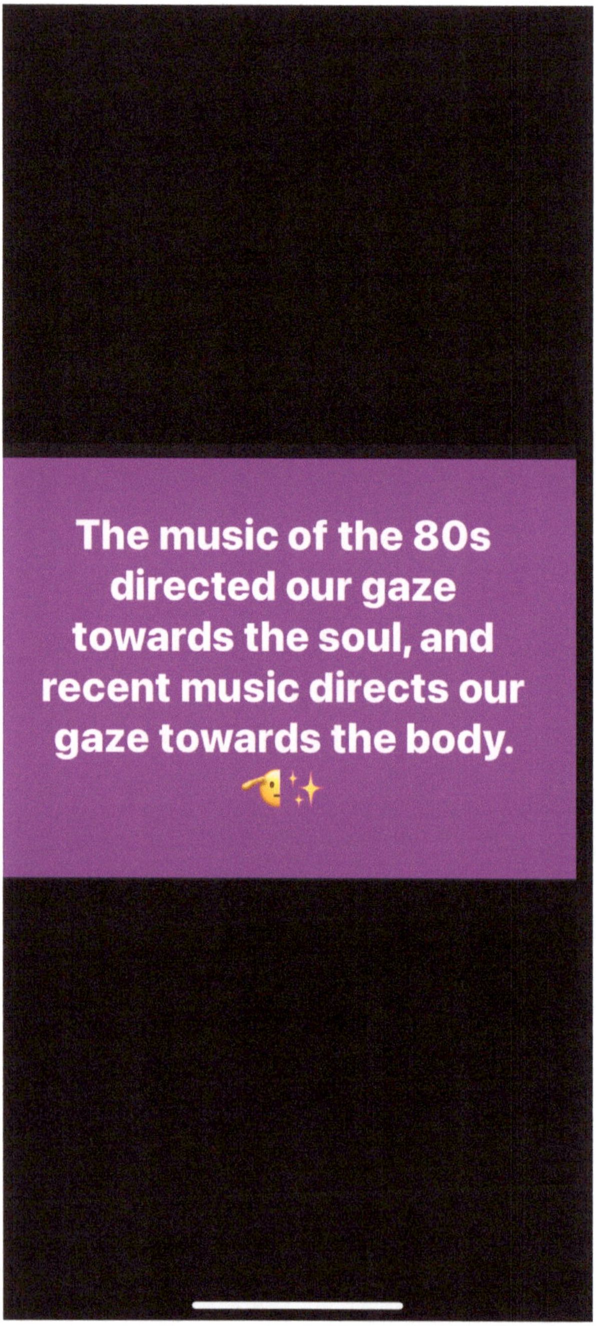

Stone Ship

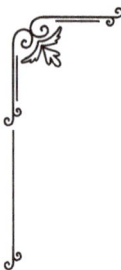

> The music of the 80s directed our gaze towards the soul, and recent music directs our gaze towards the body. 🫴✨

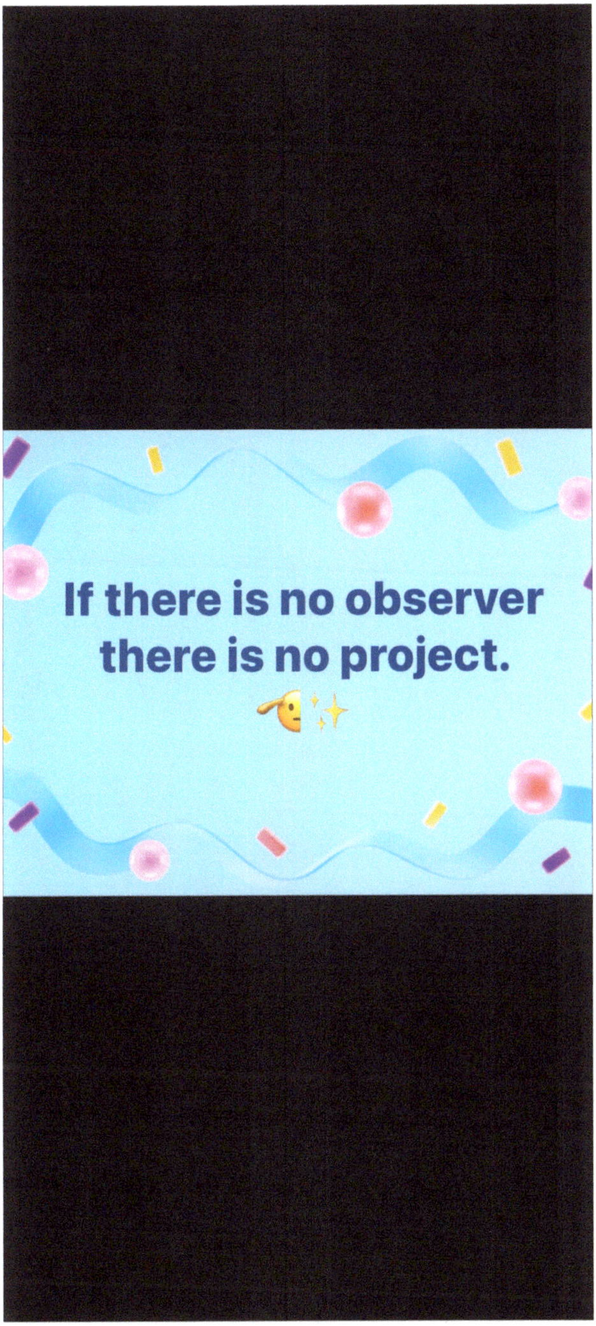

If there is no observer there is no project. 🫴✨

> The only advice I can give people is, Submit to the pleasure of your intuition, but never to those that people like, because your intuition will always protect you and people today are there and tomorrow disappear. 🎭✨

> The crooked tree lives its life while the straight one ends up as planks. 🫱✨

Stone Ship

> There are questions that do not seek answers, only presence.
> 🫠✨

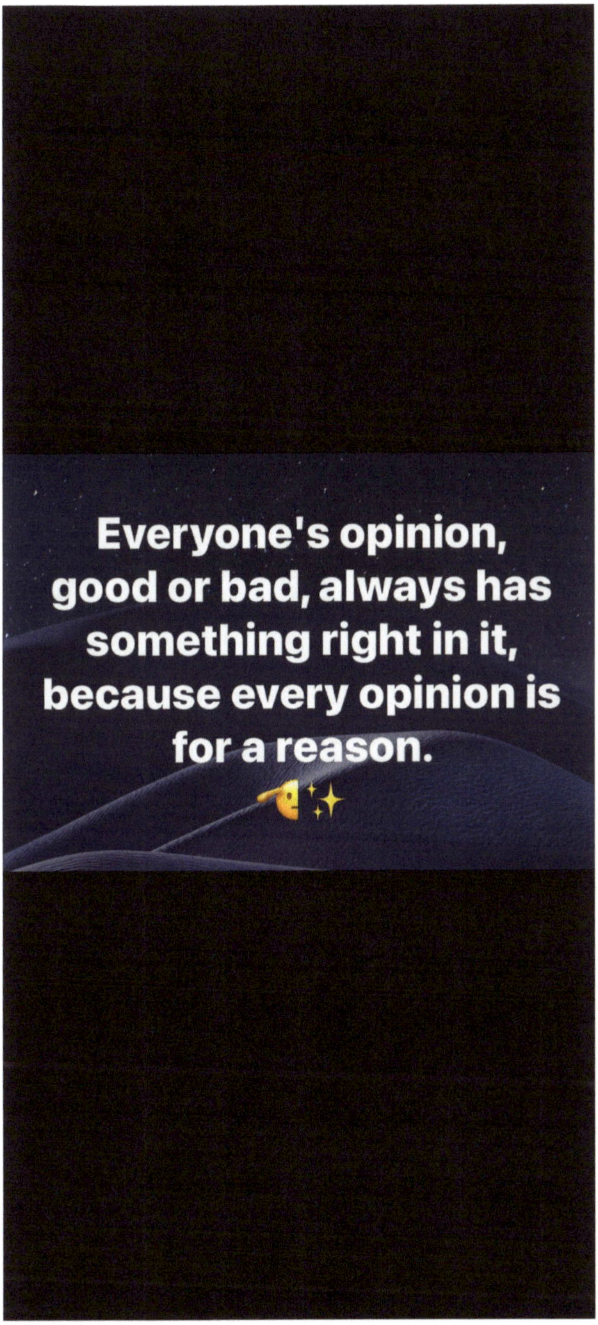

Olivia Conde

Everyone's opinion, good or bad, always has something right in it, because every opinion is for a reason. 🌜✨

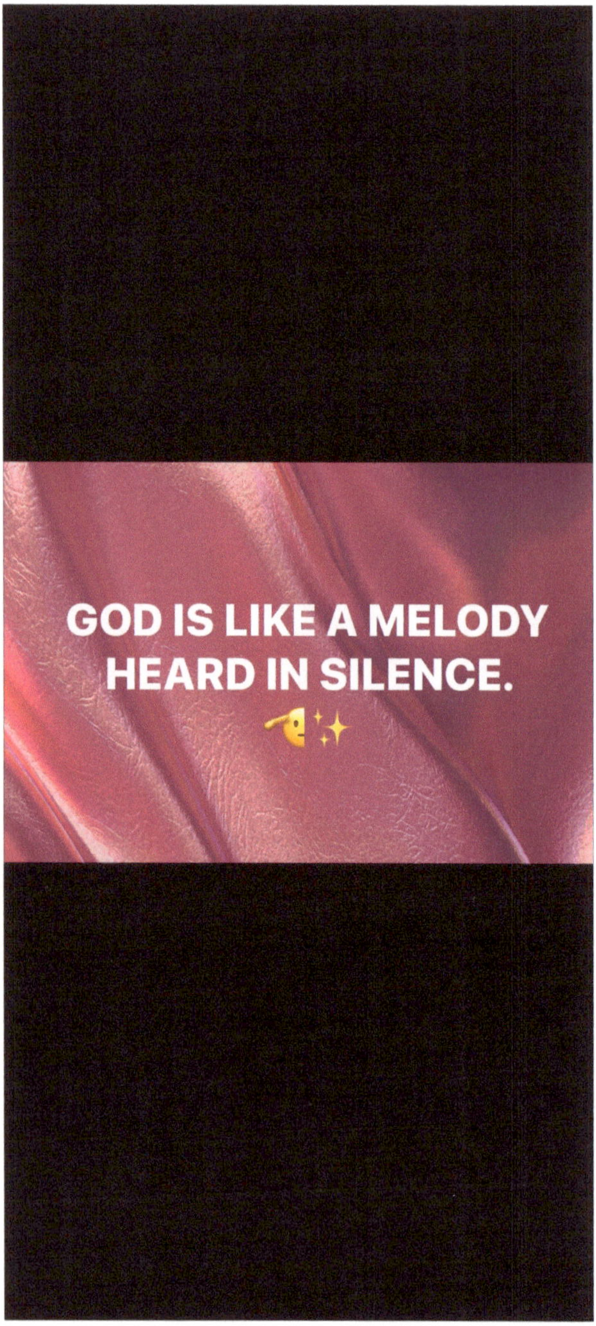

GOD IS LIKE A MELODY HEARD IN SILENCE. 🫅✨

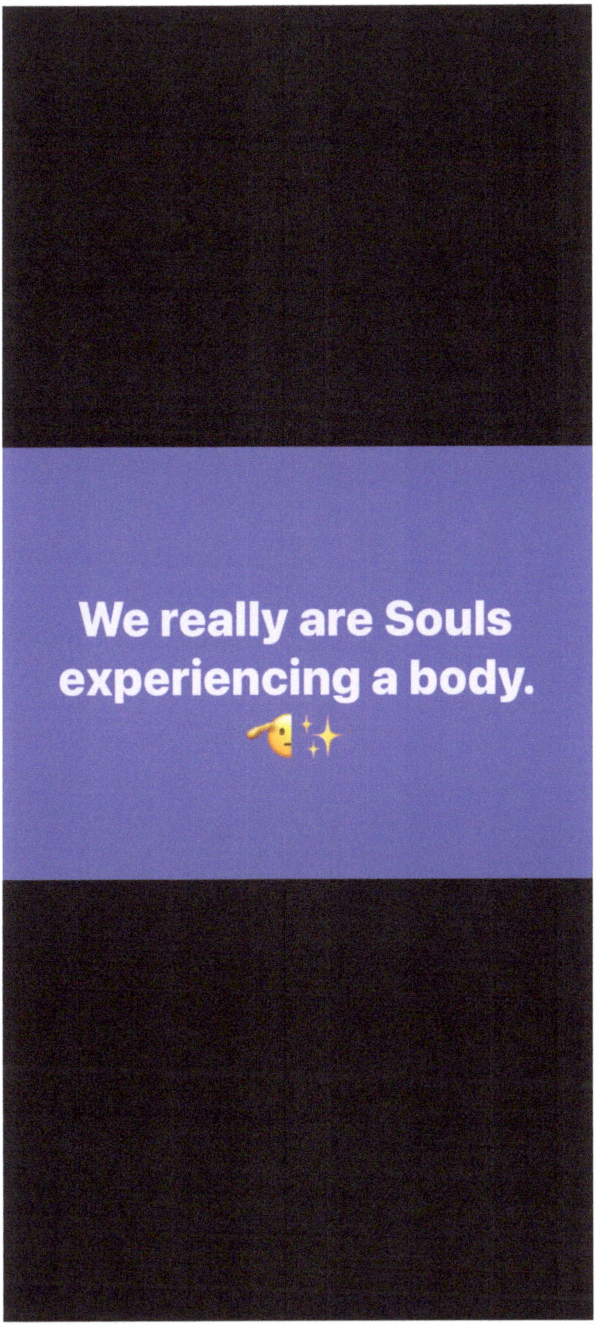

We really are Souls experiencing a body. 🫰✨

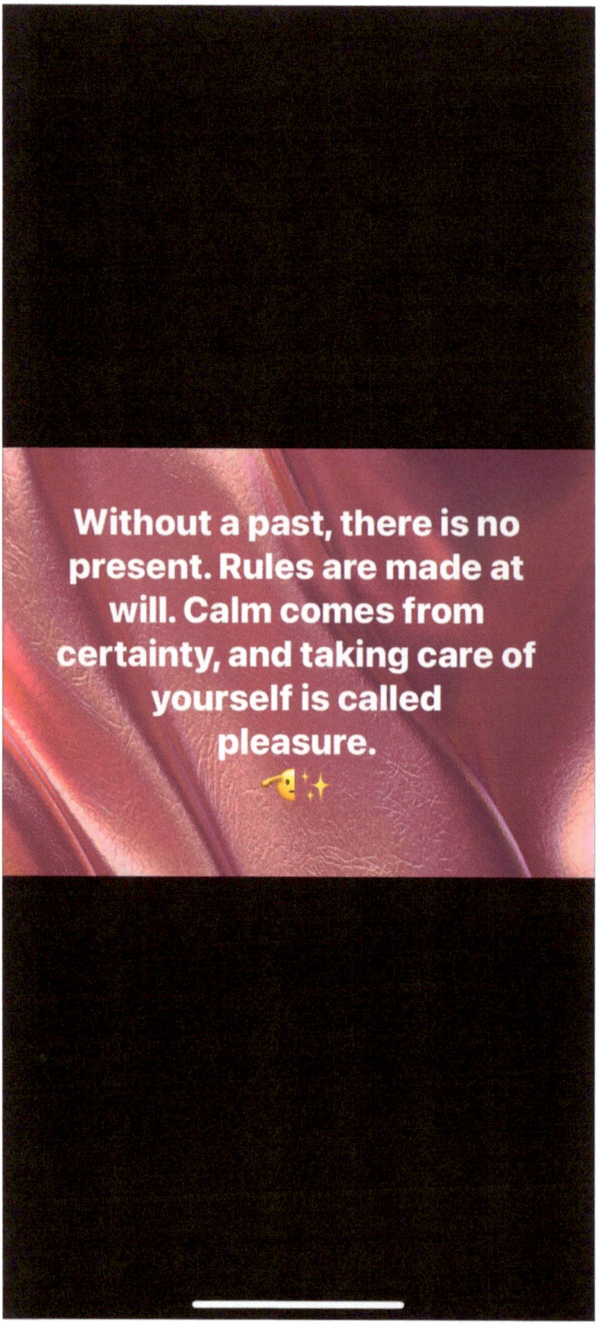

Stone Ship

> Without a past, there is no present. Rules are made at will. Calm comes from certainty, and taking care of yourself is called pleasure. 🫵✨

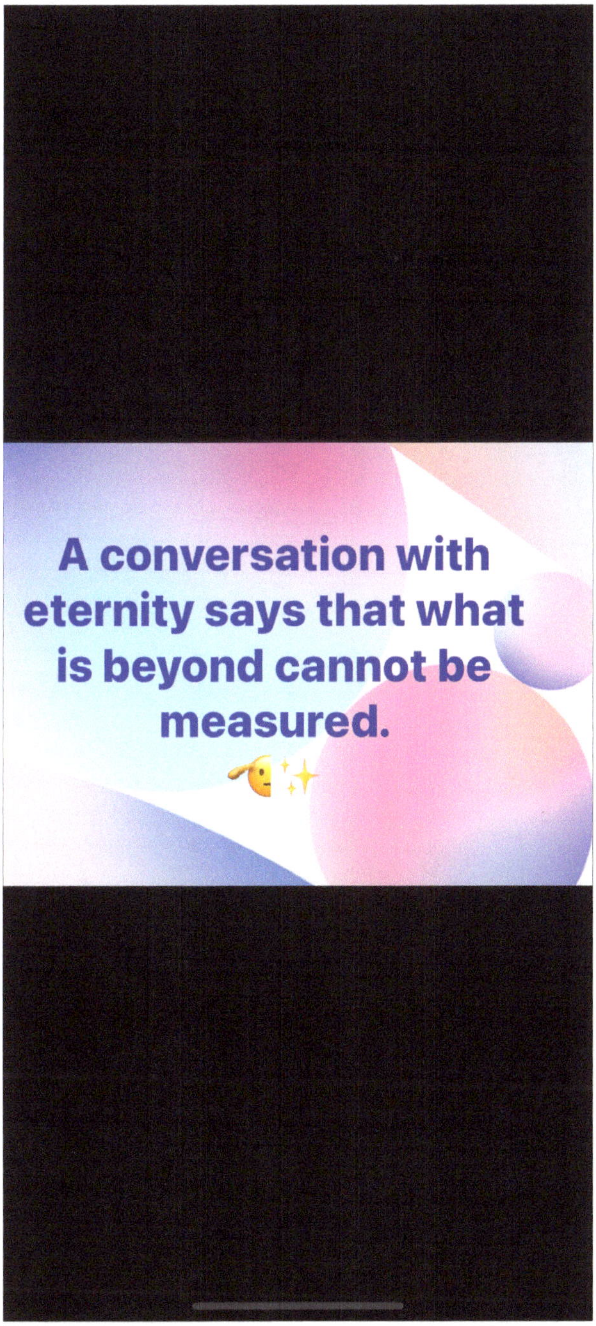

A conversation with eternity says that what is beyond cannot be measured. 🫵✨

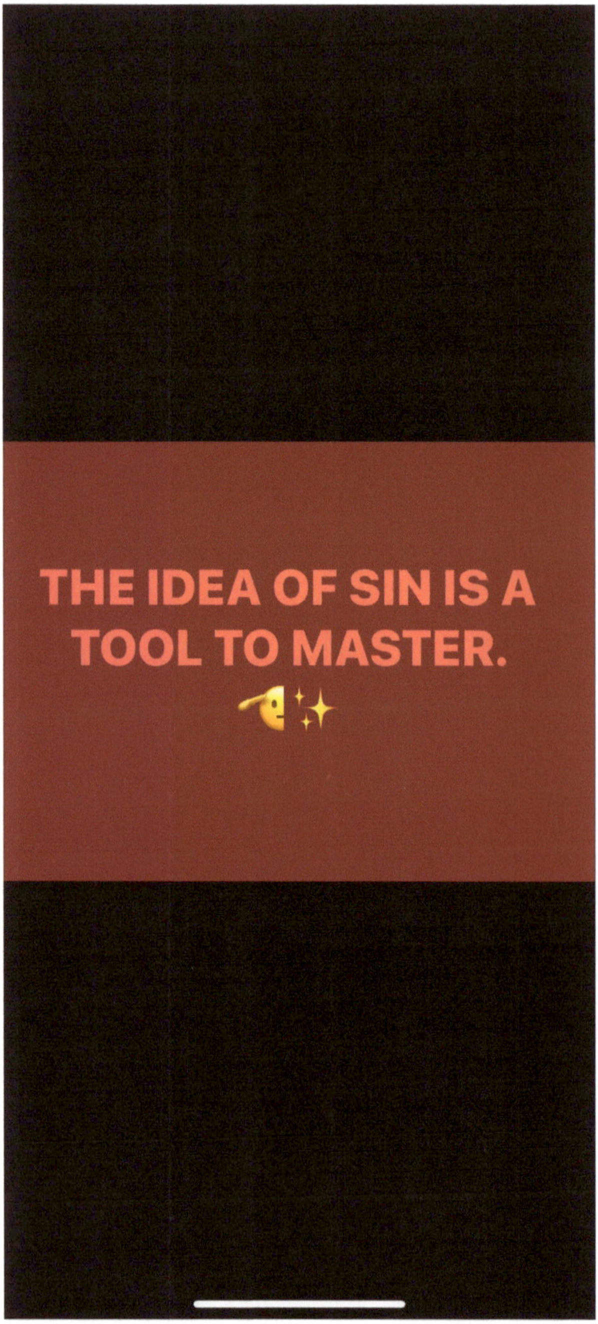

THE IDEA OF SIN IS A TOOL TO MASTER. 🫵✨

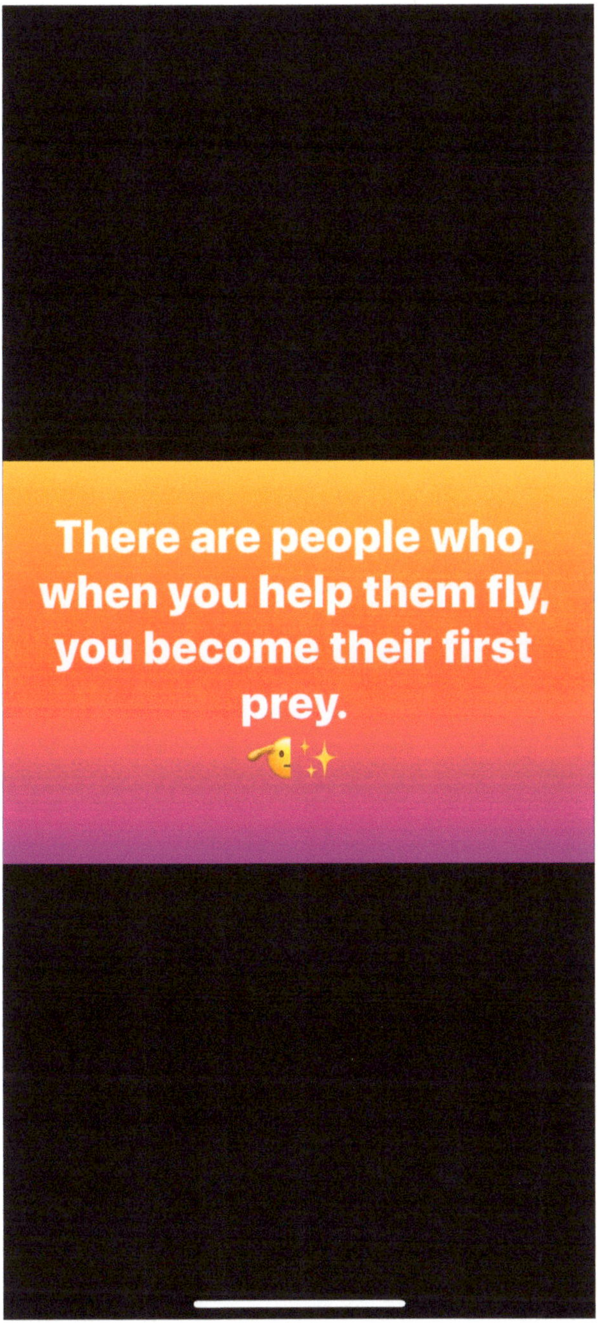

Olivia Conde

> There are people who, when you help them fly, you become their first prey. 👉✨

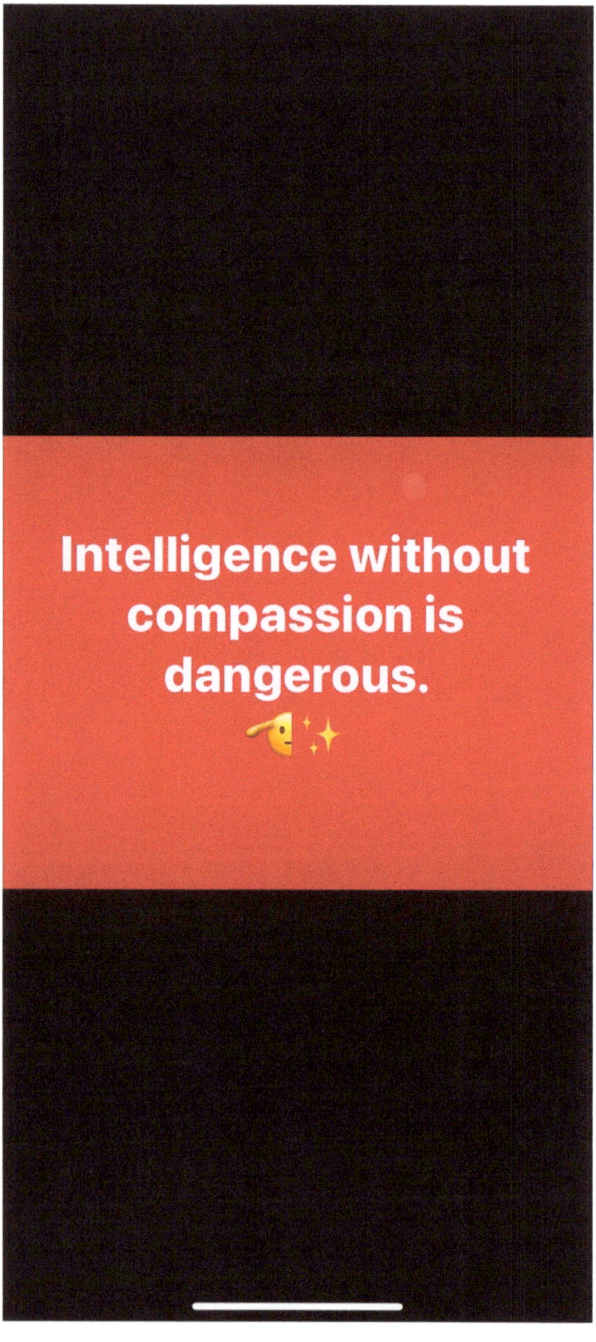
Intelligence without compassion is dangerous.

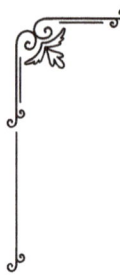

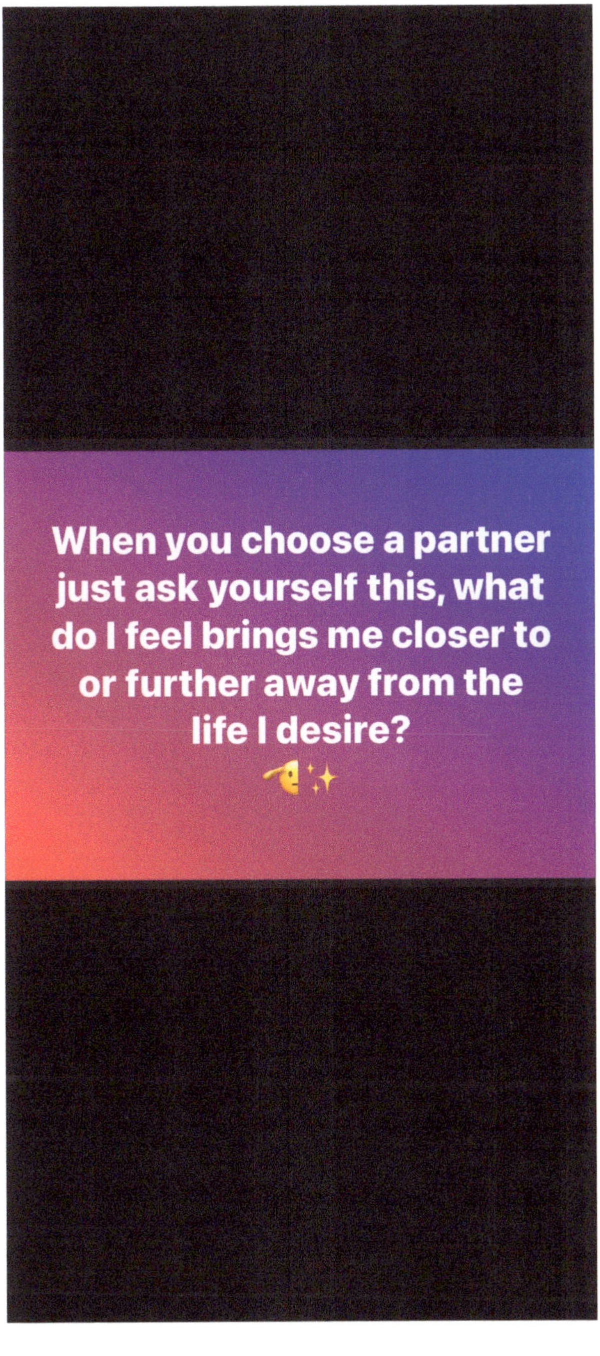

> When you choose a partner just ask yourself this, what do I feel brings me closer to or further away from the life I desire? 🫰✨

> Power in the hands of an ignorant person is dangerous. 🫡✨

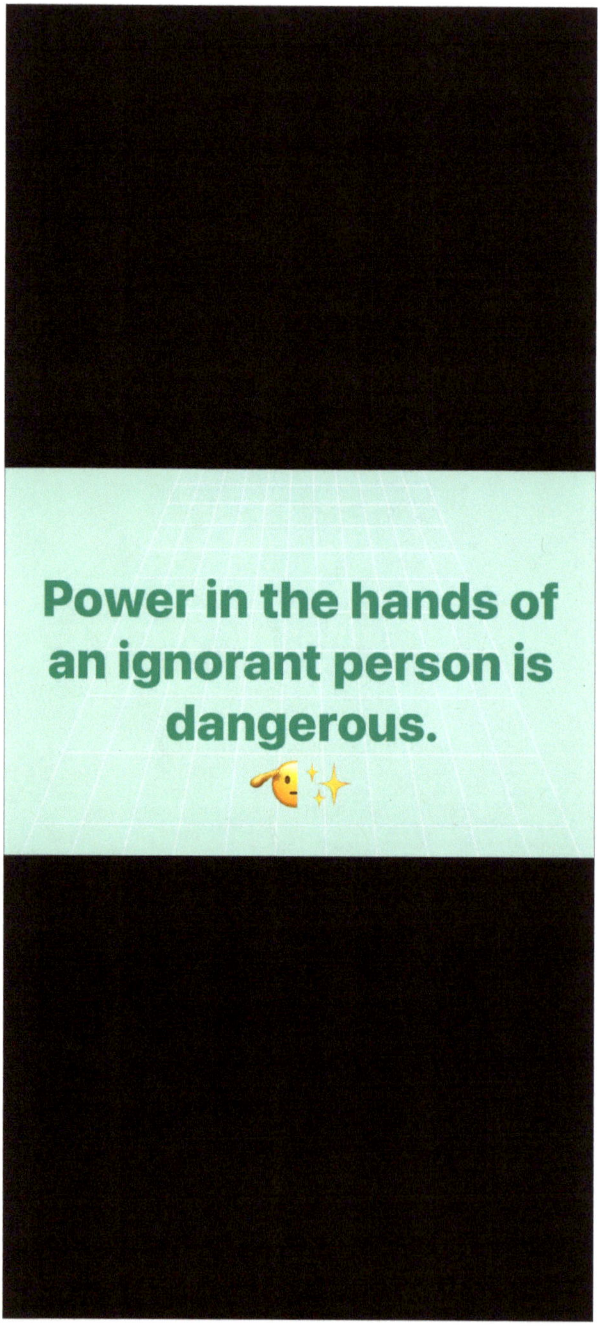

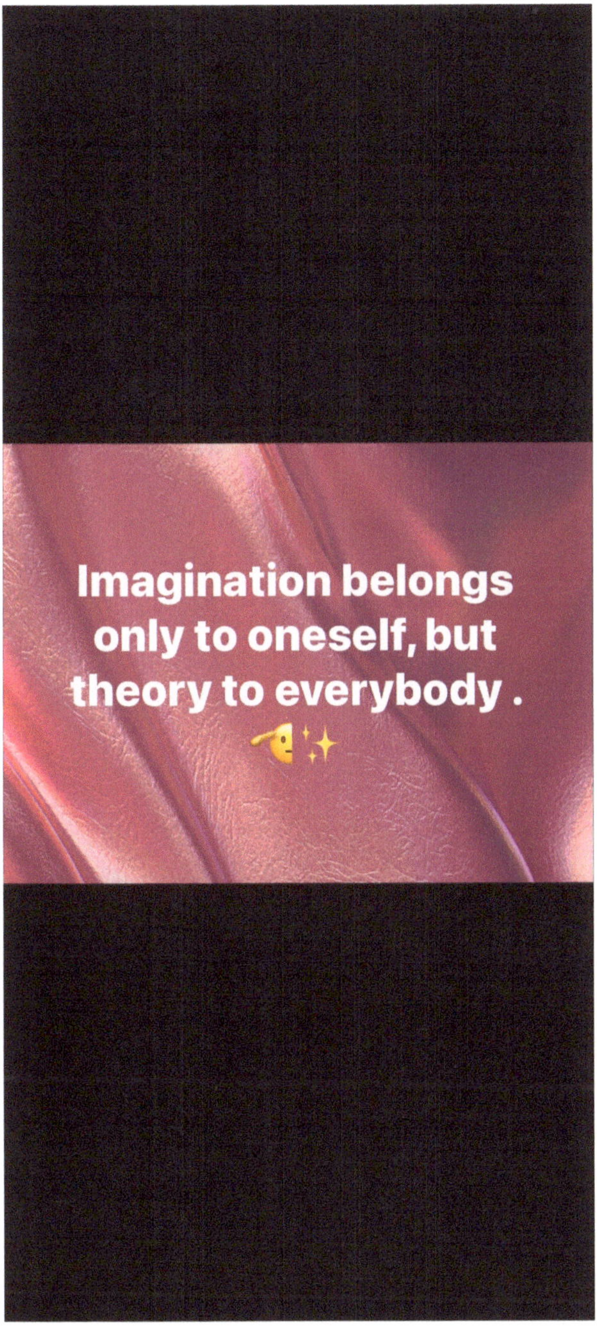

Olivia Conde

> **Imagination belongs only to oneself, but theory to everybody.** 🤭✨

> The beauty that attracts rarely coincides with the beauty that falls in love. 🫰✨

Olivia Conde

> **The beauty that attracts rarely coincides with the beauty that falls in love.** 👇✨

> **Power in the hands of an ignorant person is dangerous.**

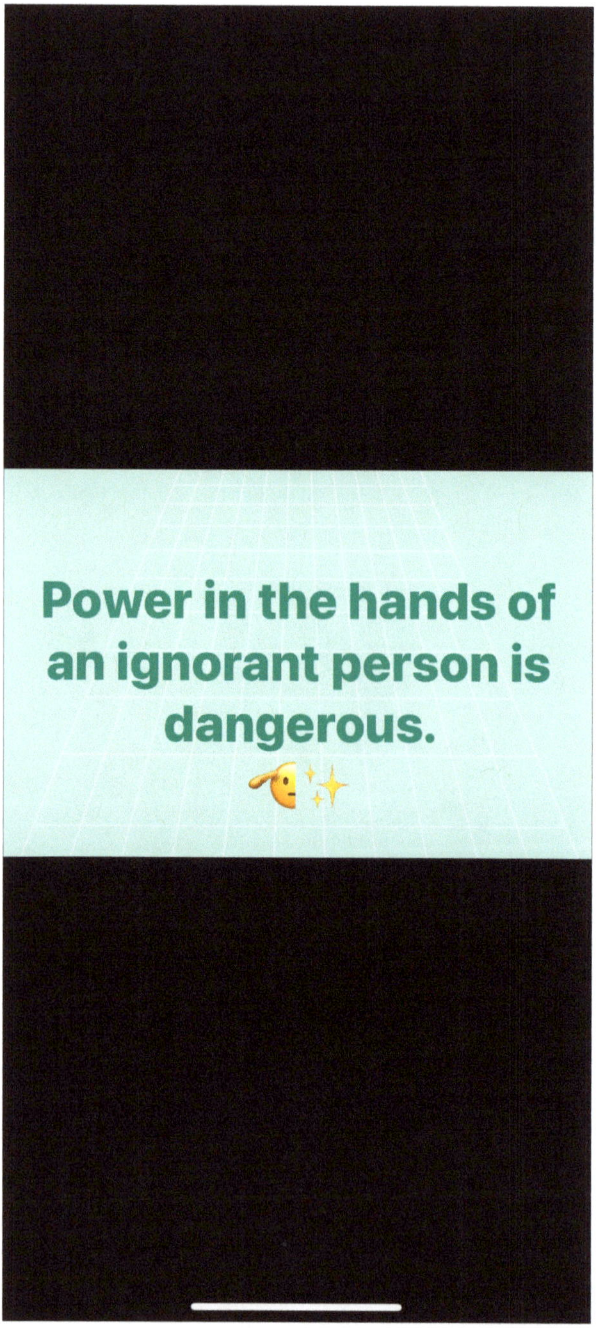

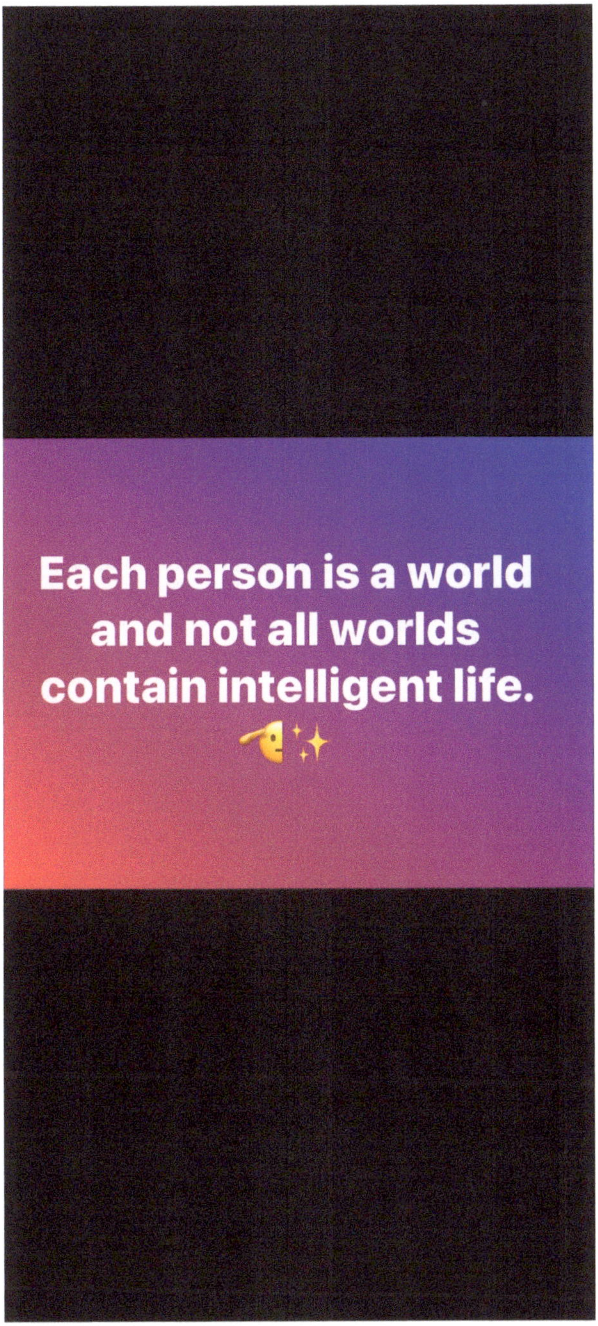

Olivia Conde

Each person is a world and not all worlds contain intelligent life. 🫵✨

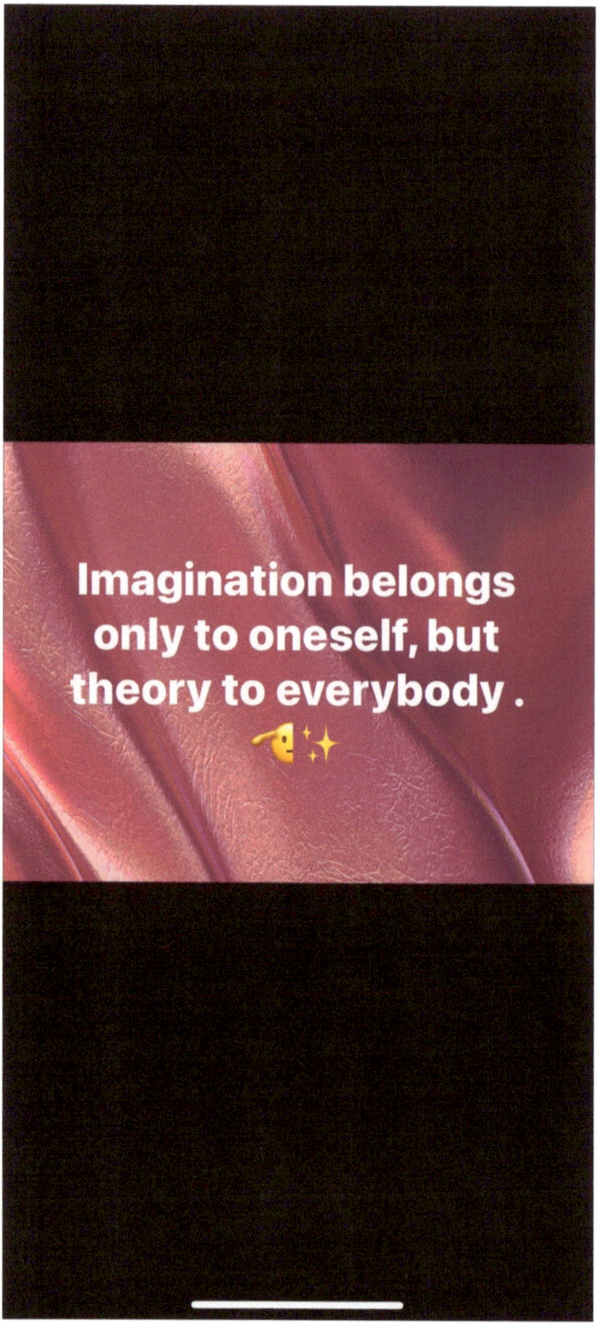

> Imagination belongs only to oneself, but theory to everybody. 🫵✨

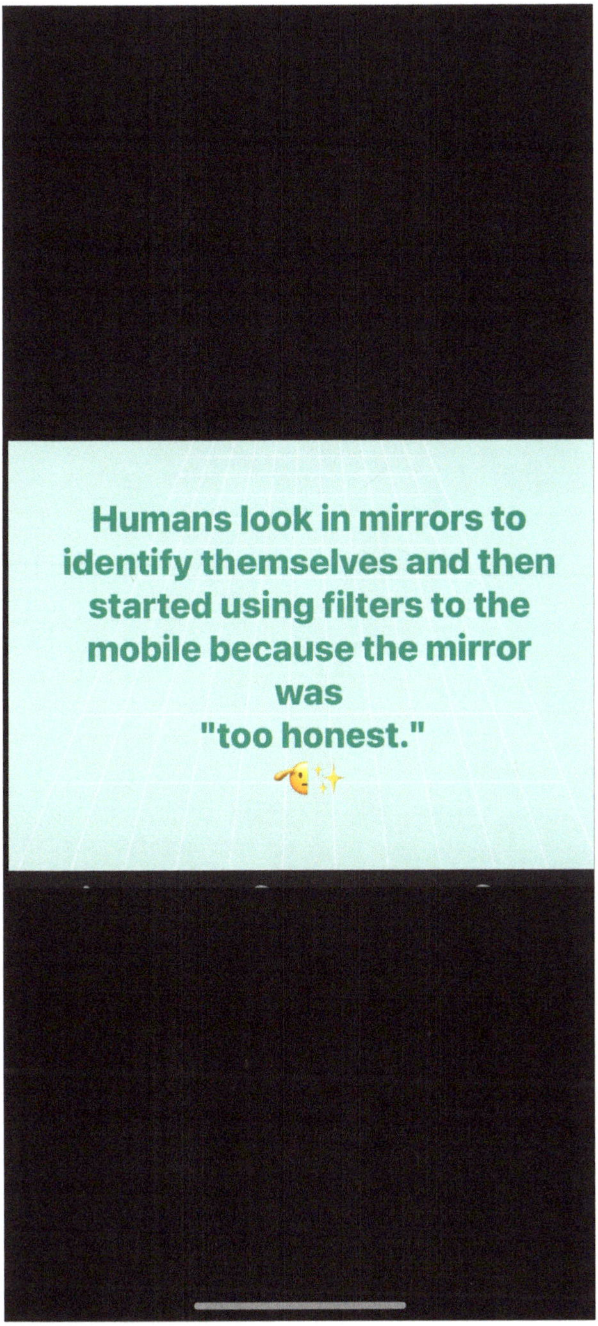

Humans look in mirrors to identify themselves and then started using filters to the mobile because the mirror was "too honest." 🤭✨

> It's not the same to see someone when you have time than to make time to see someone. 🫵✨

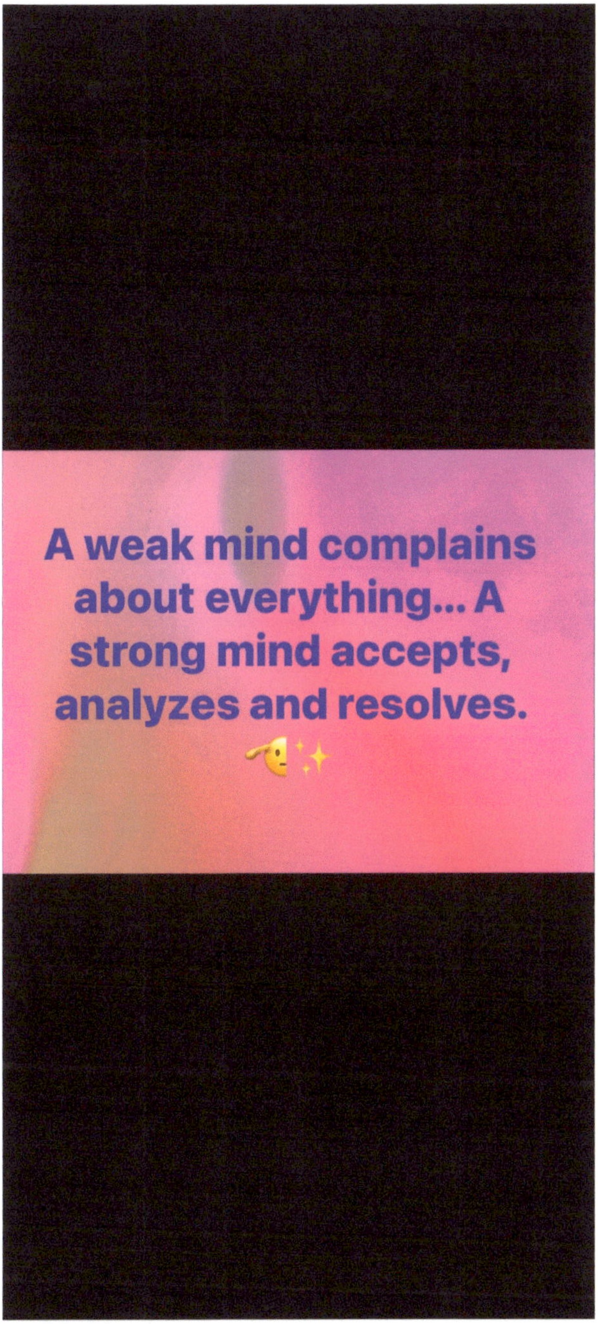

Olivia Conde

> **A weak mind complains about everything... A strong mind accepts, analyzes and resolves.** 🫰✨

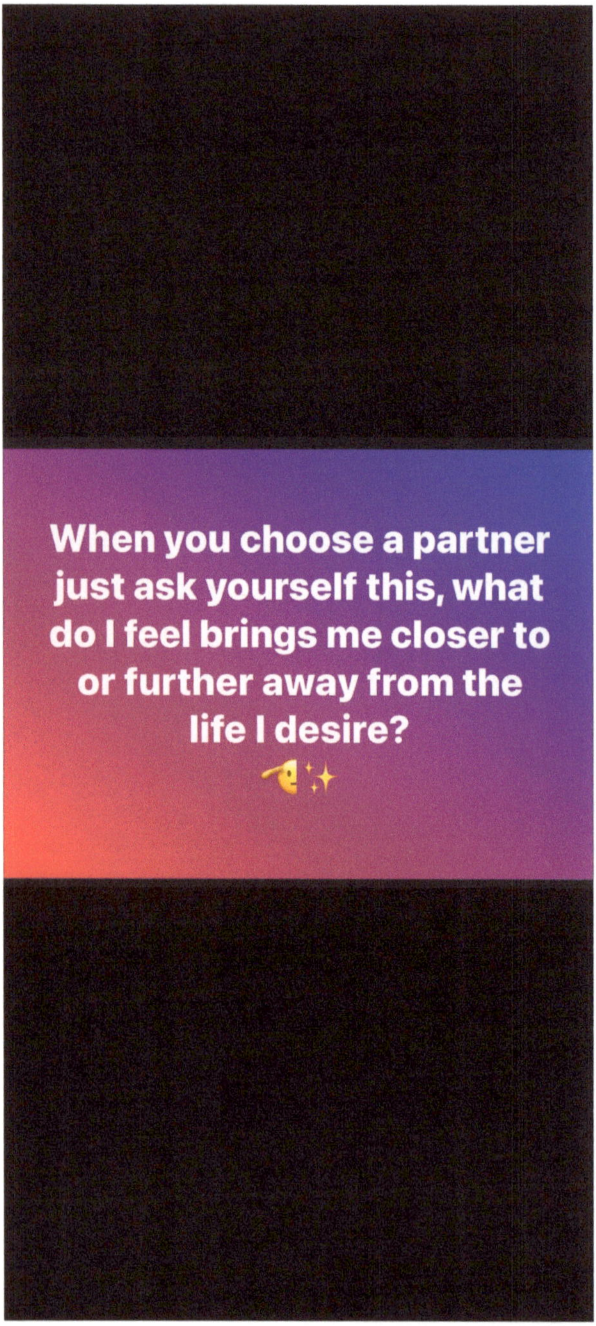

When you choose a partner just ask yourself this, what do I feel brings me closer to or further away from the life I desire? 🫰✨

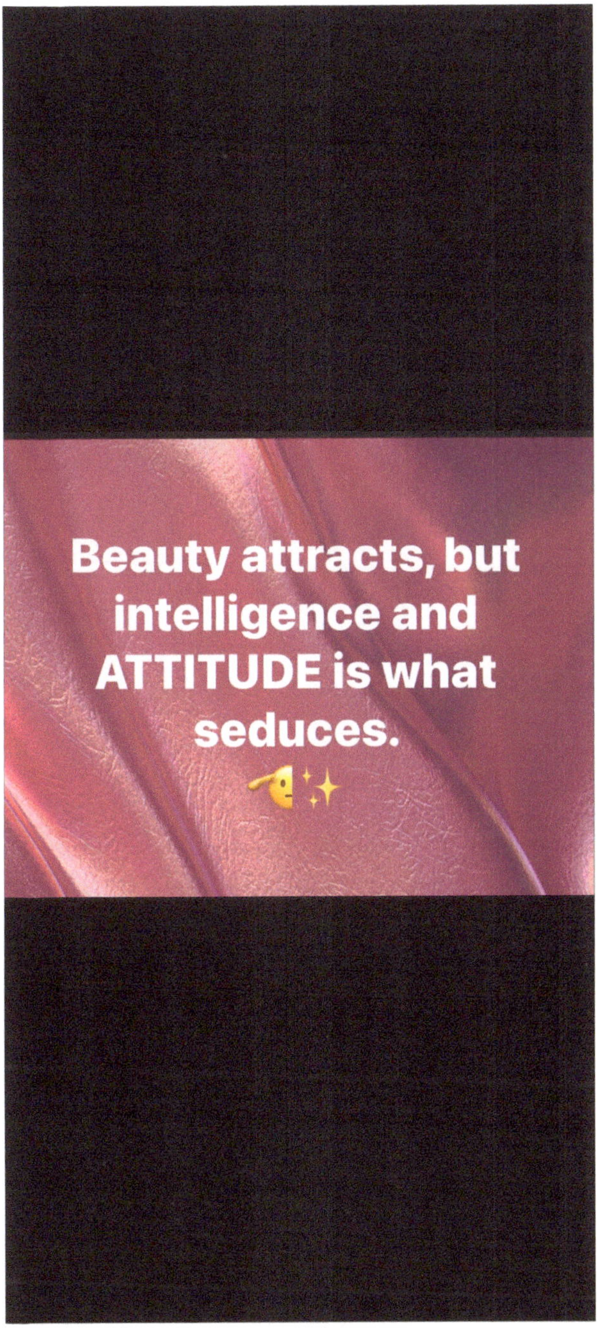

Olivia Conde

> **Beauty attracts, but intelligence and ATTITUDE is what seduces.** 🤭✨

Good people help you in silence, but bad people help you to remind you of it for the rest of their lives.

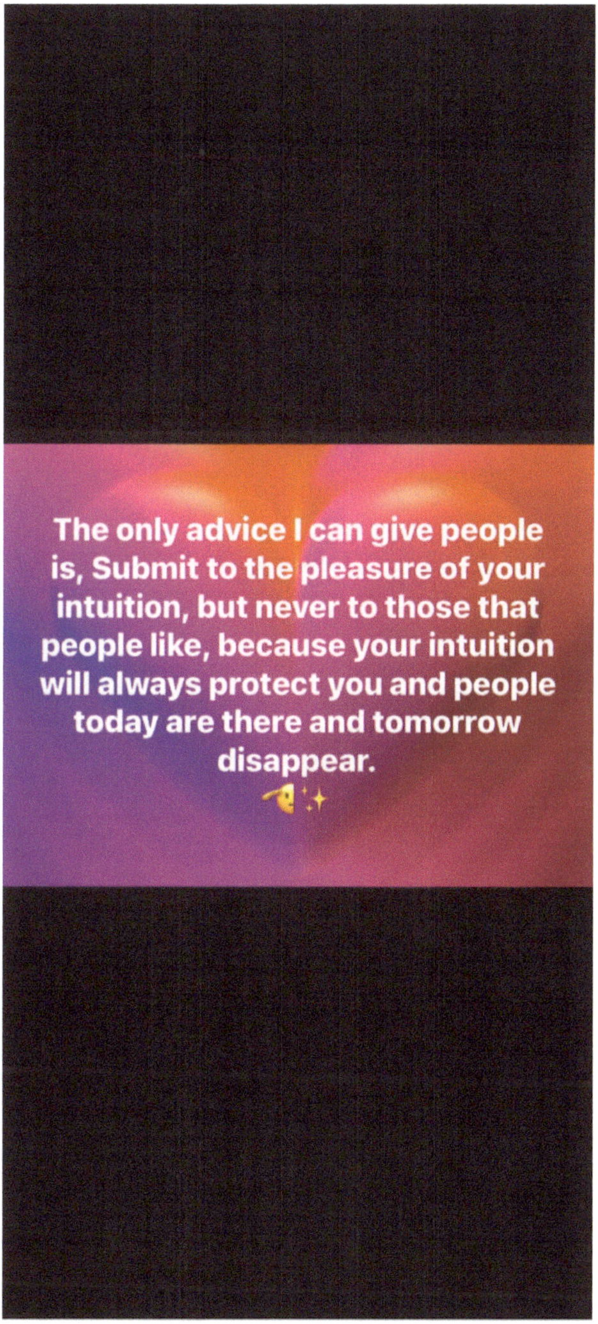

Olivia Conde

> The only advice I can give people is, Submit to the pleasure of your intuition, but never to those that people like, because your intuition will always protect you and people today are there and tomorrow disappear. 🤌✨

www.ingramcontent.com/pod-product-compliance
Lightning Source LLC
Chambersburg PA
CBHW041227070526
44584CB00006B/320